Family and Succession Law in Portugal

Family and Succession Law in Portugal

Second Edition

Guilherme de Oliveira
Paula Távora Vítor

This book was originally published as a monograph in the International Encyclopaedia of Laws/Family and Succession Law.

Founding Editor: Roger Blanpain
General Editor: Frank Hendrickx
Volume Editor: Walter Pintens

Wolters Kluwer

Published by:
Kluwer Law International B.V.
PO Box 316
2400 AH Alphen aan den Rijn
The Netherlands
E-mail: international-sales@wolterskluwer.com
Website: lrus.wolterskluwer.com

Sold and distributed in North, Central and South America by:
Wolters Kluwer Legal & Regulatory U.S.
7201 McKinney Circle
Frederick, MD 21704
United States of America
Email: customer.service@wolterskluwer.com

Sold and distributed in all other countries by:
Air Business Subscriptions
Rockwood House
Haywards Heath
West Sussex
RH16 3DH
United Kingdom
Email: international-customerservice@wolterskluwer.com

Printed on acid-free paper

ISBN 978-94-035-1341-6

e-Book: ISBN 978-94-035-1363-8
web-PDF: ISBN 978-94-035-1405-5

Printed in the United Kingdom.

The Authors

Prof. Dr Guilherme de Oliveira was born in 1947, graduated in 1972 and completed his post-graduation in 1978. He received his PhD in Civil Law in 1984 and became a Professor of the Faculty of Law at the University of Coimbra the same year. Aggregated in 1996, he has been a Professor since 1996. He is retired since 2010.

In 1988, Prof. de Oliveira founded the Biomedical Law Centre. In 1997, after some previous related academic activities, he founded the Family Law Centre, which supports post-graduate courses on Children Protection as well as post-graduate courses on other Family Law issues. Both centres have run several research projects at national and international levels. Prof. de Oliveira is a member of the expert group of the *Commission on European Family Law.*

List of Publications: *Critério jurídico da paternidade*, Coimbra, Biblioteca da Universidade, 1983; *Temas de Direito da Família*, 2nd ed., Coimbra, Coimbra Editora, 2001, ISBN 972-32-1001-0; *Temas de Direito da Medicina*, Coimbra, Coimbra Editora, 1999, ISBN 972-32-0921-7; *Curso de Direito da Família*, 5th ed., Coimbra, Imprensa da Universidade, 2016 (co-author with F.M. Pereira Coelho).

Prof. Dr Paula Távora Vítor was born in 1978, graduated in 2001 and completed her Master's in 2005. She received her PhD in Civil Law in 2017 and became a Professor of the Faculty of Law at the University of Coimbra the same year.

Paula Távora Vítor is a member of the Executive Board of Family Law Centre and of the Editorial Board of '*Lex Familiae – Portuguese Family Law Review*'.

She has participated in several projects on Persons and Family Relations and has published on these subjects, including the monograph '*A administração do património das pessoas com capacidade diminuída*' (ISBN 978-972-32-1555-7), Coimbra Editora, Coimbra, 2008.

The Authors

Preface

It has always been useful to know something about the legal systems operating in foreign countries, or at least their cultural roots. Today, it is more convenient than ever to have access to them, given the mobility that individuals currently enjoy as a result of globalization, and the surprises that this can cause in the lives of families – who lose or gain rights with a simple change of residence. Perhaps one day in the future, these various national legal systems will be brought into line in a way that protects individuals against such surprises, but that day is still far off, particularly regarding Family and Succession Law, in which most jurists still prefer to preserve their own system as a national tradition, regardless of the fact that it is inappropriate in any other country.

Unfortunately, access to the Portuguese legal system has been restricted to those few fortunate enough to understand its language. But this volume of the IEL has been conceived with those disadvantaged members of the population in mind.

In Portuguese law, readers will find influences from various European legal systems. This is because Portuguese jurists were always attentive to innovations coming from countries with which Portugal had closest ties, and the law reflects this. For example, the system of divorce used to follow the French tradition while the establishment of paternity is closer to German law.

We owe a great debt of gratitude to Professor F.M. Pereira Coelho, who made many texts available for this project; and to some other colleagues who wrote parts of the previous editions of this monograph – Nuno de Salter Cid, Rosa Martins, Joana Vicente, Geraldo Ribeiro and Rui do Carmo.

Preface

Table of Contents

List of Abbreviations

I Statutes

CC	Civil Code
CRP	Constitution of the Portuguese Republic
RJPA	Legal Regime for the Procedure of Adoption

II Organizations

EC	European Community
EU	European Union
MAP	Medically Assisted Procreation
PALOPs	Portuguese Language African Countries

III Other Terms

D.	Dom (Nobility Title)
IRS	Personal Income Tax
STJ	Supreme Court of Justice

General Introduction

Chapter 1. General Background of the Country (Demographic Data)

§1. Introduction

1. The kingdom of Portugal was formed in the eleventh century, during the period of the Christian Reconquest when the Arabs were being expelled from the Iberian Peninsula (a process which had been under way since the seventh century). It came into being with the Treaty of Zamora (1143), which recognized the independence of the earldom of Portugal (later becoming the Kingdom of Portugal) following the Battle of Ourique against the Arabs. International recognition came in 1179, when the Pope declared D. Afonso Henriques as the king and Portugal as a kingdom; finally, in the thirteenth century, the country acquired its definitive boundaries with the conquest of the Algarve (1249), the southernmost region.

2. A monarchy for more than eight centuries (it only became a Republic in 1910), Portugal's golden age was in the fifteenth and sixteenth centuries with the construction of its overseas Empire; this gave it a presence on all continents, promoting economic exchange and dialogue between different civilizations.

This movement of geographical expansion was in part motivated and conditioned by the physiognomy of the country. The territory of Portugal consists of a continental strip (of around 89,000 km^2) in the west of the Iberian Peninsula, together with the autonomous regions of the Azores and Madeira, archipelagos that have been part of the country since the mid-fifteenth century. It is characterized by an extensive coastline and by a highly differentiated and unequally divided mountainous region. There are three distinct zones: the Mediterranean South, the Atlantic North and the Northern Interior. The north is mountainous and has an Atlantic character, while the South is mostly flat with Mediterranean features.

3. Unlike Spain, France or Italy, Portugal does not have any great internal linguistic or cultural contrasts to produce divisions and tensions between different people occupying the territory. It does however have an ageing population, and there has been a constant shift of its population from the interior to the coastal strip. Despite this, the issue of regionalization has been dragging on since 1930, and various steps have been taken in that direction, ranging from the creation of legislation to initiatives promoted by different political parties; however, the regions have yet to be formally constituted. The process of regionalization is sanctioned in the Portuguese Constitution (CRP).[1]

4. Since the Revolution of April 1974 that led to the fall of the conservative authoritarian regime and to the decolonization of the African territories (Angola, Mozambique, Sao Tome and Principe, Cape Verde) and Timor, Portugal has moved on to a new stage in its history. This has had effects on all levels (political, economic and socio-cultural).

Regarding political organization, Portugal has two organs elected by direct, secret and universal suffrage (the President of the Republic, elected for a period of five years, and the Assembly of the Republic, elected for four years) and an executive organ, the Government, whose Prime Minister is appointed by the President of the Republic, taking into account the political parties represented in the Assembly and the election results. The local power, consisting of local councils, has administrative and financial autonomy in relation to the central power. They all are subject to the principles of universal suffrage, freedom of vote and secret ballot.

Internationally, Portugal is a member of the North American Treaty Organization (1949), the United Nations (1955), the Organisation for European Economic Co-operation and Development (1962), the Council of Europe (1976), the European Union (EU) (1986) and the Community of Portuguese-Speaking Countries (1996).

§2. Demography

5. The Portuguese population is approximately 10.3 million (in 2001, it was 10,356,117 of which 5,000,141 were men and 5,355,976 were women, representing a 0.7% increase compared to the previous year and 5% compared to 1991; in 2017, it was 10,300,300 of which 4,877,100 were men and 5,425,200 were women). In general terms, the 1970s was a period of rapid growth within the context of Europe, while the 1980s were marked by global stagnation and the 1990s by very slight growth.

The population density in Portugal is about 114.5 inhabitants per km^2, with the largest concentrations in the coastal cities (2011 data). The urban network is polarized in the large centres of Lisbon and Oporto, which has contributed to higher population densities along the coast in relation to the interior, and in the North as opposed to the South. The Alentejo, which occupies almost a third of the national territory, is the region with the lowest population density, with around twenty-four inhabitants per km^2.

The Portuguese population increased from 5.4 million in 1900 to 10.3 million in 2001 and to 10.5 million in 2011. However, at the present, the population has decreased to 10.3 million (2017 data). For more than two decades, the growth rate has substantially declined. The main cause is a drop in fertility levels. While in 1960 Portuguese women of childbearing age had on average 3.2 children each, in 2000,

1. Article 255 of the Portuguese Constitution.

they had only 1.5, a reduction of more than half, and in 2014, the number was 1.23. This change in fertility may be explained by several factors, such as: changes provoked by the revolution of 25 April 1974; access to mass media, leading to cultural and social expansion; the gradual entry of women into the workforce; the spread of efficient contraception and family planning; the recognition of education as a factor contributing to quality of life; the disappearance of religious attitudes towards childbearing; and finally, the environment as a social factor. In addition, couples are now delaying having children until later. While in 1976, the average age of the mother at first birth was 23.7 years old, in 2009 the average age was around 28.6, in 2014, it was 30.0 and in 2017, it was 30.3.

6. The age structure of the Portuguese population reveals that the ageing process has taken place in two dimensions. At the base of the pyramid, the proportion of young people declined from 20% in 1991 to 16% in 2001 and 5.1 in 2011 as a result of the dropping birth rate (the birth rate was 20 births in 1970, 15 in 1980 and 10.9 in 2001, 9.2 in 2011); while in 1981 there were 45.4 elderly persons for each 100 young persons, in 2001 that number rose to 101.6, in 2011 it reached 125.8, in 2014 it was 138.6 and in 2017 it was 156.2.

In a recent past, the increase in the Portuguese population had resulted mainly from immigration. The proportion of foreigners more than doubled between 1991 and 2001. In 1970, Portugal had 30,000 people of foreign nationality. In 2001 there has been a significant rise in the number of foreign population (about 68.8%). Such rise that took place between 2001 and 2002 is partly due to an extraordinary period of legalization. In 2003 the foreign population increased more than 100%. However, since 2011 there has been a decrease in immigration and in 2014 the migration rate has been negative (–30.1 thousands), but in 2017 it was 17.3. The immigrant population includes people from the former Portuguese colonies in Africa (PALOPs), Brazil, countries of the EU and today also from Eastern Europe. This last group is the most recent one in Portugal and is on average slightly older, a fact probably associated with the higher level of education of its elements.

7. The infant death rate, according to the most recent data from 2017 is 2.6/1,000 (2.6 deaths of children under the age of 1 year per 1,000 live births). This is a significant indication of demographic and social change (it was as high as 77.5/1,000 in 1960, falling to 24.3/1,000 in 1980 and to 5.5/1,000 in 2000) and confirms the improvement of living conditions in Portugal.

Chapter 2. Historical Development of Family and Succession Law

§1. Introduction

8. Family law is a branch of civil law that is particularly affected by political, social and economic change. The solutions adopted for problems such as the religious or secular nature of marriage, the admissibility of divorce, the situation of children born out of wedlock, etc. have naturally depended upon social and economic conditions and upon choices made in religious and political matters. The historical and religious traditions of each era are reflected in the system of family law adopted.

Following the founding of the nation, the Portuguese family was for many centuries modelled upon the Christian family of the medieval era. It was an institution with its own characteristics, influenced by Roman and Germanic legislation and by canon law. Thus, in the thirteenth century, there were family matters covered not only by ecclesiastical jurisdiction but also by the civil courts (canon law being the source of subsidiary law). Even during the fifteenth century, when the State began to take control of various aspects of the family and of succession through the Afonsine, Manueline and Filipine Ordinances, none of these radically altered the medieval model.

From the sixteenth century on, a crisis gradually developed in the medieval family model. The Protestant Reformation, the Gallican theologians and the writings of the philosophers of natural law shook the dogma underlying the notion of the medieval family, namely the religious basis of marriage. In Portugal, the first large-scale impact came when the Civil Code (CC) of 1867, known as the Code of the Viscount de Seabra, came into force. Clearly influenced by the political and social transformations taking place since the French Revolution, the new code introduced civil marriage alongside the traditional Catholic marriage.

The second great change came with the legislation resulting from the setting up of the Republic in 1910. Numerous statutes inspired by the new ideology were published, revealing a marked tendency towards secularization. The most prominent were the divorce laws, legislation dealing with kinship relations and the regulation of civil registers, which from then on became compulsory.

When the 1966 CC came into force, the legal regime regulating the institution of family was characterized by a new model based upon legal and social parity between spouses, each of whom was attributed different functions. Although this legislation recognized the full capacity of married women, some inequalities still persisted, and the representation of the family in some matters continued to be entrusted to the husband (preventing the introduction of foreign elements into the family), such as the administration of community assets, resolution of conflicts within the family in matters of residence, education of children.

The last great change came with the 1977 Reform, following the revolution of 1974, which installed democracy in Portugal and introduced the new Constitution of 1976. There was a clear tendency then for the family to become more nuclear, and it could be formed, according to the legislation, almost exclusively by spouses, ascendants and descendants, which was especially relevant for matters of succession. The same reform re-established the principle of the dissolubility of marriage, irrespective of the manner by which it had been celebrated, increasing the range of causes that could be used as grounds for litigious divorce and for admitting divorce by mutual consent. In addition to these alterations, the 1977 Reform also sanctioned the principle of complete equality between spouses as to rights and duties, and the principle of joint orientation of the family,[2] a corollary of the first principle.

Finally, there was an attenuation of the family hierarchy, manifested in the lowering of the age of majority from 21 to 18 (which reduced the period under which children were subject to the 'sovereignty' of the family) and in the understanding of the institution of parental responsibilities as a cluster of rights and duties that should necessarily respect the personality and autonomy of children.

§2. Marriage

9. Before being officially recognized by the Church, the 'Christian marriage' did not exist: it carried the weight of Roman and Jewish traditions, and there were many kinds of matrimony. In the eleventh century, the Catholic Church claimed total control of marriage in most European countries. Following a series of resolutions and decrees, the Church created a body of universal legal rules (matrimonial law) which would regulate marriage as a homogeneous, coherent, solemn, religious, indissoluble and heterosexual institution. This was the dominant model until the eighteenth century in Catholic countries, including Portugal.

From the sixteenth century on, Protestant movements and later philosophers of natural law and the encyclopaedists of the eighteenth century, in defending the principles of State secularization and religious freedom, came to consider marriage as a simple civil contract. Through this influence, civil law was recognized in France in 1791 (although it had already been recognized in the Low Countries in 1580 and in England in 1653).

In Portugal, the system of the 1867 CC was confusing and contradictory. Articles 1057 and 1072 seemed to admit civil marriage only for non-Catholics. The initial idea was to permit civil marriage only for foreigners living in Portugal and for non-Catholic Portuguese citizens residing in the colonies. However, in practice, it was extended to everyone. In the absence of any prior control over the religion of the parties concerned, they could freely choose between civil or religious marriage; the two institutions were regulated by different legal systems (civil law and canon law respectively) that diverged on issues such as the capacity of the parties contracting the marriage, consent, the nullity of the act, the form and the proofs.

With the proclamation of the Republic in 1910, Decree No. 1 of 25 December made marriage into a purely civil contract, in a process of true secularization. The Portuguese would celebrate marriage before the respective official of the registry office, under the conditions and in a form established in civil law, and only this would be valid. In order to prevent religious ceremonies occurring without any civil confirmation, the Code of Civil Registry of 1911 established the compulsory precedence of civil marriage over the religious one. This was the Portuguese system for thirty years.

2. Article 1671 of the CC.

In 1940, with the signing of the Concordat between the Portuguese Government and the Holy See, the system of optional civil marriage was re-established, but with some differences. Although Catholic marriage remained distinct from civil marriage as an institution, the legislation of the Concordat drew closer to the latter in three aspects – it has submitted itself: (1) to the rules of civil matrimonial impediments; (2) to the need for the preliminary publishing of banns, used by civil law; and (3) following the Additional Agreement of 1975 to the dissolution of marriage, both civil and Catholic, in the civil courts. However, Catholic marriage maintained its autonomy in matters of consent, form, causes of nullity of marriage and also in its own cause for dissolution, namely the dispensation of a marriage confirmed as unconsummated.

The general outlines of the Portuguese matrimonial system remain the same today. However, according to the Law of Religious Freedom of June 16/2001, Decree Law No. 324/2007 made some adjustments. Until then, only Catholics could choose between a Catholic and a civil service. Civil marriage was compulsory for other religions (such as Protestants, Jews, Muslims), since the law did not recognize their respective religious ceremonies, contrary to the principle of equality that excluded any kind of privilege as a result of religious persuasion. Today, according to those two laws, the civil effects are recognized of all marriages celebrated by means of a religious ceremony presided over by a minister of a church or religious community based in the country, a qualification considered necessary by the Government in view of the number of believers and the history of their presence in Portugal. That is to say, for Catholics, it is possible to choose between two different institutions regulated by different legal systems (despite their gradual approximation); for members of other religious faiths, there are only two ways to celebrate marriage, civil marriage or marriage according to the form of their professed religion, with the latter entirely subject to the law of the State, except in the form of its solemnization.

There have been important changes in patterns of engagement and marriage in Portugal over the last decades. Statistically, since the end of the 1970s, there has been a decrease in the number of marriages, with Catholic weddings declining in relation to civil ones. This decrease in the number of occurrences and form of solemnization continued in the 1990s, to become even more pronounced at the beginning of the twenty-first century. From 1992 to 2000, the marriage rate dropped from 7.0 to 5.4 marriages per thousand inhabitants. In 2017 there have been 21.803 civil weddings, 11.153 catholic weddings. As for the civil weddings that are celebrated according to the rites of other religions, in 2017 they were 155. The highest proportion of Catholic weddings was recorded in 1960, when it was around 90% of the total, dropping to 62.5% in 2001. In 2016, however, the proportion of Catholic weddings was 64.7%.

Moreover, since the beginning of the 1990s, the Portuguese are also marrying later. Most people now marry between the ages of 25–29, with a decrease in those celebrating nuptials between 20 and 24, while the 30–34 age-band is also starting to become significant. In 1992, 22.7% of men and only 15% women married over 30 years of age; in 2002, this figure rose to around 33.3% for men and 23.5% for women. Young adults are postponing marriage and starting a family in order to further their academic and professional life. In 2017 the average age of men marrying was 33.2 years old, while for women it was 31.6 years old.

10. Finally, there has also been an increase in other forms of conjugality, such as de facto union, both as an experimental phase and as an alternative to marriage. This rose from 381.120 cases in 2001 to 729.832 situations in 2011. This is not a recent situation; what is new is the degree of social recognition and legitimacy that it now enjoys.

It is important to note that many of these changes to the family and forms of conjugality occurred late in Portugal in comparison to other European countries, where they had been in evidence since the 1960s. Only in the 1970s, after the 1974 Revolution, conditions laid down for the economic and cultural change would enable this to happen.

§3. Divorce

11. The indissolubility of marriage was accepted without question for centuries by Europeans, especially from the ninth to the eighteenth centuries, in accordance with the model of matrimony imposed by the Catholic Church. The movement against the religious nature of marriage set in motion in the first half of the sixteenth century by the Protestant Reformation and continued during Enlightenment and Encyclopaedism culminated in the full restoration of divorce with the revolutionary law of 20 September 1792 in France. Sanctioned in much more moderate terms in the French CC of 1804, divorce gradually spread to other countries.

In Portugal, divorce was introduced by the Decree of 3 November 1910, which allowed not only litigious divorce but also divorce by mutual consent, irrespective of whether it was a Catholic or civil marriage. Litigious divorce was admitted in very broad terms for the era, based not only on subjective causes (adultery, desertion of the family home, ill treatment, serious affronts) but also on objective causes (de facto separation for a minimum of ten years, absence without notice, incurable insanity). This was strongly contested in Catholic circles, and consequently, on 7 May 1940, a Concordat was celebrated between the Holy See and the Portuguese State, restricting the possibilities of divorce to civil marriages.

The CC of 1966 maintained the Concordat regarding divorce, nevertheless making it more difficult. The judge could refuse the application and decree only judicial separation, if he/she considered that the circumstances of the case militated against the non-dissolution of the marriage. Objective causes were eliminated, and the possibility of directly applying for divorce by mutual consent was suppressed.

With the fall of the dictatorship in 1974, the Holy See once more proclaimed the doctrine of the indissolubility of marriage, and the duty of Catholics not to apply for divorce, in a new agreement appended to the Concordat. However, it then became a pure duty of conscience before the Church and not before the State.

The tendency of subsequent legislation has been to liberalize divorce. The 1977 Reform gave preference to divorce over personal separation, particularly divorce by mutual consent, suppressing the minimum ages of the spouses. In addition, a general clause dealing with the violation of conjugal duties as grounds for litigious divorce, and some of the objective causes of divorce admitted in 1910 were revived.

After the Reform, the most significant alterations in the divorce laws were: in the case of divorce by mutual consent, the application and decision would be dealt with by civil registry offices rather than courts;[3] there was a suppression of the minimal period of duration of marriage before divorce could be applied for;[4] in litigious divorce, the periods established for divorce grounded in objective causes were reduced; and the article that permitted the judge to refuse a divorce grounded on an alteration of mental faculties was revoked, considering that this would considerably aggravate the mental condition of the spouse concerned.[5] A major new reform has been made in 2008.[6]

12. Statistically, there has been a decline in the number of legal separations and an exponential rise in the number of divorces. Between 1991 and 2001, there was an increase of 104.2% in the number of divorcees. In 2002, there were a total of 27,960 divorces, approximately 9,000 more than in the previous year (19,044), with the vast majority divorcing by mutual consent (25,418). Amongst these statistics, the difference is narrowing between dissolutions of civil (11,456) and Catholic (16,504) marriages. In 2016 there were 22,340 divorces. Those that concerned civil weddings were 10,063 and those that pertained to catholic weddings were 12,241. The 2001 census also recorded for the first time reconstituted nuclear families; that is, families consisting of a couple married by law or de facto with children of whom at least one is the child of only one of the members of the couple, issue of a previous marriage. This suggests that divorce tends to be a temporary situation.

§4. Succession Law

13. Portuguese succession law is an individualist system mitigated by some components from the family system and, to a much lesser extent, from the socialist influence. The law of succession is closely connected to the economic and social organization of each country, particularly regarding the form of appropriation of the means of production and the detention of political power.

Portuguese law of succession is therefore a mere corollary of the principle of autonomy and of the right of property. Inheritable estate is all private property without restriction; public assets are not eligible for transfer by private individuals. Testators enjoy the broadest powers with which to dispose of their property, if they do not have forced heirs (i.e., those heirs to whom the law grants a certain reserved portion of the inheritance), in favour of family members or other people outside the family. Testamentary heirs are, under Portuguese law, completely equal to blood heirs, with some exceptions resulting from 'necessary succession'.

3. Decree Law No. 131795 of 6 June and Decree Law No. 272/2001 of 13 October.
4. Law No. 47/98 of 10 August.
5. Law No. 47/98 of 7 March.
6. Law No. 61/2008 of 31 October.

The law today establishes a smaller circle of legal heirs than in the initial version of the 1966 CC, according to which collateral relatives had inheritance rights to the sixth degree (which, in its turn, had altered the 1867 Code, where relatives succeeded heirs to the tenth degree). The 1977 Reform reduced the family nucleus, for the effects of succession, to the fourth degree in the collateral line. In the absence of these relatives, rights of succession are attributed to the State.

The Code is also mitigated by some components from the family system, these considerably more significant. In Portuguese succession law, necessary (or forced) succession has substantial autonomy before legal and testamentary succession. It includes a portion in favour of certain closest family members (spouse, descendants and ascendants), the disposal of which is forbidden to the testator (legitime – *quota legitimária*).

The 1977 Reform also brought two important alterations. First, there was the valuing of the heir position of the surviving spouse. In previous legislation, the surviving spouse was not a necessary heir and, for long historical periods, the spouse had only a very remote right in legal inheritance. In the 1867 Code and still in the first version of the 1966 CC, siblings, nephews and nieces were placed before the surviving spouse. Before the Reform of 1977, the spouse was fourth in line for inheritance, after descendants, ascendants, siblings and nephews/nieces, although if the latter were to succeed, the law conceded the spouse the right of usufruct over the inheritance. Today, with both necessary and legal suppletory succession, the spouse is first in line for inheritance along with descendants, and in second place, when there are no descendants but there are surviving ascendants. In addition, the spouse is treated more favourably, since, in certain situations, he/she is entitled to a larger share than the other legal and forced heirs[7] and has the right to be appropriated in the family home, without prejudice to the eventual restitution to the co-heirs.[8]

Second, the wording of Article 36, No. 4 of the 1976 Constitution sanctioned the principle of non-discrimination between children born in and out of wedlock, particularly for the effects of succession. Before 25 April 1976, illegitimate children had the right to only half the portion of legitimate offspring in the partition of estate. Article 36, No. 4 had immediate application, revoking preceding legislation that gave better rights of succession to legitimate relatives, both in the sense of absolute preference (exclusion of 'illegitimates')[9] and in the sense of a relative preference (illegitimate family was disadvantaged in the partition).[10]

7. Articles 2144 and 2157 of the CC.
8. Article 2103 – A of the CC.
9. Articles 2041, No. 1, 2143, 2144, 2149, 2150 of the CC.
10. Articles 2139, No. 2, 2140, No. 2, 2158, No. 2, 2159 of the CC.

Chapter 3. Sources of Family and Succession Law

§1. Constitution

14. The CRP sanctions a number of principles that define the ambit in which the ordinary legislator may move within the domain of Family and Succession Law. Rules that infringe the constitutional principles of Family and Succession Law (irrespective of their nature, form, source or hierarchy) are unconstitutional under the terms of Article 277 of the CRP. If the issue of unconstitutionality is raised in a case and granted in the decision, these rules cannot be applied by courts that are or become aware of that particular case. If the issue of the constitutionality of rules is raised directly, and not within the context of a particular case, the Constitutional Court may declare the rule generally unconstitutional, binding all constitutional organs, courts and administrative authorities. The declaration turns effective from the moment the rule that has been declared unconstitutional comes into force, and leads to the restitution of the rules that it would eventually have revoked.

When the 1976 Constitution came into effect, the sanctioning of principles like the non-discrimination between offspring born in and out of wedlock[11] or the equality of spouses[12] made some of the rules of the CC unconstitutional, such as those which benefited children born within wedlock and which disadvantaged the married woman in relation to her husband. This led to the disappearance of the so-called marital power and to the prohibition upon a wife trading without her husband's consent; parental responsibilities over a child born within marriage is today exercised by both parents, contrary to the situation in the 1966 Code, when it was exercised by the father, and the mother had only the right to be heard.

Other constitutional principles include: the right to celebrate marriage;[13] the right to constitute a family;[14] the admissibility of divorce for any marriage;[15] the protection of adoption;[16] and the protection of the family,[17] childhood, paternity and maternity.[18]

15. Within the domain of succession, Article 62, No. 1 of the CRP guarantees the right to private property and to its transfer in life or upon death under the terms of the Constitution. This precept implies recognition of the right to private succession, with a constitutional prohibition upon the exclusive right of succession of the State. The aim of the constitutional legislation is to allow each individual the possibility of disposing of his/her patrimony as he/she would, which demonstrates a clear preference for the freedom to bequeath as the expression of autonomy of will. Article 67 of the CRP establishes the family as the basic element of society, and the

11. Article 36, No. 4 of the Portuguese Constitution.
12. Article 36, No. 3 of the Portuguese Constitution.
13. Article 36, No. 1, 2nd part of the Portuguese Constitution.
14. Article 36, No. 1, 1st part of the Portuguese Constitution.
15. Article 36, No. 2, 2nd part of the Portuguese Constitution.
16. Article 36, No. 7 of the Portuguese Constitution.
17. Article 67 of the Portuguese Constitution.
18. Article 68 of the Portuguese Constitution.

relevance attributed to it in the Portuguese law of succession (mainly through necessary and legal suppletory succession) contributes greatly to its protection. Finally, the principle of equality[19] imposes a prohibition upon discrimination between children born in or out of wedlock for the purposes of inheritance. This prohibition applies immediately to successions that took place after the Constitution came into force, on 25 April 1976. Thus, since then, there has been equality amongst all descendants, whether born in or out of wedlock; in the absence of relatives of the descending line, siblings and their descendants become entitled to equal shares, whether born in or out of wedlock; persons that have been fully adopted and their descendants, in and out of wedlock, could now inherit equally, amongst other alterations.

§2. Legislation

16. There is a large number of statutes that regulate family and succession relations or which are relevant for these legal relations.

I. Civil Code

17. The CC is undoubtedly the most important law for family and succession law.

Family law occupies Book 4 (Articles 1576–2020) of the CC, which was altered profoundly by the 1977 Reform (Decree Law No. 496/77 of 25 November). This is where matters such as matrimonial law, parenthood law, guardianship, adoption and maintenance obligations are regulated.

Following the 1977 reform, Book 4 was altered further by the following statutes: Decree Law No. 185/93 of 22 May; Decree Law No. 227/94 of 8 September; Decree Law No. 163/95 of 13 July; Law No. 84/95 of 31 August; Decree Law No. 329-A/95 of 12 December; Decree Law No. 36/97 of 31 January; Decree Law No. 120/98 of 8 May; Law No. 21/98 of 12 May; Law No. 47/98 of 10 August; Law No. 59/99 of 30 June; Law No. 135/99 of 28 August; Decree Law No. 272/2001 of 13 October; Law No. 31/2003 of 22 August; Law No. 61/2008 of 31 October; Law No. 9/2010 of 31 May, Law No. 23/2010 of 30 August, Law No. 23/2013 of 5 March, Law No. 122/2015 of 1 September, Law No. 137/2015 of 7 September, Law No. 143/2015 of 8 September, Law No. 5/2017 of 2 February, Law No. 8/2017 of 3 March, Law No. 24/2017 of 24 May and Law No. 48/2018 of 14 August. That is to say, it was altered several times, which demonstrates the extent to which family law is susceptible to political and social change.

Succession law occupies Book 5 (Articles 2024–2334) but does not reveal the same degree of susceptibility as family law, despite the modifications mentioned above. However, recently, it has also been updated by Law No. 23/2013 of 5 March, Law No. 82/2014 of 30 December and Law No. 48/2018 of 14 August.

19. Article 36, No. 4 of the Portuguese Constitution.

II. Code of Civil Procedure

18. Another statute that contains many provisions that are important for family and succession law is the Code of Civil Procedure, approved by Law No. 41/2013 of 26 June and subsequently altered by Law No. 122/2015 of 1 September, Law No. 40-A/2016 of 22 December, Law No. 114/2017 of 29 December and Law No. 48/2018 of 14 August.

Most important of all are the provisions referring to maintenance obligations, divorce and separation, without the consent of one of the spouses or by mutual consent, provisions for spouses and their children, the family council.

III. Statutes Concerning Child Protection

19. In matters concerning child protection, there are essentially six statutes in force:

(a) the Law of Protection of Children and Young People in Danger– approved by Law No. 147/99 of 1 September, updated by Law No. 31/2003 of 8 August, Law No. 142/2015 of 9 September, Law No. 23/2017 of 23 May and Law No. 26/2018 of 5 July – regulates intervention in situations in which the upbringing and development of children and young people are in danger;
(b) the Law of Educational Tutelage – approved by Law No. 166/99 of 14 September, altered by Law No. 4/2015 of 15 January – regulates intervention in situations involving children aged 12–16 who reveal delinquent behaviour, with a view to inserting them into the community;
(c) the Law of Maintenance Obligations towards Children – approved by Law No. 75/98 of 19 November, altered by Law 66-B/2012 of 31 December and Law No. 24/2017 of 24 May – to guarantee the punctual payment of maintenance obligations to minors by the State, in the event of failure to comply on the part of the person responsible;
(d) the Law of Adoption – approved by Law No. 31/2003 of 22 August – establishes an improved legal regime of adoption;
(e) Law of *Apadrinhamento Civil* – approved by Law No. 103/2009 of 11 September – creates a new legal bond inspired by the catholic godparent-godchild relationship;
(f) General Regime of Civil Tutelage – approved by Law No. 141/2015 of 8 September, updated by Law No. 24/2017 of 24 May. It has revoked the Child Protection Act (Decree Law No. 14/78). It regards, namely, guardianship of children and administration of assets, regulation of parental responsibilities, maintenance obligations, contact and *apadrinhamento civil.*

IV. Code of Civil Registry

20. There are also several issues regulated by the Code of Civil Registry, approved by Decree Law No. 131/95 of 6 June and revised several times – marriage, the establishment of maternity and paternity, the preparation of birth certificates, etc.

V. Criminal Code

21. The Criminal Code, approved by Decree Law No. 400/82 of 23 September, several times revised, mainly by Decree Law No. 48/95 of 15 March and Law 59/2007 of 4 September, regulates crimes against the family, such as bigamy, falsification of marital status, the unlawful withholding of a child, violation of the obligation to provide maintenance. The family is also relevant for many other provisions of the code, both increasing punishment due to a higher culpability (murder, ill treatment, crimes against freedom and against sexual self-determination), as softening punishment due to a lower culpability (infanticide, theft, abuse of trust).

VI. Tax Law and Labour and Welfare Law

22. Finally, the family is relevant in the ambit of:

(a) tax law: such as in the area of personal income tax, which sanctions the taxation of the family unit and permits the deduction of non-reimbursable amounts expended upon healthcare and other expenses of the individual and other members of the family;
(b) labour law and welfare law: in compliance with constitutional principles, the most important of these are: the law protecting maternity and paternity, approved by Law No. 4/84 of 5 April, updated by Law No. 17/95 of 9 June, Law No. 102/97 of 13 September, Law No. 18/98 of 28 April, Law No. 118/99 of 11 August, Law No. 142/99 of 31 August and Decree Law No. 70/2000 of 4 May. Law No. 99/2003 of 27 August, (that has approved the Labour Code), has revoked this act, depending on the approval of its regulatory rules. Law No. 35/2004 of 29 July has regulated the Labour Code and thus revoked Law No. 4/84, with the exception of Articles 3º–8º and 31º; legislation guaranteeing equality of opportunity for women and men in the workplace; the attribution of maternity benefits, paternity benefits for adoption and financial support for sick children; the award of death grants and survivors' pensions for the families of social security beneficiaries, under the terms of Decree Law No. 322/90 of 18 October, updated by Decree Law No. 141/91 of 10 April, Decree Law No. 265/99 of 14 July, Law No. 23/2010 of 30 August, Decree Law No. 133/2012 of 27 June.

VII. Other Statutes

23. The following should also be mentioned:

(a) the Law of Religious Freedom (Law No. 16/2001 of 22 June, updated by Law No. 91/2009 of 31 August, Law No. 3-B/2010 of 28 April, Law No. 55-A/2010 of 31 December and Law No. 66-B/2012 of 31 December);
(b) Decree Law No. 272/2001 of 13 October, on the dejudicialization of divorce by mutual consent (updated on this subject by Law No. 61/2008 of 31 October);
(c) the Law that adopts measures protecting de facto unions (Law No. 7/2001 of 11 May, updated by Law No. 23/2010 of 30 August and Law No 2/2016 of 29 February);
(d) the Law that adopts measures protecting people living together with shared resources (Law No. 6/2001 of 11 May, updated by Law No. 7-A/2016 of 30 March).

§3. External Sources

I. International Conventions

24. Portugal has signed the following International Conventions:

(a) Conventions celebrated within the United Nations Organization.
(b) Declaration of the Rights of the Child (1959).
(c) Declaration of the social and legal principles protecting the child (1985).
(d) Convention of the United Nations Organization of 20 November 1989 on the Rights of the Child – in force in Portuguese law since 21 October 1990.
(e) Convention on the rights of persons with disabilities (2006).
(f) Convention on jurisdiction and the recognition and enforcement of judgments in civil and commercial matters (2007).

Particularly important is the work carried out at the Hague Conference with a view to harmonizing the rules concerning jurisdiction, applicable law and recognition of decisions in matters of family relations:

(a) Hague Convention on the Law Applicable to Matrimonial Property Regimes of 1978 – signed but not ratified by Portugal.
(b) Hague Convention of 17 July 1905 concerning conflicts of laws with regards to the effects of marriage upon the rights and duties of spouses in their personal relationship and with regard to their estates.
(c) Hague Convention of 12 June 1902 relating to the settlement of the conflict of laws and jurisdictions regarding divorce and separation.
(d) Hague Convention of 1 June 1970 on the recognition of divorces and legal separations – in force in Portuguese law since 9 July 1985.

(e) Hague Convention of 1961 regarding the powers of authorities and the law applicable in respect of the protection of minors.
(f) Hague Convention of 19 October 1996 on Jurisdiction, Applicable Law, Recognition, Enforcement and Co-operation in Respect of Parental Responsibility and Measures for the Protection of Children.
(g) Convention of 25 October 1980 on Civil Aspects of the International Child Abduction in force in Portuguese law since 1 December 1983.
(h) Conventions of 2 October 1973 on the Law applicable to maintenance obligations and on the recognition and enforcement of decisions relating to maintenance obligations – in force in Portuguese law since 1 August 1976 and 1 October 1977 respectively.
(i) Conventions of 15 November 1965 relating to jurisdiction, applicable law and recognition of decrees relating to adoptions, and of 29 May 1993 on the protection of children and cooperation in respect of inter-country adoption, not yet ratified by Portugal.
(j) Convention of 1973 concerning the International Administration of the Estates of Deceased Persons, ratified in 1975.
(k) Convention of 23 November 2007 on the International Recovery of Child Support and Other Forms of Family Maintenance (ratified by the EU).
(l) Protocol of 23 November 2007 on the Law Applicable to Maintenance Obligations (associated with Council Regulation (EC) No. 4/2009 of 18 December 200, whose protocol determines the applicable law).

Under the aegis of the Council of Europe, various conventions and agreements have been established that affect the very diverse matters connected to fundamental rights, especially of children:

(a) European Convention for the Protection of Human Rights and Fundamental Freedoms (1950) approved by Portugal in 1978.
(b) European Convention on Adoption (1967) – in force in Portuguese law since 24 July 1990.
(c) Convention on the Legal Status of Children born out of Wedlock (1975) – in force in Portuguese law since 8 August 1982.
(d) European Convention of 20 May 1980 on the Recognition and Enforcement of Decisions concerning the Custody of Children and the Restoration of Custody of Children (1980) – in force in the Portuguese legal system since 1 September 1983.
(e) New Convention relating to personal relations regarding children – determines the general principles to be applied to contact rights and guarantees the correct procedure for the visit and the immediate surrender of the child after the established period is over.
(f) European Convention on the Exercise of Children's Rights (signed on 6 March 1997, ratified on 31 March 2014 and in force since 1 July 2014).

There are also a number of bilateral agreements between the Portuguese State and other subjects of international law:

(a) Concordat between the Portuguese State and the Holy See of 18 May 2004 – published on 16 November of the same year.
(b) Luso-French Convention on legal cooperation regarding minors (1983) – in force in Portuguese law since 1 October 1984.
(c) Luso-Luxembourg Convention relating to legal assistance in matters of child custody and contact rights (1992) – in force in Portuguese law since 1 June 1995.
(d) Convention on maintenance obligations between the Portuguese Republic and the Democratic Republic of Sao Tome and Principe (1984).
(e) Agreements concerning maintenance obligations between the Portuguese Republic and Cape Verde (1982), in force since 19 April 1990, and with the Government of the United States (2000), approved in 2001.
(f) Cooperation Agreement in the area of jurisdiction and legal matters between the Portuguese Republic and the Republic of Angola (signed on 30 August 1995, in force since 5 May 2006).
(g) Cooperation Agreement in the area of jurisdiction and legal matters between the Portuguese Republic and the Republic of Mozambique (signed on 12 April 1990, in force since 22 February 1996).

It should also be noted that the approval phases of international conventions are not uniform: the solemn treaties established on matters of jurisdiction reserved for the Assembly[20] are always subject to approval by the Assembly of the Republic, followed by ratification by the President of the Republic;[21] other agreements are generally subject to approval by the government, with the signature of the President, although the Government may, if it seems fit, submit it for the approval of Parliament.[22]

Although the so-called general International Law or *iuscogens international* (e.g., Universal Declaration of Human Rights and other universal or with universal value international treaties) forms an integral part of Portuguese law,[23] the rest of conventional international law is only in force in internal Portuguese law upon verification of the regularity of the process and after publication in the official journal.[24]

II. European Law

25. The construction of the EU as a truly European legal space has stimulated national legal systems to converge on many issues, including family law. Undoubtedly, family law is profoundly influenced by national traditions, and for this reason has always resisted efforts of unification. This implies a true political transfer of jurisdiction in a domain so connected to sovereignty such as family law, especially when extra patrimonial.

20. Article 161, subpara. i) of the Portuguese Constitution.
21. Article 134, subpara. b) of the Portuguese Constitution.
22. Article 161, subpara. i), final part of the Portuguese Constitution.
23. Article 8, No. 1 of the Portuguese Constitution.
24. Article 8, No. 2 of the Portuguese Constitution.

The diversity that exists amongst European versions of family law has always contrasted sharply with the relative similarity of the laws that regulate commercial exchange, banking, transport and insurance. However, national traditions within Europe have also modified with time and have permitted some basic convergences in matters of marriage, divorce, maintenance obligations, status of offspring and parental responsibilities. Portuguese family law has been able to accompany this convergence, as a result of its present state of development and the capacity for change that the country has revealed.

The construction of the EU has also provided some technical tools. Unequivocally, efforts have been made regarding legal cooperation in civil matters on the part of European institutions in recent years. There has been a true standardization of the rules of private international law of Member States. Determining the competencies of jurisdictions on the level of Member States and facilitating the rapid recognition and enforcement of legal decisions throughout the whole of the EU territory are fundamental objectives. In this regard, it is necessary to mention the landmark of Regulation (EC) No. 44/2001 of the Council of 22 December 2000, concerning legal jurisdiction, recognition and enforcement of decisions in civil and commercial matters, which replaced the Brussels Convention of 1968 amongst countries of the EU.

However, the EU has wanted to extend these objectives to family matters and on 1 March 2001, the Council Regulation (EC) No. 1347/2000 of 29 May 2000 came into force in Portugal, regarding the jurisdiction, recognition and enforcement of decisions in matrimonial matters and the regulation of parental responsibilities in relation to common offspring of the couple. The regulation, which was applicable to civil processes relating to divorce, separation or to the annulment of marriage and other processes recognized by Member States, did not prejudice the Concordat between Portugal and the Holy See and prevails over the Hague Convention of 1970 on the recognition of divorce and separation of persons. Meanwhile, Council Regulation (EC) No. 1347/2000 has been repealed by the Council Regulation (EC) No. 2201/2003 of 27 November 2003 concerning jurisdiction and the recognition and enforcement of judgments in matrimonial matters and the matters of parental responsibility, that regulates matters regarding (a) divorce, legal separation or marriage annulment; (b) the attribution, exercise, delegation, restriction or termination of parental responsibility.

Within EU Law, it should be mentioned, additionally:

(1) Council Regulation (EC) 4/2009 on jurisdiction, applicable law, recognition and enforcement of decisions and cooperation in matters relating to maintenance obligations.
(2) Regulation (EU) No. 650/2012 of the European Parliament and of the Council of 4 July 2012 on jurisdiction, applicable law, recognition and enforcement of decisions and acceptance and enforcement of authentic instruments in matters of succession and on the creation of a European Certificate of Succession.
(3) Council Regulation (EU) No. 2016/1104 of 24 June 2016 implementing enhanced cooperation in the area of jurisdiction, applicable law and the recognition and enforcement of decisions in matters of the property consequences of registered partnerships.

(4) Council Regulation (EU) No. 2016/1103 of 24 June 2016 implementing enhanced cooperation in the area of jurisdiction, applicable law and the recognition and enforcement of decisions in matters of matrimonial property regimes.
(5) Council Regulation (EU) No. 1259/2010 of 20 December 2010 implementing enhanced cooperation in the area of the law applicable to divorce and legal separation.

Also relevant is the Council decision (2003/93/CE) of 19 December 2002, which authorizes Member States to sign the 1996 Hague Convention, in the interests of the EC, regarding jurisdiction, applicable law, recognition, enforcement and cooperation in matters of parental responsibility and child protection measures.

Finally, there is a note of concern from the EU regarding the social and political regulation of the family-work relation. Numerous directives and resolutions have been passed dealing with the balanced participation of women and men in professional activity and family life.

§4. Jurisprudence

26. From the legal and institutional perspectives, some reasons still persist today for maintaining the relative autonomy of the Civil and Common Law systems. The Portuguese legal system follows the Civil Law tradition. This legislative approach has its roots in the Middle Ages and, with modern legal rationalism, has come to be identified with continental European law. While Common Law is polarized in the concept of the *binding precedent*, which postulates the analogical approximation of cases presented in the Courts (with due attention to the respective *rationes decidendi*, of course), in Civil Law systems, legislation continues to be the most relevant means of constituting law.

27. Like all the legal systems that make up the great family of Civil Law, the Portuguese system has tried to avoid the risks that jurisprudence brings for the security and certainty of law, understood as a purely legalistic positivist concept, today already outdated. This it did by means of an institution that is specifically Portuguese: the system of *assentos*.

The *assentos* system was instituted after the Procedural Reform of 1926 (although it had had historical roots in the *assentos* of the House of Pleading in the fifteenth and sixteenth centuries and in the Law of Good Reason – *Lei da Boa Razão* – of 1769), and passed almost entirely into the Codes of Civil Procedure of 1939 and 1961. The *assento* was the prescription of a definitive and general legal solution issued by the Supreme Court of Justice (STJ), whenever there was a conflict in jurisprudence between two judgments on the same legal question and within the ambit of the same legislation.

At first (1939), *assentos* were compulsory for all lower courts unless they had been altered by other Supreme Court judgments; then from 1961, the Code of Civil Procedure eliminated the possibility of modifying them; and in 1966, they became generally legally obligatory (Article 2 of the CC).

The institution of *assentos* could be criticized on many scores, from the point of view of both doctrine and jurisprudence. It effectively involved the exercise of a legislative function by a non-legislative constitutional power (the judicial power), which was ultimately unconstitutional in the light of the principle of separation of powers, the significance of state functions and the provisions of Article 112, No. 6 of the CRP.

The 1995 Code of Civil Procedure finally did away with the institution, following a strongly contested judgment from the Constitutional Court (Judgment No. 810/93). When the general binding force of the *assentos* had been broken by constitutional jurisprudence and the principal of broad revisibility imposed, the institution seemed to become redundant; the normal authority and persuasive force of the Supreme Court decision obtained in the present *julgamentos alargados de revista* (decision of an appeal by the full bench of the Civil Chamber of the Supreme Court) (Article 732-A and B of the Code of Civil Procedure, presently Articles 686 and 687 of the Civil Procedure Code) was deemed sufficient to ensure the desirable unity of jurisprudence, without the rigidity and generalization that characterized the *assentos*.

Chapter 4. The Courts

§1. The Different Courts

28. Various courts have jurisdiction on questions of family law. A special position is given to the Constitutional Court, which is responsible for 'administering justice on matters of constitutional nature', this being its main function. Of the thirteen judges making up the Tribunal, ten are directly selected by the Assembly of the Republic, with the other three co-opted by the judges already selected. The tribunal is composed only by jurists: six are necessarily chosen from courts and the rest amongst jurists.

One of the most important functions of this jurisdiction (though not the only one) is controlling the constitutionality of rules. Within the ambit of family law, the Constitutional Court has declared some relevant rules unconstitutional, a declaration that is generally binding. For example, Article 1793, No. 1 of the CC, was judged unconstitutional in the interpretation according to which the regime of protection of the family home was not applicable to situations when a de facto union terminated even though there were children resulting from that union.[25] Similarly, the Constitutional Court has judged Articles 1860, paragraph (e) and 1864, first part, of the CC, former wording, unconstitutional. The judgment understood that the right to the knowledge and acknowledgement of paternity, a corollary of the right to personal identity, is a fundamental right and may only be restricted under the conditions established in Article 18 of the Constitution, which does not cover the possibility of that right becoming dependent on the verification of material conditions, such as those referred to in Article 1860 of the CC.[26] The Constitutional Court has already pronounced in one case in which the unconstitutionality of Article 1781, a) of the CC was alleged (which allows either of the spouses, even the guilty one, to apply for divorce grounded on de facto separation) due to the violation the principle of human dignity. The Constitutional Court did not deem it unconstitutional, considering that a rule that obstructs that possibility would be contrary to the right to free development of personality and even to the right to contract marriage.

29. There are judicial courts, organized hierarchically in the form of a pyramid with the STJ at the top and with the trial courts (Courts of First Instance) at the bottom. This hierarchy is only justified for purposes of appeal, with the upper court(s) responsible for reviewing the process:

- the STJ: it is the highest court in the hierarchy of judicial courts, that based in Lisbon, and which, except in cases laid down by law, deals only with matters of law;
- second instance courts or Appeal Courts – the courts are based in Coimbra, Évora, Lisbon, Oporto and Guimarães – and form the middle section of the pyramid and deal with matters of fact and law;
- Courts of First Instance – it is in these courts that claims are usually issued.

25. Judgments of the Constitutional Court No. 359/91 of 9 July and No. 1221/96 of 4 December.
26. Judgment of the Constitutional Court No. 694/95 of 5 December.

30. The Judicial Organization Law and its regulatory act[27] have created family and juvenile specialized departments within the district courts (first instance), with the exception of Bragança, Guarda and Portalegre, which are responsible for preparing and judging issues of family law, relating to spouses and ex-spouses and also to minors and offspring who have attained majority. Only in districts where there is no family and juvenile court, the Court of First Instance will be the district court (i.e., it will transform itself into the family and juvenile court).

31. The Judicial Organization Law does not establish courts of specialized jurisdiction to deal with questions of succession. For these issues, the district courts are (generally) competent. The court in the district where the will is to be read, that is, at the place of final residence of the *de cuius* (Article 2031 of the CC), is competent for the inventory, to name someone as beneficiary and also for the process of disclaimer or acceptance by an heir of the estate. In the event that the will is to be read abroad, the court in the place where the estate (real or movable) is situated will be competent, or, if there is none, the court of the area of residence of the applicant.

§2. Family and Juvenile Courts

32. The family and juvenile specialized departments within the district courts deal with the following matters referred to in Articles 122º–125º of the Judicial Organization Law:

- prepare and hear processes relating to spouses and former spouses, such as actions of judicial separation and divorce, inventories in case of separation or divorce, declarations of the inexistence or annulment of marital status, attribution and enforcement of maintenance obligations, cautionary procedures. They may also try matters of civil tutelage, that is, suits of regulation or deprivation of parental responsibilities, the institution of guardianship, adoption, official inquiry of maternity or paternity, judicial authorizations, etc.
- are responsible for the judicial process of promotion and protection of children and young people in danger, such as decreeing measures relating to minors that have been victims of ill treatment, have been abandoned or whose health, safety or education are in danger. In addition, they also practise various jurisdictional acts of educational tutelary procedure directed at children between 12 and 16 years of age who have committed crimes, with a view to applying tutelary measures such as admonition, educational accompaniment, internment in educational establishments.

33. In this area, as regards to the juvenile law, inter-disciplinary and inter-institutional participation is essential. Therefore, the system created for the protection of children and young people in danger (from ill treatment, family dysfunction,

27. Law No. 62/2013 of 26 August, and Decree Law No. 49/2014 of 27 March.

para-delinquency, etc.) involves a pyramid-shaped and subsidiary scheme of intervention. At the base of the pyramid are those public and private bodies whose function includes working with children, in matters of education, health or social action. These include hospitals, schools, the Institute of Solidarity and Social Security, private welfare institutions, the police. In the middle section, there are Protection Committees, official but non-judicial institutions of heterogeneous composition, responsible for intervening at a local level. These bodies are autonomous and may deliberate on protection measures and act with exemption and impartiality. Decisions of such bodies must arise from an agreement reached by the persons involved in the case. At the top of the pyramid, there are the courts, whose intervention is subsidiary. Intervention with children revealing delinquent behaviour also requires the application for educational tutelary measures in conjunction with various institutions such as the services of Social Rehabilitation, centres for professional training, educational centres.

The interface between the judiciary and the social services is occupied by the Public Prosecution Service. This is a magistracy that operates parallel to the judicial magistracy, with special functions. The Public Prosecution Service represents the interests of the child or young person and defends them legally. It intervenes in different areas:

– it takes initiative and is heard in various civil tutelary procedures;
– it monitors the activities of local protection committees, appreciating and controlling the legality and suitability of measures; it represents children and young people in danger, proposing actions and applying for the necessary provisions in defence of their rights;[28]
– it plays an important role in educational tutelary intervention, directing the phase of investigation of the crime, promoting the enforcement of tutelary measures, carrying out visits to educational centres;[29]
– in cases of divorce and separation by mutual consent, it has the power to pronounce upon the exercise of parental responsibilities over children that are minors;[30]
– in adoption processes, the Public Prosecution Service is a constant presence, from the 'administrative' phase to the judicial phase itself, as well as in incidents of revocation, revision and extraordinary appeal of a final judgment.[31]

34. The family and juvenile court generally functions with a single judge. However, in cases related to the promotion and protection of children's rights and in educational tutelary cases in which a measure of institutionalization is considered for application, the judgment is carried out by a court constituted by a trial judge and two social judges, who are specially selected.[32]

28. Article 72 of the Protection Law.
29. Article 40 of the Educational Tutelary Law.
30. Article 14 of Decree Law No. 272/2001 of 13 October.
31. Articles 26 and 27 of the Adoption Process Legal Regime, adopted by Law No. 143/2015 of 8 September.
32. Article 115 of the Protection Law and 30 of the Educational Tutelary Law.

Inter-disciplinary and inter-institutional participation, and the particular involvement of technicians from many different areas (such as Medicine, Psychology, Education, Social Services) enable magistrates today to have a better knowledge and understanding of social and legal questions that may arise. The law itself points increasingly towards the need for specialized jurisdiction and for specific training of judges placed in these courts. For example, in civil tutelary processes, the judge may appoint technical consultants in order to assist with the investigations, clarify certain issues, perform tests or provide opinions.

35. A final word on the importance of mediation and on the role of the lawyer in family conflicts. In civil tutelary procedures (especially those that involve family conflicts, such as the regulation of the exercise of parental responsibilities), the judge has the power, at any stage of the process, officiously or at the request of the parties concerned, to request the intervention of mediation services.[33] The intervention of a third person who is neutral and impartial may indeed bring many advantages in this kind of conflict, preventing hasty decisions on the part of the people involved, re-establishing communication between them, and promoting a greater flexibility within the family organization and relations.

This mediator role should be asked of the lawyer in conflicts between spouses, especially when the interests of children are at stake. The lawyer must not selfishly take into account only the interests of his/her client, but must constantly attempt to consider the perspective of the other party and reinforce a spirit of reconciliation. Taking into account the status of the child/young person as the subject of rights in the ambit of modern juvenile law, the lawyer also plays an important role in furthering those interests on the level of the promotional, civil tutelary and educational procedures. In civil tutelary processes, the constitution of a lawyer is not compulsory, except in the appeal stage and whenever the child's interests and those of their parents or legal representatives are incompatible.[34]

In processes of promotion and protection of children in danger, the child or young person has the right to be heard individually or accompanied by his/her parents or a lawyer;[35] when there is conflict with the parents, and if there is maturity, they may choose their own lawyer. It is today recognized that the lawyer has a more dynamic and active role in the promotion of the child's interests.

In educational tutelary processes, there are situations in which it is compulsory to have a defending lawyer (hearing and detention of a minor), and this will be preferentially someone with specific training in that area.[36] The role of the defence lawyer is to assist the minor and also to closely observe the family environment.

33. Article 24 of the Civil Tutelary Process Legal Regime.
34. Article 18 of the Civil Tutelary Process Legal Regime.
35. Article 84 of the Law of Protection.
36. Article 46 of the Educational Tutelary Law.

§3. PROCESSES OF VOLUNTARY JURISDICTION

36. A significant number of actions brought to family and juvenile courts (or to district courts) take a special form, that of processes of voluntary jurisdiction, as laid down in Articles 986 onwards of the Code of Civil Procedure. The main characteristic of voluntary jurisdiction is the existence of a single fundamental interest protected by law, which the court will ensure is realized in accordance with equity, adopting for each particular case the solution that seems the most convenient and opportune in the light of the interests in question.

It operates this way in the case of suits dealing with separation or divorce by mutual consent, the establishment of maintenance obligations towards children that have attained majority or emancipation, the allocation of the family home, the conversion of separation into divorce, the process of regulation of parental responsibilities, etc. The same applies in matters of succession, in actions relating to abeyant inheritance and in the exercise of executorship.

37. There are four main fundamental principles characterizing voluntary jurisdiction. Regarding the powers of the court, the principle of inquisition prevails; that is to say, the judge may freely try facts and is not limited to those brought by the parties in the process.[37] Regarding the criteria of the trial, equity predominates over rules of law. The judge does not have to act according to strict rules of law. The solution should be adopted that is deemed most convenient and opportune in each case, even if this does not strictly observe the law. What is being highlighted here is the creative role of the jurisdictional function: the judge may not only adapt legal rules to the particularities of individual cases, but may also create totally new criteria for decisions about concrete problems.[38] The principle that allows the free amendment of decisions[39] is translated into the possibility of modifying resolutions whenever circumstances particularly justify it.

Finally, since the court is not subordinated to the strict rule of law, but can rather decide on the basis of equity, appeals to the STJ are not admissible; as we have seen, only the violation of substantive law constitutes specific grounds for appeal to that court.[40]

38. One of the paradigmatic cases in which the special nature of voluntary jurisdiction is felt is, undoubtedly, the process of regulation of the exercise of parental responsibilities in cases of divorce or legal separation. The criteria governing the new regime for the exercise of parental functions, established by agreement between the parents or by judgment, are the interests of the minor and take into account three fundamental issues: the residence of the children, contact rights and maintenance obligations. The interest of the child is by nature a nebulous concept, and it is therefore up to the judge to specify and define this for each particular case, opting for the most convenient and opportune solution in the light of such interest.

37. Article 986, No. 2 of the Code of Civil Procedure.
38. Article 987 of the Code of the Civil Procedure.
39. Article 988, No. 1 of the Code of Civil Procedure.
40. Article 988, No. 2 of the Code of Civil Procedure.

There has been a curious development in Portuguese jurisprudence as to criteria employed in the attribution of child custody in the event of divorce or separation. Until 1930, the custody of the child was generally entrusted to the 'innocent' spouse. With the significant increase in the number of divorces from the 1980s onwards, judgments became usually grounded on Principle VI of the *Declaration of the Rights of the Child* (1959), according to which 'The child of a young age should not, except in exceptional circumstances, be separated from the mother.' More recent jurisprudence has criticized this maternal preference: 'Given the principle of equality between citizens, the specific issues justifying the claim that a woman always cares better for a young child than a man would seem out of step'[41] This alteration in jurisprudence, namely the understanding of the superior interest of the child as a prevailing principle, is grounded on Article 9 of the 1989 Convention on the Rights of the Child. The regulation of the exercise of parental responsibilities should take into account: the state of physical and psychic development of the child; his/her age and real affective and material needs; and the ability of each parent to satisfy those needs. It is up to the judge to order all the inquiries that are, in his/her view, necessary to arrive at a full understanding of those interests, such as the hearing of the minor, in accordance with the current view of the child as the subject of their own rights.

The way that the issue of contact rights is treated in jurisprudence has also undergone some evolution. The system of contact may not be seen as a right of parents or of their interests, but rather as a way of satisfying the real interests of the child and of contributing to his/her healthy emotional and psychological development.

39. The establishment of maintenance obligations is another chapter in which the principle of equity and the alterability of decisions prevail. The criterion established by law for the calculation of the average amount to be paid is indeterminate and flexible, and is gauged in accordance with the possibilities of the parent concerned and with the child's needs. It should take into account the means and expenses of the parent concerned, and, given the cost of living and prices of objects, all expenditure necessary for the physical and intellectual development of the child. It is the judge, always guided by common sense, who will establish the amount to be paid in maintenance, and also alter it, if necessary.

A large number of applications for alterations in parental responsibilities in Portugal deal with modifying maintenance arrangements, or with the failure to comply with maintenance obligations or with the contact regime established in a previous decision. This demonstrates that these two aspects of the regulation of parental responsibilities are the source of great instability, and a great deal of perspicacity is required from the judge not to overlook the higher interests of the child in a situation of conflict between parents.

41. Judgement of the Oporto Court of Appeal of 18 November 1999.

Part I. Persons

Chapter 1. The Status of a Person

§1. Definition of a Person

40. Under legal terms, a *person* is either a human being or an organization that are holders of rights and obligations. Legal personality consists, therefore, in the possibility to actually have rights and obligations. The acquisition and termination of legal personality and the particularities worth mentioning within this field will be better understood if the two basic kinds of legal entities (legal *persons*) provided for in Portuguese law – *physical or natural persons* and *juridical persons* – are analysed separately.

41. Human beings are deemed to have legal personality the moment they are completely born and alive.[42] Thereafter they shall be designated as *physical or natural persons* (in Portuguese *pessoas singulares* – literally 'singular persons'). Notice of birth shall be given within a short term, for civil registration purposes, even if it takes place during a journey.[43]

42. The law entitles rights to *nascituri* (*lato* and *stricto sensu*), but the actual acquisition of such rights depends on them being born alive. Either *nasciturus stricto sensu* (already conceived) or *nodum conceptus* (not yet conceived) may acquire rights by donation or by succession (testate or contractual succession), as far as they are the children of a specific person who is alive at the time the donator has made his/her statement or at the time the succession is open.[44] Under legal provisions, the *nasciturus* who has already been conceived at the time of succession opening has 'beneficiary capacity' – understood as the expectation to be called upon

42. Article 66, No. 1 of the CC. According to law, 'birth of an alive child applies to the expulsion or complete emergence from the body of its mother, regardless of the stage of gestation, of the fecundation product that, after such a separation, breathes or shows any vital signs, such as heart or umbilical cord beatings, or actual contractions in any muscle subject to will power, whether the umbilical cord has been cut or not, and whether the placenta is retained or not'; 'the product of a birth under such circumstances is named born alive' (Law No. 44 128 of 28 Dec. 1961, Art. 2). The expression 'born alive' is mainly used for demographic statistical purposes.
43. Articles 96–111 of the Code of Civil Registry.
44. Articles 66, No. 2, 952, No. 1, and 2033, No. 2, a), of the CC.

intestate succession when attaining his/her legal personality – and the voluntary acknowledgement of the *nasciturus* is valid, as long as the father identifies his/her mother.[45]

The conceived *nasciturus* (*en ventre de sa mère* or *foetus*) is also protected by criminal law, that criminalizes the practice of inducing abortion, either performed by the pregnant woman or by a third party, with or without her consent. Nevertheless, in certain cases 'pregnancy termination' is not criminalized, provided that it is carried out by a physician or under his/her supervision, in a health care institution or otherwise legally licensed institution, with the pregnant woman's consent. Thus, having the afore conditions been complied with, the induced abortion is not punishable: whenever it is the only way to remove danger of death or of serious and irreversible damage to the pregnant woman's body or health (either physical or mental); whenever it is considered adequate to avoid danger of death or of serious and lasting damage to the pregnant woman's body or health, as long as it is performed within the first twelve weeks of pregnancy; whenever it stands firm that the child to come will suffer from a particularly serious condition considered as incurable or from a congenital malformation, as long as it is performed within the first twenty-four weeks of pregnancy; whenever the *foetus* is not viable; whenever the pregnancy results from a crime against sexual freedom and self-determination, as long as it is performed within the first sixteen weeks of pregnancy; or whenever it is performed by option of the pregnant woman within the first ten weeks of pregnancy.[46]

43. Legal personality of physical persons terminates with their death. Nevertheless, both civil law and criminal law protect the memory of the deceased person against offences.[47]

The death must be medically certified, apart from exceptional cases of legal declaration of death *in absentia*; it must as well be noticed within a short period of time

45. Articles 1854–1855 and 2033, No. 1 of the CC. As to the assessment of the moment of conception, *see* Arts 1798 and 1800 of the same Code. There is a consensus concerning the right of the *nasciturus,* once born, to be compensated for prenatal damages, right to be claimed by his/her legal representatives as soon as he/she has legal personality In a judgment of 29 Jan. 2013 (Proc. 475/04.9TBANS.C1) the Coimbra Appeal Court considered that the presumed father has the right to receive the compensation due for non-patrimonial damages endured by the loss of life of the *nasciturus* in a car accident, compensation to be added to the one that is due to the same parent for the grief that he suffered with the death of the *foetus*. In a judgment of 3 Apr. 2014 (Proc. 436/07.6TBVRLP1.S1) the Supreme Court held that an individual's daughter deceased in a car accident is entitled to be compensated for her moral damages relating to the death of his father occurred before her birth.
46. Articles 140–142 of the Criminal Code, Arts 2–6 of the Law No. 16/2007 of 17 April (amended by Law No. 136/2015 of 7 September) and Order (*Portaria*) No. 741-A/2007 of 21 June. The legal provision in order not to be punishable the induced abortion performed by option of the pregnant woman within the first ten weeks of pregnancy resulted from a legislative amendment made in 2007, after a referendum with a favourable but not binding result.
47. Articles 68, No. 1 and 71 of the CC and Art. 185 of the Criminal Code. This Code, under the heading 'crimes against life in society', lays out 'crimes against respect due to deceased' (Arts 253–254); however, such crimes are foreseen to protect collective moral feelings.

for the death to be legally registered.[48] When the production of a certain legal effect depends on a person surviving another and doubts arise as to the time of death, the presumption is taken that both died at the same time. According to law, a person is considered to be dead whenever the corpse has not been found or recognized, as long as his/her disappearance has taken place under such circumstances that no doubts can be risen about his/her death. Nevertheless, the law also provides for the possibility of death being presumed in case of a long absence, as we will refer to *infra* in a more detailed way.[49]

44. Organizations aimed to the fulfilment of collective purposes, once legally constituted, and in certain cases registered, or upon their administrative assessment, also have legal personality; in Portuguese language they are named *pessoas colectivas* (literally 'collective persons'), but from now on we will name it *juridical persons*. They may be either public or private, according to their scope and to their legal status. This issue shall be slightly dealt with, in view of the necessity to make a short exposition.

45. Public *juridical persons* may be territorial or non-territorial. The first ones are attached to the State (*stricto sensu*), the Autonomous Regions, the Municipal Authorities and the Parishes;[50] the latter comprise Public Institutes, Organizational Public Entities and Public Associations.[51]

46. Private corporation entities fall normally under one of the following categories: associations; companies or civil partnerships under commercial statutes; as

48. Law No. 141/99 of 28 August, Art. 12 of Law No. 12/93 of 22 April (amended and republished in Annex to Law No. 22/2007 of 29 June), Statement of Physicians Order dated 1 Sep. 1994, in *D.R.*, I-B Series of 11 Oct. 1994, Order 14341/2013 of 19 October, in *D.R.*, 2nd Series of 6 Nov. 2013, and Arts 192–208 of the Code of Civil Registry.
49. Articles 68, Nos 2 and 3, and 114 of the CC.
50. Several constitutional rules refer to the State as a public entity (e.g., Arts 22, 48, No. 2, 82, No. 2, 103, No. 1, 269, Nos 1 and 2) and Art. 199, c), attaches it as a public juridical person, likewise several rules of ordinary legislation. Under article 227, No. 1 of the Constitution, Autonomous Regions are classified as territorial juridical persons, likewise article 235, No. 2 of the Constitution applying to Local Autarchies (only Municipal Authorities and Parishes are to be considered, since administrative regions, though provided for the Mainland, are not set up). As to the powers and performance of the Municipal Authorities and Parishes bodies, *see* Law No. 169/99 of 18 September, in large part repealed by Law No. 75/2013 of 12 September, and *see* especially this Law No. 75/2013, with latest amendments made by Law No. 69/2015 of 16 July.
51. Public institutes are a heterogeneous assembly of public juridical persons carrying out different activities, such as: providing services to the community; financial or technical support to either private or co-operative sectors; carrying out scientific and technological research; upper teaching; developing conditions to enable the development of certain activities and/or supervising their performance. Law No. 3/2004 of 15 January (with latest amendments made by Decree Law No. 96/2015 of 29 May) is the legal framework for public institutes. As regards the Public Business Sector *see* Decree Law No. 133/2013 of 3 October (amended by Law No. 75-A/2014 of 30 September). Professional associations with the responsibility of the fulfilment of public interest are, among others, Public Associations; the Bar Association (which new Statutes passed by Law No. 145/2015 of 9 September) is one of them.

well as foundations.[52] The legal qualification of cooperatives has been subject to discussions as to whether they are companies or associations; the Co-operative Code designates them as 'autonomous *juridical persons*'.[53] Under Portuguese law, most of the civil partnerships do not have legal personality as such, despite of having, for some purposes, a legal regime similar to the one applicable to the *juridical persons*. In addition, the CC rules governing juridical persons are applicable to such partnerships 'whenever the analogy of the situations so justifies'.[54]

47. Under the provisions of the Concordat signed on 2004 between the Holy See and the Republic of Portugal, legal personality is recognized to the Catholic Church, to the Portuguese Episcopal Conference (in accordance with the statutes approved by the Holy See), to the dioceses, parishes and other ecclesiastical jurisdictions (provided that the constitutive act of its canonical legal personality is notified to the competent body of the State) and to other entities recognized as canonical legal persons by the competent ecclesiastical authority (once entered in the Register of the Canonical Legal Persons).[55] As to other churches and religious communities, the law provides for religious juridical persons to be created and legal personality is attached to these entities through registration with a specific registry.[56]

48. The public juridical persons cease through a ruling act.[57] Private juridical persons, as a rule, cease through decision of the adequate body, through expiring or by judicial decision, without prejudice both to other causes foreseen in the specific regime concerned and to the necessity of patrimonial liquidation.[58] The extinguishment of the dioceses, parishes and other ecclesiastical jurisdictions, as well as of the other canonical legal persons, is done in a form similar to that used for its constitution.[59]

52. Articles 157–194 of the CC and Arts 1 and 5 of the Companies Code (passed by Decree Law No. 262/86 of 2 September, and amended several times since then, lately by Decree Law No. 148/2015 of 9 September).
53. Cf. Art. 2, No. 1 of the new Co-operative Code (Law No. 119/2015 of 31 August).
54. Articles 157 and 980–1021 of CC.
55. Articles 1, No. 2, 8, 9, No. 2, and 10 of the aforementioned Concordat, signed on the 18 May 2004 and published in the *D.R.*, I-Series, 16 Nov. 2004, and Decree Law No. 19/2015 of February.
56. Article 33 of the Religious Freedom Act (Law No. 16/2001 of 22 June, with latest amendment introduced by Law No. 66-B/2012 of 31 December) and Decree Law No. 134/2003 of 28 June (amended by Decree Law No. 114/2011 of 30 November).
57. *See*, for instance, Art. 16 of Law No. 3/2004.
58. Articles 182–184 and 192–194 of the CC, Arts 112, 120 and 141–165 of the Companies Code, 112–114 and 118 of the new Co-operative Code and Art. 42 of the Religious Freedom Act (*see*, as well, Art. 44 of this Act).
59. Article 9, No. 3 of the aforementioned Concordat of 2004 and Art. 9 of Decree Law No. 19/2015 of 3 February.

§2. Capacity

49. As far as legal capacity is concerned, it is also advisable to analyse physical persons and juridical persons separately. And applying to both, it is convenient to refer to the *capacity to enjoy rights* and to the *capacity to act in legal terms.*

50. As a rule, all physical persons can have any rights and obligations. Therefore, they may, in principle, be a part of any legal relationship; exceptions are to result from the law. We hereby refer to the capacity to enjoy rights and emphasize the quantity (variable) of rights and obligations they may have. Restrictions may result from various reasons or circumstances, namely nationality, age, mental disability, civil status or gross misconduct.[60]

51. The capacity of physical persons to act in legal terms consists in their possibility of exercising, either personally and freely or through a representative appointed by them, the rights and obligations they have.

52. Minors not emancipated are, as a rule, considered not to have the capacity to act in legal terms. A person only becomes of full age on his/her eighteenth birthday; nevertheless, if a minor whose age is between 16 and 18 years gets married, he/she becomes duly emancipated and therefore able to act in legal terms as if he/she were of full age, except if he/she did not get the necessary and previous consent to get married (granted by either his/her parents or by the guardian, or granted by the Civil Registrar); under these circumstances, regardless of being emancipated, he/she continues to be considered a minor for certain patrimonial purposes.[61]

Under legal provisions, since the minor has limited capacity to act in legal terms, representation is exercised in the context of parental responsibilities and, subsidiarily, of guardianship.[62] Nevertheless, law provides several exceptions to such incapacity of non-emancipated minors. While approaching the theme of acts and contracts carried out by minors, some of these exceptions shall be pointed out; others shall be pointed out at this moment, also showing that law takes into account several degrees of maturity of the minors. Thus, for example: regardless of the fact that non-emancipated minors ought to obey their parents (or guardian) 'as long as no illicit or immoral issues are concerned', the latter, in view of the minors' maturity, shall listen to their opinion when important family issues arise and shall give them the possibility to be independent in their personal life; regarding the adoption

---

60. Article 67 of the CC, Art. 15, No. 2 of the Constitution and, e.g., Arts 1601 (absolute impediments to marriage), 2189 (incapacity to make one's will; *see* as well 2182, No. 1) and 2034 (unworthiness to succeed) of the CC. As to nationality *see*, however, Nos 1, 3, 4 and 5 of Art. 15 of the Constitution; as to ordinary legislation *see* Law of Nationality (Law No. 37/81 of 3 October, lately amended by Organic Law No. 9/2015 of 29 July) and Regulation on Portuguese Nationality (approved by Decree Law No. 237-A/2006 of 14 December and amended by Decree Law No. 43/2013 of 1 April).
61. Articles 122, 123, 130–133, 1604, a), and 1649, CC. Concerning the legal proceeding for the exemption of the consent for minors' marriage, *see* Arts 255–257 of the Code of Civil Registry.
62. Articles 124, 1877–1920-C and 1921–1950 (but *see also* Art. 1954) of the CC.

of a child over 12, his/her consent shall be obtained (except if it is a child with cognitive impairments that hinder that possibility or if there is a great difficulty to consult him/her); the adopters' children over 12 are as well to be consulted as to the adoption of the new child; if parental responsibilities are held by both parents, as it normally happens while they are still married or cohabit, and either parent may require the intervention of the Court in order to solve disagreements between them over highly important issues, whenever no judicial conciliation has been achieved, the child over 14 shall be heard before a decision is taken (except 'when serious circumstances advise otherwise'); before a guardian is nominated, any child over 14 shall be heard about it by the Court; as from the age of 16, minors have legal capacity to acknowledge paternity without their parents' (or guardian's) consent, and they are also totally autonomous as to religion matters.[63]

53. Within the scope of the capacity to act in legal terms, reference shall be made to the new legal status of adults with cognitive impairments and the regime of custodianship (*acompanhamento*), that does not necessarily encompass lack of capacity to act (*See infra* §7).

54. Pursuant to the Constitution, juridical persons are entitled to the rights and are subject to the duties suited to their legal nature. According to ordinary legislation, their capacity covers only the rights and obligations necessary or adequate to the achievement of their purposes (principle of the speciality), and they cannot have, obviously, rights and obligations prohibited by law or adjacent only to the legal personality of a physical person. The juridical persons are represented by those who are designated by the law or by its statutes (or, might no statutory clause exist on that matter, by the members of the board or by someone to be nominated by the board).[64]

§3. Absentees

55. Under legal terms, a person is considered an absentee when he/she has disappeared, his/her whereabouts are unknown and doubts arise about him/her being alive.

The substantive legal regulation on this issue is divided in three sets of main rules, developed in accordance with the solidity of the absence, that is to say, the

---

63. Articles 128, 1850, 1878, No. 2, 1886, 1901, 1931, No. 2, 1935, 1981, No. 1, a), and No. 3, a), and 1984, a), of the CC. Beyond civil scope, *see*, for instance, Art. 38, Nos 1 and 3 of the Criminal Code: the consent of a minor above 16 years old, and with enough maturity to evaluate the meaning and target of such a consent upon giving it, excludes the illicit character of a criminal fact, if it concerns freely available legal interests and as far as it does not offend public morality.

64. Article 12, No. 2 of the Constitution, Arts 1, 3, No. 1, a), and 5, No. 1, a) and b), of the Statutes of the Public Prosecution Service (Law No. 47/86 of 15 October, with latest amendments introduced by Law No. 9/2011 of 12 April), Arts 18, No. 1, a), and 35, No. 1, a), of Law No. 75/2013 of 12 September, Arts 160 and 163 of the CC, Arts 24 and 25 of the Code of Civil Procedure and, e.g., Arts 6, No. 1, 192–193, 252, 260–261, 408–409 and 470 of the Companies Code, Art. 2, No. 1, 9, 47, g), 49 and 50 of the new Co-operative Code, Arts 34, h), and 43 of the Religious Freedom Act and Arts 14 and 21, No. 3 of the Law No. 3/2004.

higher or lesser probability of the absentee returning or, otherwise, of him/her being really dead: provisional curatorship; final curatorship; and presumed death.[65] Two additional substantive provisions are added complementing the aforementioned sets of rules.[66] There are also several relevant proceeding rules[67] which shall not be particularly dealt with.

56. Might it be necessary to deal with the administration of the absentee's assets, and arising the case of him/her not having a legal representative or not having appointed an attorney who may perform such duties, the Court shall appoint a provisional curator to act on his/her behalf; might the circumstances so demand, there can also be appointed a special curator to handle certain legal affairs. The provisional curatorship may be required either by the Public Prosecution Service or by any person interested in the preservation and administration of the absentee's assets.

The absentee's spouse, one of the absentee's presumptive heirs or someone interested in the preservation of the assets shall be chosen as provisional curator. However, might there be any clash of interests between the absentee and the curator or between the absentee and the curator's spouse, ascendants or descendants, a special curator shall be appointed. Except in an emergency, a list of the absentee's assets shall be made before their being delivered to the curator, and he/she shall pay the bail which was assessed by the Court; might the curator not make the mentioned bail, somebody else shall be appointed by the Court.

The provisional curator is subject to the legal regime of general mandate concerning whatever is not against the specific applicable standards; it is up to him/her to require preventive judicial proceedings and bring judicial actions that shall not be postponed in order to protect the absentee's interests; he/she is also entitled to represent the absentee in any judicial action brought against the latter. Only under judicial consent – not to be granted but in special circumstances – may the curator transfer or encumber an estate, precious objects, bonds, stores and any other assets whose transfer or encumbrance does not fall within acts of administration. Anyway, he/she shall give action of the accounts before the Court (once a year or whenever he/she is required to); upon decision of final curatorship, the curator shall give action of the accounts to the final curators. The provisional curator is entitled to receive 10% of the net amount that he/she has accomplished.

The provisional curatorship terminates whenever: the absentee returns or makes any legal arrangements about his/her assets administration; the legal representative or the attorney of the absentee shows up; the absentee's assets are handed over either to the final curators or to the administrator of the estate; or when the absentee's death is an accomplished fact.

57. The final curatorship does not imply a previous provisional curatorship, though it may occur afterwards. The only requirements to be met are the absence

65. Articles 89–98, 99–113 and 114–119 of the CC; *see* as well Art. 1781, c).
66. Articles 120–121 of CC.
67. *Maxime* Arts 21, 23, 80, No. 2, 881–890, 914, 1001, 1016 and 1021–1025 of the Code of Civil Procedure and Arts 4, No. 1, b), 7, 24, No. 2, c), 28, No. 1, and 77–78 of the Legal Regime of the Inventory Process (approved by Law No. 23/2013 of 5 March, and published as an annex to this Law.

for more than two years and the lack of a legal representative or of an attorney or, even there being any such legal representatives, the absence period being superior to five years. Might one of such situations occur, the Public Prosecutor or any of the parties interested in the legal declaration of absence – the absentee's spouse not separated of persons and assets, his/her heirs as well as anyone who is entitled to his/her assets, whose right depends on his/her being dead – may apply to Court. The proceedings start with the legal declaration of absence and usually end with the partition of the absentee's assets. After the partition, the assets shall be delivered to the absentee's presumptive heirs; until then, the assets shall be administered by the administrator of the estate. Nevertheless, the presumptive legatees or other interested parties who might be entitled to certain assets belonging to the absentee may apply to the Court for the delivery of such assets upon the legal declaration of absence (the Court will try to be aware of the contents of the will eventually left by the absentee).

After the legal declaration of absence, whenever the absentee is married, his/her spouse not being separated of persons and assets may apply for the inventory and partition and may demand the allowance for maintenance he/she is entitled to. Pursuant to the mentioned legal declaration, disclaimer of the absentee's succession or the provision of the succession rights may also be admitted, though the effectiveness of such statements of will – as well as the acceptance of the inheritance or of legacies – depends on the 'final condition' of the absentee's survival.

The presumptive heirs and other interested ones to whom the absentee's assets have been handed are appointed as final curators. The Court may require anyone or some of them to make bail, taking into account the kind and value of the assets and revenues that may, eventually, have to be returned.

The final curators to whom the assets have been delivered have rights, limitations and duties identical to the ones aforementioned relating to the provisional curator. Nevertheless, the spouse and the ascendants and descendants of the absentee who have been appointed as final curators, once the assets have been delivered, are entitled to the whole of the profits; the remaining final curators are entitled only to two-thirds of the net income of the assets which are being administered by them, since the other one-third shall be kept for the absentee.

Final curatorship ceases: if the absentee returns; having been reported that he/she is alive and where he/she is living; whenever there are no doubts that he/she is dead; or if his/her presumed death is declared. In the two first cases the absentee's assets shall be handed over to him/her upon his/her request. While such request is not made, the curatorship regime shall be in force.

58. The declaration of presumed death does not imply a previous curatorship, though it may occur afterwards. It is required that ten years have elapsed upon the date the absentee has been last heard of, or only five years if, in the meantime, might he/she be alive, he/she would have attained 80 years old. Nevertheless, such a declaration cannot be given but five years after the date the absentee, would he/she be alive, would be of full age, that is to say, before the day he/she would be 23 years old. The aforementioned declaration may be legally applied for by the *supra* mentioned persons as interested parties in the legal declaration of absence.

The declaration of presumed death has the same effects as a death actually reported, but it does not imply, *ipso facto*, the dissolution of the marriage. This legal statutory limitation is quite understandable, since, as we have noticed, the absentee's spouse is not the only illegible person to require the referred declaration. When one year has elapsed upon the absentee having been last heard of, the spouse may bring a divorce suit. However, the law gives him/her a very strange alternative: to contract a new marriage without the previous one having been dissolved. In such a case, according to the law, might the absentee return or have been reported to be alive when the new marriage was performed, the first marriage is considered dissolved by divorce on the very date the presumed death has been declared.[68]

The absentee's assets are delivered to his/her beneficiaries under the same terms provided for the final curatorship, taking into account the necessary adaptations, but no bail shall be made, and if such bail has already been made, it may be withdrawn. Might it be proved that the absentee has died on a different date from the one assessed in the declaration of presumed death, the inheritance's rights apply to those who, on that date, would be his/her beneficiaries. However, this solution is bound by two restrictions: its application cannot damage the adverse possession rules;[69] and the new beneficiaries, in relation to the previous ones, only enjoy the same rights applicable by law to the absentee, might he/she return or might he/she prove to be alive. In such cases, the absentee's assets shall be returned to him/her just as they are; there is, nevertheless, a subrogation in rem, since those assets shall include, besides what has been left over, the following: the value of the transferred assets; the assets acquired with the value of the transferred assets (if in the title-deed the origin of the money is mentioned); and the assets directly acquired through exchange for the original assets. Moreover, might it be proved that the absentee's beneficiaries have used *mala fide* – knowledge that he/she was alive at the date when he/she had been declared as presumed dead – he/she is entitled to be compensated for the damages endured.

59. Might a person, considered legally as an absentee, be entitled to rights which shall not be unless he/she is alive, those rights pass on to the persons who would be his/her heirs, might the absentee actually be dead. Nevertheless, if a provisional curatorship has been established, such a regime is not altered, and those rights are subject to it. Might a final curatorship have been assessed, the persons concerned are, for all legal purposes, considered as final curators.

---

68. Cf. Arts 115–116 and 1781, c), of the CC.
69. Under the provisions of law (Art. 1287 of CC), adverse possession is the possession of the right of property or of another property right, kept for a certain period, which enables the possessor, unless provided otherwise, to acquire the right corresponding to his/her performance.

Chapter 2. Registration of Civil Status

§1. The Civil Registration and the Civil Registrar

60. Under legal terms, registration may be defined as the record in an adequate document – kept in a specific office under the responsibility of a specialized officer – of any legal facts (*lato sensu*) which should be kept for purposes of evidence and publicity.

According to Portuguese law, the adequate offices to record the relevant facts within Family and Succession Law are, as a rule, the Civil Registry Offices and the Central Registry Office.[70] The officer we shall refer to is the Civil Registrar, and the main documentary supports of the registration are computer supports.[71] The law sets out that civil registration is obligatory and, as we shall see *infra*, there is a long list of facts subject to this registration; such facts refer to the civil status (*lato sensu*) of the physical persons.

61. As a rule, the facts deemed to be registered cannot be summoned unless they are actually registered and their evidence can only be made through the means provided for in the Code of Civil Registry.[72] The legal documents referring to the registration are deemed as authentic and, therefore, they are vested with public faith. Thus, they bear a special credibility of proof of the facts they pertain to, though this proof may be liable to be contradicted on the grounds of the forgery of the documents concerned.[73]

62. Though the items above show the importance of the Civil Registrar, we cannot help saying that this importance has greatly increased during the last few years. In order to evidence this fact, one just has to compare the Code of Civil Registry now in force (1995) with the previous one (1978)[74] and look into other three Acts: Decree Law No. 163/95 of 13 July, Decree Law No. 272/2001 of 13 October and Decree Law No. 273/2001 of 13 October. From such a comparison comes up that the Civil Registrar has been charged with many powers and responsibilities which

70. Article 8 of the Code of Civil Registry (but *see also* Arts 5–7 and 9); and *see* the Organic Law No. for the Registry Offices and Notary (Decree Law No. 519-F2/79 of 29 December, with latest amendment introduced by Decree Law No. 209/2012 of 19 September) and Statutes for the Registration Services and Notary (passed by Regulatory Decree 55/80 of 8 October, with latest amendments introduced by Decree Law No. 209/2012).
71. Articles 5, 13, No. 1, 14, 15, 17, 54 and 68 of the Code of Civil Registry and Order (*Portaria*) 1109/2009 of 25 September.
72. Articles 2, 4, 191 and 211 (*see also* Arts 266 and 270) of the Code of Civil Registry. The following cases are, among others, exceptions to the rule of the obligation of previous registration as a condition to be summoned: a previous marriage not dissolved, as an impediment to the marriage; prenuptial agreement pertaining to the spouses, their heirs and third parties of the deed where the mentioned contract was written down; furthermore, certain judicial decisions related to parental responsibilities, except when it refers to third parties *in* bona fide. *See* Arts 1601, c), 1711, 1920-B and 1920-C of the CC.
73. Articles 363, No. 2, 370, 371, No. 1, and 372 of the CC and Arts 3, No. 1, 88 and 89 of the Code of Civil Registry.
74. The Code of Civil Registry of 1978 was passed by Decree Law No. 51/78 of 30 March.

used to be within the responsibility of the Courts.[75] However, it must be said that the possibility of appeal to the latter from the decisions of the Registrar has been safeguarded, as well as the remittance to the Court of the 'proceeding for an agreement to be reached between parties', might one of them make an opposition to the application made by the other and the conciliation attempt fails to succeed.

63. The Civil Registrar plays a fundamental role in the preliminary procedures of notice which usually precede the marriage; the civil marriage is conducted before the Civil Registrar, who is charged with important tasks during the ceremony; moreover, it is up to him/her to declare that 'on behalf of both the law and the Portuguese Republic' the contracting parties are 'united in matrimony'.[76]

Under legal provisions, the common procedure of justification, either judicial or administrative, as well as the special procedures foreseen in the Code of Civil Registry cannot be carried out but in the Civil Registry Office. When it comes to judicial justification – nowadays limited to the rectification of an irregular register whenever doubts arise on the persons' identity as well as on such situations when death has occurred under special circumstances – the Civil Registrar is, however, vested with instructing competencies; the Court is only entitled to require the Civil Registry Office to complete the file with extra information (might it be considered incomplete), and it is up to the Court to give the final decision. The administrative justification proceedings – applicable to overcome the lack of register and to declare its legal inexistence or nullity – are entirely dealt with in the Civil Registry Office, although they may turn into judicial justification proceedings.[77]

The special proceedings that can be found in the Code of Civil Registry are, nowadays, the following: declaration of an impediment to marriage; exemption of impediment to marriage; substitution of the parents' consent for the marriage of minor children under marriageable age; validation of a marriage voidable due to lack of witnesses; enactment of civil status document equivalent; divorce and separation of persons and assets by mutual consent; and alteration of name. The Civil Registrar's final decisions are liable to judicial appeal or superior claim, eventually followed by judicial appeal.[78]

In the previous item reference has been made to 'proceedings for an agreement to be reached between parties'.[79] Such procedure applies to the request of commutation of a separation of persons and assets into a divorce and to the following requests: maintenance to be granted to full age or emancipated children; allocation of the family home; deprivation of one spouse to bear the other spouse's surnames;

75. For example on such issues as: ordinary proceedings of justification; overcome of consent for the marriage of minors in marriageable age; exemption of bar to marriage; divorce or separation of persons and assets by mutual consent.
76. Articles 134–155 of the Code of Civil Registry.
77. Articles 221–244 of the Code of Civil Registry.
78. Articles 245–292 of the Code of Civil Registry. As to the proceedings of divorce and separation of persons and assets by mutual consent (Arts 271 and 272–274), attention should also be paid to Arts 12, No. 1, b), 14, 17 and 21 of Decree Law No. 272/2001 and to Arts 1775–1778-A of the CC. As to the other proceedings, *see also* Arts 13, 15 and 17, Nos 2 and 3 of the mentioned Decree Law No. 272/2001.
79. Decree Law No. 272/2001, Arts 5–10.

and permission to bear the former spouse's surnames. However, in such cases, the aforementioned procedure is not applicable might the request in question be made along with others within the scope of a judicial suit or when it represents an incident or a dependence of a pending action.

The Civil Registrar is entirely and solely responsible for the following procedures: reconciliation of separated spouses; exemption of an inter-nuptial period; and separation of persons and assets or divorce by mutual consent, except if the spouses do not present all the agreements legally demanded for the procedure in the Civil Registry Office or if the separation of persons and assets or divorce results from an agreement obtained within the scope of a judicial suit of separation or divorce without the consent of one of the spouses. Nevertheless, in the cases of separation or divorce occurring in the Civil Registry Office, whenever it comes to concern the exercise of parental responsibilities, it is provided that the Public Prosecutor shall appraise the agreement; might he/she consider that such agreement does not sufficiently protect the minors and if the spouses do not wish to have it altered according to the indications they are given, the case shall be remitted to the Court, pending decision thereon.[80]

We should note, finally, that in 2011 was created a special procedure of gender change in the civil register and corresponding amendment of the forename.[81] Such Law has been revoked in 2018, by Law No. 38/2018, of 7 August, that establishes a new regime regarding gender self-determination.

64. Considering the importance of the Civil Registrar's powers and responsibilities, the law is quite demanding in relation to the requirements that must be complied with in order to join this career: a degree in Law or equivalent academic qualification; aptitude tests and complementary training, except when applying as a Doctor of Laws; internship; and final tests.[82]

§2. Facts Subject to Registration and Means for Their Proof

65. We have mentioned that law abides a long list of facts referring to the civil status (*lato sensu*) of the physical persons to be registered. We highlight here the following: birth; filiation; adoption; marriage; prenuptial agreements and amendments to the couple's property regime; parental responsibilities regulation, respective modification or ending; deprivation of parental responsibilities as well as its limiting provisions; guardianship of minors, the administration of minors' assets and the custodianship of persons with diminished capacity; '*apadrinhamento civil*' and its revocation; provisional or final curatorship of absentees and their presumed death; death; and any other facts that may determine the amendment or the ending of the facts previously referred to or that must be registered upon special legal order

80. Article 1776-A of the CC and Art. 12, Nos 4–7 of Decree Law No. 272/2001.
81. This procedure is was regulated by the Law No. 7/2011 of 15 March.
82. *See* Decree Law No. 206/97 of 12 August.

(e.g., acquisition or loss of nationality). Nevertheless, relevant facts pertaining to aliens are not subject to registration unless they take place in Portuguese territory.[83]

Criminal Code lays out the crime of 'forgery of civil status', which is punishable with either an imprisonment sentence of up to 2 years or with a fine up to 240 days. Such crime applies to anyone who may register with the Civil Registry Office an inexistent birth or to anyone who might usurp, change, presume or cover up his/her civil status or the legal family status of another person, in order to jeopardize the official checking of the civil status or of the legal family status.[84]

66. According to the Code of Civil Registry, any facts deemed to be officially registered as well as the civil status of a person can be proved through access to civil registry database or through a certificate. The Code also provides that a 'notoriety certificate' may be issued to replace missing certificates.[85] Legal rules relating to the identity card and to the citizen card (most recently created) – sufficient documents to prove the civil identity of their holders – are contained in special legislation.[86]

The certificates are the main means to give evidence of the facts subject to civil registration. The Code lays out the several kinds of certificates, specifying: both its contents and layout; the legitimacy to make an application thereon; how to apply for such documents and the deadline for its issuance. Moreover, the Code sets out the prohibition to have certificates issued from documents that are filed with the Civil Registry Office and are considered classified.[87]

67. This chapter requires some words on the entitlement to apply for civil registration certificates.

According to the Code of Civil Registry, as a rule, the judicial or police authorities, as well as the Institute of the Registries and Notaries, may always apply for a certificate of any register or document whatsoever, and anyone is entitled to apply for a certificate of the registers of the Civil Registry.[88] Nevertheless, some exceptions fall under this rules.

The exceptions provided for in the Code of Civil Registry[89] cover the following: no certificate of a full copy (or photocopy) of registers of adoptive children can be issued unless the application is made by the persons to whom the register is related to, by their descendants or heirs and by their ascendants (however, when it comes to the latter, rules imposed by the CC relating to the confidentiality of the identity of both the adopter and birth parents of the adoptee must be complied with);[90] no

83. Article 1 of the Code of Civil Registry and Arts 16–19 of the Law of Nationality.
84. Article 248 of the Criminal Code.
85. Articles 211–217, 220-A–220-F and 266–270 of the Code of Civil Registry. Cf. also Order (*Portaria*) 145/2010 of 10 March (amended by *Portaria* 286/2012 of 20 September).
86. Law No. 33/99 of 18 May (with latest amendment made by Decree Law No. 194/2003 of 28 August) and Law No. 7/2007 of 5 February (amended by Law No. 91/2015 of 12 August).
87. Articles 211–217 of the Code of Civil Registry.
88. Article 214, Nos 1 and 6 of the Code of Civil Registry.
89. Article 214, Nos 2–5 of the Code of Civil Registry.
90. According to provisions of Art. 1985 of CC: the identity of the adopter cannot be revealed to the birth parents of the adoptee unless the former declares that he/she does not oppose to such a revelation; the birth parents can oppose, through an express statement, to their identity being revealed to the adopter.

certificate of full copy (or photocopy) of a register of sex change and corresponding amendment of the forename can be issued unless the application is made by the person to whom the register relates to, by his descendants or heirs or by judicial or police authorities for the purpose of criminal investigation; during the adoption proceedings, after adoption has been decreed or if the Registry Office has been notified of a judicial or administrative awarding of the minor, certificates of his/her birth registration shall be issued taking into account the rules and decisions concerning the confidentiality of the identity; whenever the affiliation registrations are to be considered secret, no certificates thereof can be issued but to instruct preliminary proceedings of notice for marriage purposes or for maintenance action.[91]

There is one exception to the mentioned rule on the entitlement of anyone applying for a certificate, which is not provided for in the Code of Civil Registry. Whenever a defendant must go on trial for a crime he/she is charged with his/her presence is only dispensable in particular cases – and not being possible to have him/her notified thereof or to put him/her under detention or preventive arrest, the defendant is notified by posters to be present in Court, otherwise he/she will be declared contumacious. Might such a declaration be made, the Court, in order to discourage a contumacy situation, may order the defendant to be forbidden to obtain certain documents, certificates or registers.[92]

91. According to provisions of Art. 1857 of CC (voluntary acknowledgement of adult or emancipated children), the voluntary acknowledgement register is considered secret might it depend on consent and as far as such consent is not granted. But the same article lays out the possibility of invoking the secret registration of the voluntary acknowledgement in a 'preliminary process of marriage' or in a legal suit of nullity or annulment of marriage.
92. *See* Arts 335 and 337 (specially 337, No. 3) of the Code of Criminal Procedure (passed by Decree Law No. 78/87 of 17 February, subject to several amendments, the latest of which was introduced by Law No. 130/2015 of 4 September).

Chapter 3. Personality Rights

§1. INTRODUCTION

68. According to the Constitution, the Portuguese Republic is based on the dignity of the human person and on the respect for and safeguard of fundamental rights and freedoms, and ensures the construction of a free, fair and solidary society. In its international relations, Portugal is governed by the principles of human rights respect, while the rules and principles of general or common international Law are an integral part of Portuguese Law. Moreover, as it was stressed out *supra* in the General Introduction, rules derived from several international conventions and agreements shall apply in Portuguese Law, such as the Convention for the Protection of Human Rights and Fundamental Freedoms (generally known as European Convention on Human Rights) and the International Pact on Civil and Political Rights. Also according to the Constitution: the safeguard of fundamental rights and freedoms shall be the basic task of the Portuguese State; all citizens shall have the same social dignity and shall be equal before the law; the fundamental rights embodied in the Constitution shall not exclude any others resulting from the laws and applicable rules of International Law; and the provisions of the Constitution and laws relating to fundamental rights shall be interpreted and inserted in accordance with the Universal Declaration of Human Rights.[93] Moreover, the Charter of Fundamental Rights of the EU shall be taken into account.

69. Quite a lot could be said about the extensive list of fundamental rights and duties (especially rights) implied in the CRP. However, only a brief reference will be made here on 'rights, freedoms and personal safeguards' included in a chapter of the fundamental law under that very heading,[94] though it shall be previously remarked that: every constitutional rule relating to rights, freedoms and safeguards shall be directly applicable (without requiring an ordinary legal intervention, might it be feasible otherwise) and binding on public and private entities; the rights, freedoms and safeguards may only be restricted by ordinary law in those cases expressly provided for in the Constitution, insofar as it is necessary to safeguard other rights or interests constitutionally protected; any restriction thereon shall be general and abstract in character and shall neither be retroactive nor limit in extent and scope the essential content of constitutional provisions; and, except in case of a state of siege or emergency, those rights shall not be suspended.[95]

Human life is proclaimed inviolable, and it is expressly declared that in no case shall the death penalty be applicable.[96] Moral and physical integrity are also considered inviolable; therefore, no one shall be subjected to torture or ill treatment or to cruel, degrading or inhuman punishment. Under the heading 'other personal rights' it is recognized that everybody shall have the right to 'personal identity, to

93. *See* Arts 1, 2, 7, No. 1, 8, 9, b), 13, No. 1 and 16 of the Constitution.
94. Chapter I of the Title II of the Constitution (Arts 24–47).
95. Articles 18 and 19, No. 1 of the Constitution.
96. Article 24 of the Constitution. In Portugal the death penalty for 'civil crimes' was abolished by Law Charter (*Carta de Lei*) of 1 Jul. 1867.

the development of his/her personality, to civil capacity, to citizenship, to his/her good name and reputation, to his/her own image, to free speech, to privacy in his/ her personal and family life and to be protected against any discrimination whatsoever'. But all this, though being a lot, is not everything. The right to enjoy freedom and security is also contemplated; rules on preventive arrest and detention are also set up; restrictions to the ruling of criminal law are established and guarantees regarding criminal proceedings are given; Portuguese citizens shall not be expelled from the national territory, limitations to the extradition of Portuguese and foreign citizens are laid down and, in any case, extradition is not allowed, might it be for political reasons or for crimes which, under the law of the applicant State, carry the death penalty or any other sentence that may cause 'irreversible damage to the physical integrity'; the individual's home and the privacy of his/her correspondence, as well as of any other means of private communication, are declared inviolable; everyone shall have the right to find a family and contract marriage on terms of complete equality, notwithstanding that the conditions for and effects of marriage and its dissolution shall be regulated by the ordinary law; spouses shall have equal rights and duties; parents shall have the right and duty to bring up their children, and the latter shall not be separated from them, except under very serious circumstances and 'always by judicial decision'; adoption shall be governed and protected by ordinary law; freedom of both expression and information as well as press freedom shall be protected; the freedom of conscience, religion and worship shall be inviolable; the intellectual, artistic and scientific creation shall be unrestricted; the freedom to learn and teach shall be safeguarded; the right to meet and demonstrate, the freedom of association and the right to choose a profession shall be recognized. As it can be seen, it is a long list, though incomplete and restricted to a single chapter of the Constitution.

§2. Personality Rights in the Civil, Criminal and Labour Codes

70. It can be declared that personality rights are *general*, since they are common to all individuals, that they are *absolute*, since everybody must respect them, and that they are usually *extra patrimonial*, since, as a rule, they bear no pecuniary value, notwithstanding the fact that their violation may require an indemnity.

On the issue of personality rights the Portuguese CC begins with an article dedicated to the 'general safeguard of personality' and finishes with an article on the 'voluntary limitation of the personality rights'. According to these rules, law protects individuals against any illicit offence, or danger of suffering such an offence, inflicted either to their physical or moral personality, and, unaware of the liability resulting from the offender's behaviour, the offended person, or the person about to be offended, 'may require the measures adequate to the circumstances', so that the effects of the offence committed may be relieved or the practice of the imminent offence may be avoided.[97] According to the latter, might it be contrary to the 'principles of the public policy' (domestic), the voluntary limitation to the performance

97. Article 70. As to civil liability and to the indemnity obligation *see* Arts 483 onwards and 562 onwards, of the CC.

of personality rights is null, and even if it is valid it is always revocable, though the duty for a compensation for the damages such revocation may cause shall be maintained.[98]

Between the two above-mentioned rules, the Code contains articles concerning: the protection of deceased people against offences; the safeguard of the name and pseudonym; 'letters' (both confidential and not confidential), family memories and any other confidential writings; the safeguard of the reputation; and the safeguard of the privacy of personal life.[99]

71. The protection granted by the CC to personality rights is, in some cases, complemented with the protection given by criminal law. In the special part of the Criminal Code, under the heading 'crimes against persons', the following crimes, among others, are implied: against life; against physical integrity; against personal freedom; against sexual freedom and self-determination; against honour; against the privacy of personal life; and against other personal legal interests (where one's word and reputation shall be included).[100]

We have mentioned various 'rights, freedoms and personal safeguards' contained in a chapter of the Constitution under such heading. Most of them are safeguarded by the Criminal law under the mentioned heading of 'crimes against persons'. Nevertheless, it must be stated that under other headings of the special part of the Criminal Code there are provisions for crimes whose punishment reinforces the constitutional protection of some other rights and freedoms at stake. Hence, on the issue of 'crimes against cultural identity and personal integrity' the crime of racial or religious discrimination is provided, as well as crimes of torture and other cruel, degrading or inhuman treatments; furthermore, under the heading 'crimes against life in society', 'crimes against religious sentiments'[101] are also provided.

72. Personality rights are also protected by labour legislation. Under the heading 'personality rights', the Labour Code contains rules relating to: the freedom of both expression and opinion; the physical and moral integrity; the safeguard of the privacy of personal life; the protection of personal data; the biometric data; medical tests and examinations; remote surveillance means; and the confidentiality of messages and information within the private scope.[102]

§3. Special Features Relating to Minors

73. We are going to point out some features relating to minors, though it is not quite common among us to deal, within the scope of 'personality rights', with some

98. Article 81 (*see also* Arts 280 and 281) of the CC.
99. Articles 71–80 of the CC.
100. Articles 131–139 and 143–199 of the Criminal Code.
101. Articles 240, 243–244 and 251–252. *See* as well the Criminal Law about the International Humanitarian Law violation (passed by Law No. 31/2004 of 22 July and amended by Law No. 59/2007 of 4 September).
102. Articles 14–22 of Labour Code (passed by Law No. 7/2009 of 12 February and with latest amendments made by Law No. 120/2015 of 1 September).

of the matters to be addressed. We will split the following explanation in four parts, in which we will try to summarize the solutions that the Portuguese law has envisaged for several questions minority may require.

I. Minors' Acts and Contracts

74. As we have seen in Chapter 1 of Part I, concerning the capacity to act in legal terms, a minor is a person not having attained 18 years of age; the minors not emancipated (by marriage) are, as a rule, considered legally unable to act personally and freely. Nevertheless, as we also pointed out, law takes into account several maturity stages and provides for several exceptions to the mentioned legal incapacity. Some of those exceptions were already mentioned; let us refer some others.

75. The law considers valid the contracts inherent to the minor's day-to-day life that may be within his/her 'natural capacity' and implying only expenses or the disposal of assets of small value.[103]

Contracts are also valid inasmuch as they relate to the profession, art or craft the minor has been authorized to perform, as well as any contracts entered in the carrying out of such profession, art or craft. Moreover, the administration acts or assets disposal that a minor over 16 has acquired through his/her work are also valid.[104]

As a rule, no minor shall be allowed to work, regardless of the kind of work and means of payment, unless he/she has attained 16 years of age, has finished compulsory schooling or is enrolled and attending secondary level of education and possesses physical and psychological capacity adequate to his/her work. However, there are exceptions to this rule. On one hand, a minor under 16 that has finished compulsory schooling or is enrolled and attending secondary level of education may, through written consent of his/her legal representatives, perform light tasks not jeopardizing his/her safety and health, his/her attendance at school and his/her development, as long as certain other requirements related with his/her school training are met. On the other hand, might these requirements be complied with, even if the minor over 16 has not finished compulsory schooling or is not enrolled and attending secondary level of education, he/she may enter into a legal contract of employment, though also subject to his/her legal representatives' consent, in writing. Whenever the minor has reached 16 and has finished compulsory schooling, or is enrolled and attending secondary level of education, a contract of employment made directly with him/her is valid, unless his/her legal representatives oppose thereto, in writing.[105]

103. Article 127, b), of the CC.
104. Article 127, a) and c), of the CC.
105. Articles 68, 69 and 70 of the Labour Code. Law No. 85/2009 of 27 August (amended by Law No. 65/2015 of 3 July) establishes the regime of compulsory schooling for children and young people of school age (between 6 and 18 years old). Regarding the basic and secondary education *see* Arts 6–10 of the Law of Bases of the Educational System (Law No. 46/86 of 14 October, with latest amendments made by the mentioned Law No. 85/2009).

76. Whenever the contract made by a minor is not considered legally valid, such contract may be declared void, not only upon application of his/her personal representatives, but also, if he/she dies, upon application of his/her heir (but always within certain deadlines), or upon his/her own application, within one year as from the date he/she has attained majority or emancipation.[106] Nevertheless, whenever a minor has obtained an advantage by falsely stating himself/herself to be of full-age or emancipated, he/she has no right to invoke that the contract is voidable.[107]

Whenever the contracts made by a minor are voidable, such an irregularity is reparable through his/her ratification on attaining majority or being emancipated; however, it may be repaired before such a date through ratification of his/her legal representatives, might it concern a contract that could have been made by them on his/her behalf.[108]

77. Under legal terms, the attorney, while entrusted voluntarily by someone with representative powers, only needs to have the capacity to understand and act accordingly required by the kind of contract he/she has been entrusted with.[109] He/she may be a minor of any age, as long as he/she is deemed to have sufficient understanding. Needless to say that his/her performance must abide by the granted powers, that the legal effects of such a contract enter within the legal sphere of the represented – whose legal capacity and legitimacy are required to contract and that the power of attorney expresses his/her discretionary will, allegedly free and conscientious; it is also a fact that the attorney can only be substituted by another person through consent of the represented one, or might such a replacement result from the provisions of the power of attorney or from the legal relationship it is based on; the power of attorney is also freely revocable, even without cause, unless it has also been granted in the interest of the attorney or in the interest of a third party and the interested party does not agree with such revocation (in such instance a cause is required); furthermore, for the purposes of making a contract declaration null or void, the lack of or the defected will of the represented are relevant features, as well as the ignorance of the facts which may affect the results of the contract.[110] Anyway, a minor having the legal possibility to be the attorney at power of an adult is quite interesting.

78. Like anyone 'of sound mind and memory' minors may acquire possession. And, such as adult persons, though they may not be 'of sound mind and memory', they can acquire possession of assets that may be subject to occupation.[111]

---

106. Article 125, No. 1 of the CC. *See* Art. 287, No. 2, which provides that, while the voidable contract is not completed, its irregularity can be applied for regardless of the term.
107. Article 126 of the CC.
108. Article 125, No. 2 of the CC.
109. Article 263 of the CC.
110. Articles 258, 259, No. 1, 262, No. 1, 264, No. 1, and 265, Nos 2 and 3 of the CC.
111. Article 1266 of the CC. Possession is the power or control similar to lawful ownership (Art. 1251 of the CC); except for some legal restrictions, animals and other movable assets may be acquired by occupation as far as they have never had any owner or have been abandoned, lost or hidden by their owners (Art. 1318 of the CC).

Minors, as well as other persons that do not have full legal capacity to act, may come to acquire it through acquisitive prescription.[112]

79. For both sexes marriageable age is legally set at 16. A minor who has attained the age of 16 may get married, notwithstanding the fact that he/she must obtain his/her legal representatives' consent.[113] Nevertheless, the Civil Registrar may remove such requirement, as long as he/she considers that the minor is sufficiently mature both physically and psychologically, and that there are reasons strong enough to justify the marriage.[114]

80. A minor under 14 is entitled to be a member of youth associations if his/her legal representatives grant their consent in writing; a minor above 14 may, without previous consent, either be a member of those associations or form new ones and be a member of their bodies.[115]

II. Minors' Responsibility for Torts

81. Concerning civil responsibility for illicit facts, Portuguese law applies a general principle according to which anyone who, with intent or through mere fault (by negligence) violates, in an illicit way, somebody's rights or any legal rule aimed at protecting third party's interests, must pay the victim a compensation for the torts resulting from such violation. As a rule, it is up to the victim to prove the offender's fault, unless there is a legal presumption of fault. And, where there is no other legal criteria (specific), the guilt shall be appreciated by the 'diligence of a *bonus pater familias*', taking into account the circumstances of each case; that means: the guilt is predicated (in abstract) taking into account the behaviour to be expected from a normal diligent person, might he/she be faced with the circumstances of the particular case. Nevertheless, no liability shall be entitled to the person who, at the very moment of the fact that caused the damage, had no ability of understanding or of willing without being to blame for such condition (might it be transitory).[116]

82. Minors, as well as adult persons, are liable for torts, unless they are in a situation in which they cannot be held responsible for damages they caused; such situations refer to persons who have not yet reached the age of seven and to those who are, by any cause, unable to think and act freely, unless this is a temporary situation and it has been caused by that same person and without this being his/her fault.[117] Nevertheless, two important rules shall be taken into account in this area: according

112. Article 1289, No. 2 of the CC. As to the presumption of absentees' death reference was made *supra* to the legal concept of adverse possession (Art. 1287 of the CC).
113. Articles 1601, a), and 1604, a), of the CC.
114. *Ibid.*, and Arts 255–257 of the Code of Civil Registry.
115. Article 2 of Law No. 124/99 of 20 August. Law No. 23/2006 of 23 June establishes the legal regime of young people's associations.
116. Articles 483, No. 1, 487 and 488, No. 1 of the CC.
117. Articles 488, No. 2, and 350, No. 2 of the CC.

to one of them, anyone who by law or by contract is bound to supervise other persons, due to their natural condition is liable for any damages caused on a third party, unless he/she can prove having accomplished his/her surveillance duty or give evidence that, regardless of having fulfilled that duty, damages would have been inflicted anyway; according to the other one, regardless of the fact that the unlawful fact causing damages has been committed by a person considered not to be responsible, this person may, for equity reasons, be condemned to repair those damages, though insofar as the adequate indemnity cannot be obtained from the persons charged with the duty of his/her surveillance.[118]

Whenever not only one but several persons are considered liable for the damages inflicted (e.g., both the offender and the persons in charge of his/her surveillance, or only the latter, e.g., the parents), there is a joint liability; therefore, the compensation may be entirely demanded from only one of them. Nevertheless, law grants the right of recourse from the others, according to each one's fault and according to the pursuant consequences, and presumes that the fault of each one was equal, though it may be proved otherwise. Therefore, the person from whom the whole compensation, which was to be shared among the others, has been required may demand from each one of them the share he/she is liable for.[119]

III. Minors' Responsibility for Crimes

83. It is obvious that minors, as any other individuals, can commit acts qualified by law as a crime. Might it be the case, the provisions of the law to be applied depend on the age group the minor falls in. Therefore, the situation shall be dealt with inasmuch as the minor is under or over 16; might he/she be under 16 there will still be a distinction for an age comprised between 12 and 16, or under 12. Anyway, the only hypothesis we shall consider applies to minors who are not psychologically impaired in such a way that turns them criminally not imputable.[120]

We shall make a brief reference to the system in force, though it shall be previously noticed that, in this area, Portugal has created, as from 1911, a body of legal statutes applying to minors under 16.[121]

84. According to law only minors under 16 are in a situation of incapacity due to minority.[122] Nevertheless, there is a special legislation providing for crimes committed by someone whose age is comprised between 16 and 21 that establishes a special system for young adults. Thus, for the purposes of that legislation, young

118. Articles 491 and 489, No. 1 of the CC.
119. Articles 497 and 350, No. 2 of the CC (*see also* Arts 524 and 526).
120. It is criminally not imputable the person (adult or minor) that, due to psychical impairment, is unable to judge that the fact qualified as a crime is illicit or cannot behave according to an accurate evaluation (Art. 20, No. 1 of the Criminal Code).
121. Childhood Protection Act (or Children's Protection Act) of 27 May 1911 ('Decree with force of Law' published in the *Government Gazette* No. 137 of 14 Jun. 1911; *see* in particular Arts 1 and 62 and following ones).
122. Article 19 of the Criminal Code.

people (minors) of 16 or 17 are embraced.[123] According to this legislation, the possibility of a special mitigation of the punishment (might the penalty be imprisonment) is provided for and shall be determined whenever the judge seriously considers that such mitigation will be advantageous to the social reintegration of the young offender. As to minors of 16 or 17, might the crime be punishable with a sentence of imprisonment up to two years, the judge, taking into account the personality of the young person and the circumstances of the fact, may order several measures, sole or jointly: admonition; entrusting the minor to his/her parents, to his/her guardian or to the person responsible for his/her custody; imposition of behaviours or duties; placing the minor under educational supervision; submission to assistance regime; entrusting the minor to a 'fit family', placing him/her in education or re-education institutions, under a regime of apprenticeship or labour, in a day-boarding school, or in a medical-psychological institute. Whenever the measures 'semi-boarding school or medical-psychological institute' have been ordered, the judge, upon application of the minor, after having heard the principal of the institution and considering that it is unquestionably advantageous for the minor's education and training, may authorize his/her staying there until he/she has achieved 18, but never beyond the date he/she has attained 21.

85. Whenever the facts legally qualified as crimes are committed by minors aged between 12 and 16, another special legislation shall apply: the 'Educative Tutelary Act' (*Lei Tutelar Educativa*).[124] Pursuant to the provisions of this law, might the minor have committed only one of such acts, the Court shall sentence him/her to one 'protective educational measure'; might he/she have committed more than one, the Court will sentence him/her to one or several 'protective educational measures'. All these measures, shortly designated as 'protective measures', 'aim at educating the minor for law abiding and for his/her integration, in a dignifying and responsible way, within the community life'. The enforcement of the 'protective measures' can be extended until the young man/woman has completed 21 years old, at which time it must cease.

The law foresees nine 'protective measures': admonition; denial of the right to drive motorcycles or to get permission to drive such vehicles; order a fine to be paid to the offended person; providing services or tasks for the benefit of the community; imposing rules of behaviour; imposing obligations; attendance of training programmes; educational monitoring; and internment in educational centres (either in a day regime, half-boarding or boarding regime). Among the measures that might prove adequate and sufficient for the applicable case, the Court may give priority to the one which shall reveal to be less restrictive to the minor's autonomy of life and capable of being better accepted by the minor and by his/her parents, his/her guardian or by the person who has his/her custody. Whatever the case might be, the selected measure must be suited to the seriousness of the offence and to the objectives of the sentence. Moreover, the duration of the internment in educational centre

123. Article 9 of the Criminal Code and Decree Law No. 401/82 of 23 September (Arts 1, 4 and 5).
124. The 'Educative Tutelary Act' was passed by Law No. 166/99 of 14 September and profoundly altered by Law No. 4/2015 of 15 January, which has republished the Law No. 166/99 as an annex.

cannot, in any case, exceed the maximum sentence of imprisonment legally foreseen for the type of crime correspondent to the fact in question.

Whenever the Court considers that several protective measures shall be imposed on the same minor (who has committed more than one crime) the Court shall order its simultaneous abiding, might it consider them as compatible; might it decide otherwise, and after the Public Prosecutor being consulted, the Court shall replace the whole or some of the measures by others or decide that they are to be abided successively, as long as certain terms are abided by.

86. Minors under 12 who have committed facts legally qualified as crimes shall neither be treated like criminals nor be subject to 'protective measures'. They shall be considered children in danger, therefore, subject to adequate dispositions foreseen in the 'Protection of Children and Young People in Danger Act', which actually does not provide for specific rules embracing the possibility of the minor having committed one or several of such facts.[125]

IV. Crimes Against Minors

87. Minors can, obviously, be victims of the most different crimes. In this explanation, however, we shall not deal but with crimes specifically foreseen to protect, directly or indirectly, the minors. However, we will take the opportunity to refer to some crimes (not all) with specific relevance when the victim is a minor.

88. The crime of 'domestic violence' is committed by who, repeatedly or not, inflicts to certain people physical or mental ill treatment, including corporal punishment, deprivation of liberty and sexual offences. In the absence of special aggravation of the penalty by the severity of the physical injury or by the death of the victim (cases in which the penalty shall be, respectively, of two to eight years and three to ten years of imprisonment), the offender is punished with one to five years of imprisonment, but if the offender commits the act (without qualification) against a minor, in the presence of a minor, in the common residence or in the victim's home, the penalty shall be of two to five years of imprisonment; and, regardless of any other accessory penalties (such as the prohibition of contact with the victim), who is convicted for the crime of 'domestic violence' can be deprived from the exercise of parental authority (parental responsibilities) or guardianship for a period of one to ten years. The crime of 'ill treatments' applies to anyone who, having the duty of care towards a minor (or another person particularly defenceless), his/her custody, being responsible for his/her upbringing or control, or being his/her employer, has the following behaviour: mistreats him/her, either physically or psychologically, or treats him/her in a cruel way; charges him/her with dangerous, inhuman or prohibited activities; or overcharges him/her with excessive work. For such a crime a penalty of one to five years' imprisonment is foreseen, if to the offender

125. The mentioned Protection Act was passed by Law No. 147/99 of 1 September (with latest amendments made by Law No. 142/2015 of 8 September) and partially complemented by Decree Law No. 332-B/2000 of 30 December.

doesn't fit more severe punishment foreseen in another legal rule; and in case of severe physical injury or of death of the victim the imprisonment penalty will be, respectively, of two to eight years and three to ten years. According to the legal rule concerning the crime of 'human traffic': who, by any means, conscripting, entice, transporting or host a minor, or deliver, offer or accept him/her for the purpose of exploitation is punishable with a penalty of three to ten years of imprisonment (or three to twelve if the offender does it professionally or with lucrative intent); and who upon payment or other consideration, offer, deliver, solicit or accept a minor, or obtains or provide consent to his/her adoption, is punished with imprisonment from one to five years. The consent of the victim of these crimes does not preclude in any case the illegality of the fact.[126]

89. The Criminal Code foresees seven crimes against minors, concerning 'sexual self-determination': sexual abuse of children; sexual abuse of dependant minors; sexual acts with adolescents; using prostitution of minors; incitement to prostitution of minors; pornography of minors; and enticement of minors for sexual purposes.

The crime of sexual abuse of children refers, first of all, to someone who practices a 'relevant sexual act' with or on a child under 14 or leads the child to commit such an act with somebody else. Such an offence is punishable with a penalty of one to eight years' imprisonment. The law does not specify the meaning of 'relevant sexual act', but it seems that the sexual act shall be qualified as 'relevant' for the purpose of this kind of crime, whenever its nature, contents or meaning should be considered relevant according to the victim's sexual determination, from an objective point of view. That shall not be the case, as a rule, might the act be, for instance, a mere kiss, but it shall fall under this crime, if, for instance, the offender masturbates the victim or leads the victim to masturbate him or if he leads the victim to practice such acts with somebody else. Besides the law states expressly that if the relevant sexual act consists in copula, anal or oral coitus, or vaginal or anal introduction of body parts or objects, the offender shall be punished with a penalty of three to ten years' imprisonment. Furthermore, the following acts shall be punished with a sentence of imprisonment up to three years (or from six months to five years, whenever a pursuit of gain is implied): might the offender perform exhibitionistic acts before the victim or acts upon the victim through pornographic conversation, writing, spectacle or object or if he/she entice the victim to witness sexual abuse or sexual activities.

The crime of sexual abuse on dependent minors aims at the same behaviours but relating to minors whose age is comprised between 14 and 18, and who have been entrusted with the offender for the purposes of education or support. The penalty foreseen for the two first groups of acts is comprised between one and eight years' imprisonment. The other behaviours are punishable with a sentence of imprisonment up to one year or, when a lucrative intent is implied, up to five years.

The crime of sexual acts with adolescents occurs when a person of full age, and taking advantage of the inexperience of the victim, practices a 'relevant sexual act'

126. Articles 152, 152-A (and *see* Art. 144) and 160 of the Criminal Code.

with a minor whose age is comprised between 14 and 16 or leads the victim to practice such an act with others. In these cases, the offender shall be punished with a penalty of imprisonment up to two years. However, if the 'relevant sexual act' consists in copula, anal or oral coitus, or vaginal or anal introduction of body parts or objects, the offender shall be punished with imprisonment up to three years. The criminal action for the crime of sexual acts with adolescents depends on complaint, unless suicide or death of the victim occurs.

The crime of using prostitution of minors is committed by whom, being a person of full age, and upon payment or other consideration, practice a 'relevant sexual act' with a minor between 14 and 18 years old. The offender shall be punished with imprisonment up to two years, but a more severe penalty shall be applied (imprisonment up to three years) if the 'relevant sexual act' consists in copula, oral or anal coitus, or vaginal or anal introduction of body parts or objects.

The crime of incitement to prostitution of minors is committed by who promote, favour or facilitate the activity of prostitution by a minor or entice a minor for that end. This crime is punishable with imprisonment from one to eight years. However, if the offender uses violence, serious threat, trick, fraudulent manoeuvre, abuse of authority resulting from a family relationship, from guardianship or curatorship, or from hierarchical dependency, or if he/she acts professionally or with lucrative intent, or taking advantage of the psychological incapacity or some other special vulnerability of the victim, the penalty shall be comprised between two and ten years of imprisonment.

The crime of pornography of minors is committed by whoever: (a) use a minor in a pornographic spectacle or entice a minor for that end; (b) use a minor in a photo, film or recording, or entice a minor for these purposes; (c) produce, distribute, import, export, disclose, display or in any way transfer such materials; (d) or acquire or hold such materials with the purpose of its distribution, importation, exportation, disclosure, displaying or transference. The penalty will be of one to five of imprisonment, but if the offender performs the acts in question professionally or with lucrative intent, or if he/she practices the acts specified in (a) or (b) using violence or serious threat, the penalty shall be of one to eight years of imprisonment. If the acts mentioned in (c) or (d) are committed using pornographic material with realistic representation of a minor the offender shall be punished with imprisonment up to two years.

The crime of enticement of minors for sexual purposes is committed by whom, being a person of full age, and by using information and communication technologies, entice a minor for an encounter aiming the practice of certain acts of sexual abuse or of pornography of minors. This crime is punishable with imprisonment up to one year or, if the mentioned enticement is followed by material acts conducive to the encounter, up to two years.

The law also provides for aggravation punishment for the above-mentioned crimes against the 'sexual self-determination' (and for crimes against the 'sexual freedom') in view of the relationship between the victim and the offender, the especially harmful result of the crime, the age of the minor and the simultaneous verification of more than one relevant circumstance. However, in the field of the crimes against sexual freedom and sexual self-determination of a minor, if there is no aggravation of the penalty by the result of the crime, the Public Prosecutor, considering the interest of the victim, can determine the 'provisional suspension of the process' (up to five years), provided that a similar measure for a crime of the same nature has not been previously applied.

In accordance with the seriousness of the fact committed and its connection with the function exercised by the offender, whoever is punished for a sexual crime (any sexual crime), if the victim is not a minor, can also be convicted, for a period of two to twenty years, in the accessory penalty of prohibition to exercise a profession, an employment, functions or activities that involve having regular contact with minors and also in the accessory penalty of prohibition to have a minor under his/her legal care. However, these accessory penalties shall be fixed for a period between five and twenty years if the victim is a minor. And whoever is punished for a sexual crime (any sexual crime) against his/her descendant or against descendant of his/her spouse (or descendant of the person with whom the offender maintains a similar de facto relationship) shall also be punished with the accessory penalty of deprivation from the exercise of parental responsibilities for a period between five and twenty years.[127]

90. The Criminal Code foresees the crime of 'the minor being taken away'. Certainly, foreseeing and punishing such a crime aims at protecting the status of the minors' legal representatives or of the persons or institutions to which the minors were entrusted. But it is also certain that this protection aims, in the end, to safeguard the minor's well-being, since it is taken for granted that such powers are given having the minor's interests in mind. Such a crime shall apply to the person that: takes the minor away; leads the minor to run away, through violent means or threatening him/her in a very malicious way; or, repeated and unjustifiably, does not comply with the rules established in the regulation of parental responsibilities, by refusing, delaying or hindering significantly the delivery or acceptance of the minor. The penalties foreseen are a maximum of two years of imprisonment or a fine up to 240 days, but in the latter case mentioned the penalty will be especially attenuated when the conduct of the offender has been constrained by respect for the wishes of the child over the age of 12 years.[128]

91. Finally, we consider pertinent to refer the crime of 'violation of maintenance obligation'. Such a crime applies to a person who is legally obliged to maintenance and, though being able to do so, does not comply with this obligation within two

127. In the Criminal Code: these accessory penalties are foreseen in Arts 69-B and 69-C; the mentioned seven types of crimes against 'sexual self-determination' are provided in Arts 171–176-A; the other sexual crimes (against sexual freedom) are foreseen in Arts 163–170; the aggravations of the penalties for sexual crimes are provided in Art. 177; and the hypothesis of provisional suspension of the process is foreseen in Art. 178, Nos 3 and 4. We should mention that, according to Art. 118, No. 5, in case of crimes against sexual freedom and sexual self-determination of minors, as well as in the crime of female genital mutilation (foreseen in Art. 144-A), being the victim a minor, the criminal procedure does not become extinct, by effect of prescription, before the victim has completed 23 years old. Law No. 103/2015 of 24 August created a 'registration system of criminal identification of convicted for crimes against sexual self-determination and sexual freedom of a minor' (system published as an annex to the same law).

128. Article 249, No. 1 of the Criminal Code.

months following the due date. The offender is punished with a fine penalty of up to 120 days or, if he practice repeatedly the crime, with a penalty of imprisonment up to one year or a fine up to 120 days. However, if the failure to comply with the maintenance obligation endangers the satisfaction, without a third party's aid, of the needs of the person entitled to the maintenance, the penalty shall be of imprisonment up to two years or a fine up to 240 days. The same penalty shall be applied to whom, with the intention not to comply, puts himself/herself in the impossibility to comply and fails to comply creating the mentioned danger. The object of setting down this crime is not only the protection of minors, but it is a fact that they are most frequently the great victims of such behaviour. Nevertheless, if such obligation is complied with, the Court may discharge the sentence the offender has been charged with, or may abolish, on the whole or partially, the pending sentence.[129]

92. Portuguese Law has created a system whose aim is safeguarding the maintenance owed to minors.[130] According to this legislation, whenever a person judicially bound to maintenance to a minor living in Portugal fails to comply with such a duty by his/her own freewill, might it not be possible to get the arrears through any other means provided for in the law, and if the minor neither gets a net income superior to the social support index nor receives some other income through the person he/she is entrusted with, it is up to the State to ensure the payment of the arrears at stake up to the time the maintenance duty is complied with. The amounts to be paid by the State shall be set up bearing the following in mind: the economic situation of the household the minor is inserted in; the outstanding maintenance; and the specific needs of the minor. The law lays down a maximum limit for the amounts to be paid by the State. At present, they shall not exceed the amount of EUR 42,890 a month, for each debtor.

129. Article 250, Nos 1–4 and 6 of the Criminal Code.

130. Law No. 75/98 of 19 November (cf. Arts 1 and 2, as amended by the Law No. 66-B/2012 of 31 December). Besides the rest of this law, *see* as well the inherent regulation: Decree Law No. 164/99 of 13 May, with latest amendments introduced by Law No. 64/2012 of 20 December.

Chapter 4. Names

§1. The Right to a Name

93. Names are designed to identify a person in birth records. They form the main means by which people are individualized, in isolation and in relation to the family to which they belong.

The Law cannot deprive a person of the protection due to his/her name, upon which very legitimate interests converge. The name does not only serve the interests of the individual, by affirming his/her personal identity, but also serves a community interest, a social need to individualize its citizens. The name may also be a factor of integration of the individual into the family society (as in the case of adoption, for example), a source of economic or social interests (as with the former spouse that keeps the other's name for professional purposes) or even a manifestation of a sentimental bond between the individual and the moral patrimony of the family clan.

Article 26, No. 1 of the Constitution establishes that everyone has the right to a personal identity. The name now constitutes the core of this personal identity. In Article 72, No. 1 of the CC, the right to a name has been legislatively sanctioned as a right of personality: 'every person has the right to use their name, in its complete or abbreviated form, and to oppose any illicit use of it for their identification or for any other purposes'; while No. 2 establishes the name holder's limitations, stipulating that it may not be used 'in a way that hinders the interests of anyone who has the same name or a similar one'. The right to a name is protected both in private law (through the specific means of safeguarding the right to a name) and by the general means of protection of any right of personality (as in the public sphere), whether the regulation processes are instigated through official initiative or by criminal action, such as when a false name has been used or when the name has been illegally altered.

§2. Composition of the Name

94. The system of naming used in Portugal has traditionally been the so-called peninsula system (also adopted in Spain and in some South American countries), in which the given name is followed by surnames from both lineages, paternal and maternal. It is distinguished from the European system, which consists of a given name (or Christian name) followed by a surname from only one line, normally the paternal, and which constitutes the matrimonial name.

Before the 1977 Reform of the CC, each name had to contain a maximum of six words, consisting of up to two given names and four surnames from both family lines, the last being one of the father's surnames or one to which he/she has a right. The father had priority regarding the choice of name, and, while the mother had the right to be heard, the father's will would prevail in the event of disagreement, as a corollary of marital power.

With the 1977 Reform, the children could use surnames from both lines or only from one, at their discretion, and it was no longer mandatory that the last surname should be from the paternal line; in the event of disagreement between the parents, it would be up to the judge to decide in the interest of the child.[131]

Thus, in the light of the Code of Civil Registry (which thoroughly and systematically regulates the name of natural persons), the complete name of a person should consist of a maximum of six words, simple or compound, of which only two may correspond to the given name and four to the surname.[132] The complete name will generally be attributed by the person making the declaration for the birth records, or by the registrar in the case of abandoned children. In this last situation, the registrar should preferably choose names that are in common usage and also try to avoid ambiguous names or anything that might recall the child's abandoned condition.

95. As to given names, the choice is free in principle, though observing the restrictions of Article 103 of the Code of Civil Registry. Given names should be Portuguese whenever the child being registered is the offspring of Portuguese parents; it should appear in the national or adapted onomasticon, be graphically and phonetically adapted to the Portuguese language, and should not lead to confusions about the sex of the child. This does not invalidate the long-term custom in Portugal of including Maria in the formation of male names, when preceded by another masculine name (e.g., Francisco Maria, Luís Maria) or of forming female names with male ones (e.g., Maria Manuel, Maria João).

96. The same given name may not be given to siblings, unless one of them has died. Foreign names are admitted if the child being registered is foreign or if it has a nationality other than Portuguese. The words 'Júnior' or 'Sénior' are not part of the traditional national onomasticon, and some doubts therefore exist as to their admissibility. They are normally used as adjectives in everyday language or at the end of the name, to distinguish son and father respectively. A decision at the STJ in 2002 allowed a father to attribute Júnior to his son as the second given name. After all, it is a word of Latin root, adopted directly by the Portuguese language; it is not aberrant, comical or offensive to the general susceptibility of Portuguese people, and as such is able to express the constant evolution of the onomasticon, as an important aspect of the living language.

As for surnames, these are chosen from amongst those that belong to both or to only one of the parents or from surnames to which they have a right. This rule applies to both children born to married parents and to those who are not; all that is required is that on the date the birth records are drawn up maternity and/or paternity is legally established. There is no preference for children born to unmarried parents to take the mother's surname. The child's name may not therefore include surnames belonging to others (unless the parents have no surname).

An individual that is the child of unknown parents or who has been abandoned will be given surnames by the registrar. Here, the acquisition of surnames is grounded in an act of concession of public authority, of constitutive effect.

131. Article 1875, Nos 1 and 2 of the CC.
132. Article 103, No. 2 of the Code of Civil Registry.

The repetition of surnames is only admissible when both branches – paternal and maternal – have the same surname.

Finally, in cases where paternity is not established, the CC[133] allows for the child to be given the mother's husband's surnames, if both the mother and her husband declare before an employee of the registry office that this is their will, in flagrant breach of the principle of biological truth.

§3. Alteration of Name/Surname

97. One of the characteristics of personal names in the Portuguese system is their immutability, from the moment they are attributed and established in the respective birth records. This is justified by the private interest in the identification of individuals and by the social and public function that the name plays.

This immutability should be seen only as a tendency, since there have been various justifications presented to diverge from this principle. Thus, we can distinguish.

I. The Alteration of Name upon a Process of Ministerial Authorization

98. The name established in the birth records may be modified upon authorization from the Ministry of Justice.[134] This alteration may consist of an addition, suppression, substitution or simple change in the order of names, but it can never violate the legal principles underlying the composition of the name. The reasons invoked for the alteration are taken into account in a discretionary manner.

A judgment from the STJ in 2002 illustrates this situation. The applicant, who had lost surname x as a result of the removal of paternity, had applied for authorization to recover that name (to which surnames of the mother and the biological father would be added), grounded in the right to personal identity that covers not only the right to the name but also the right to a personal history; this was not granted by the court, which concluded that an alteration could not be authorized that did not comply with the respective legal framework.

II. Alteration of Name Through Change of Status

A. *Alteration Through Marriage*

99. The fundamental rule is laid down in Article 1677 of the CC, according to which spouses retain their own surnames but may add surnames of the other, up to a maximum of two.[135] The legislator has made the spirit of individualism prevail over the institutional and unitary image of the family. The woman may add some of her husband's surnames to her own (which is what occurs most frequently today) or

133. Article 1876, No. 1 of the CC.
134. Article 278 onwards of the Code of Civil Registry.
135. Article 103, No. 2, subpara. a) of the Code of Civil Registry.

inversely, the husband may add to his name some of his wife's surnames. It is still literally possible to do both at the same time, that is, for both spouses to add surnames from the other (rare possibility). Today, it is becoming more frequent for women to keep only their maiden names, for professional and other reasons.

B. Alteration Through Death of Spouse and Second Marriage

100. Spouses that have added their husband's or wife's name to their own retain those names upon widowhood. If they marry again, they may retain the surnames from the first marriage, if the intention to do so is declared before the new marriage is celebrated,[136] although in this case, they may not add surnames from the second marriage.[137] If they do not make this declaration before the second marriage is contracted, the widow or widower will lose the surnames that they adopted in the first marriage, being then able to add surnames from the second one.

C. Alteration in the Event of Separation or Divorce

101. When separation has been decreed, each spouse retains the other's surnames if these have been adopted. However, nothing prevents them from renouncing to their spouse's surnames, under the general terms of the Code of Civil Registry.[138]

In the case of divorce, each spouse will, in principle, lose any surnames that they have adopted from the other. However, if for any reason they wish to retain the surnames of the other spouse (such as in situations in which the name of the other spouse has been used in specific commercial, literary or artistic circles, or if the court has been awarded the custody of children who use the father's name), that spouse will have to give his/her consent or it will have to be authorized by the court, taking into account the reasons invoked.[139]

It should also be remembered that, in the event of the death of one of the spouses, from whom a separation or divorce has been decreed, the spouse that retains the surnames of the other may be deprived by the court of the right to use them if that usage could seriously harm the moral interests of the other spouse or of his/her family.[140]

136. Article 1677-A of the CC.
137. Article 103, No. 5 of the Code of Civil Registry.
138. Article 103, No. 2, subpara. d) of the Code of Civil Registry.
139. Article 104, No. 4 of the Code of Civil Registry.
140. Article 1677-C of the CC.

D. Alteration of Name on the Grounds of Adoption

102. A child does not usually have the right to determine his/her own name. However, when adoption has been decreed, the adoptee loses his/her original surnames, and a new name is constituted based on the surname(s) of the adopter(s).[141] The adoptee effectively acquires the status of son or daughter of the adopter and becomes a member of his/her family, extinguishing all family relations with their natural ascendants. The adoption is registered in the birth records,[142] and certain requirements must be met concerning the need to maintain the identity of the adopter and of the adoptee's natural parents a secret.[143] Exceptionally, upon application by the adopter, the court may modify the child's given name, if this safeguards his/her interests, such as the right to a personal identity, and facilitates integration into the family.[144]

On the other hand, in the case of simple adoption, the adoptee does not lose his/her original surnames, although the judge may, on the request of the adopter, also attribute some of the adopter's surnames, which will be joined to those of the natural family.[145]

E. Alteration of Name in Situations of Gender Self-Determination

103. Until 2011, the procedures for changing gender and name derived from general rules: the interested party had to adopt the physical characteristics of the intended gender, through surgery, and file a court action against the state, to correct the gender assigned by the civil registry office at birth – male or female – as it did not correspond to the actual physical characteristics of their body; and submit a change of name accordingly. In 2011, Law No. 7/2011 of 15 March was the first *specific* law to regulate the issue. The essential traits of this legal change were: courts gave way to the civil registry office; access was only granted to adult persons; a medical report was required proving gender identity disorder or transsexualism. Under this Law, applicants, apart from applying for a declaration that they were of the opposite sex, would also apply for a rectification of all records containing their name, indicating the name that they wished to use and applying for a new birth certificate expressing the new sex.[146] However, this Law has been revoked by Law No. 38/2018 of 7 August that adopted a new paradigm and established a new regime. The new paradigm highlights the psychosocial nature of gender definition and understands change of gender within the context of protecting fundamental rights, particularly the right to free development of personality.[147]

141. Article 1988, No. 1 of the CC.
142. Article 69, No. 1, subpara. f) of the Code of Civil Registry.
143. Article 13, Nos 2 and 3 and Arts 214, Nos 2 and 3 of the Code of Civil Registry.
144. Article 1988, No. 2 of the CC.
145. Article 1995 of the CC.
146. Article 3, No. 1, a) of Law No. 7/2011.
147. Articles 2 and 3 of Law No. 38/2018.

104. The question of transsexuality or transgenderism has only been focused by Portuguese jurists in recent decades. The first legal decisions on this matter took place in the 1980s, when the legal recognition of sex change raised difficulties on various levels. The immediate issue was of its admissibility. The counter position invoked the principle of the immutability of sex, of sex as part of a person's status, and therefore unchangeable. Admissibility of sex changing is nowadays a solved issue, although the question of the requirements may still be subject to debate.

105. Regarding the procedural means for achieving legal recognition of sex change, the traditional way involved a status suit with ordinary proceedings, in which an application was made to the court to declare that the individual had a different sex to that registered in the records.[148]

Law No. 7/2011 allowed the application to be made at the Civil Registrar from the beginning, avoiding any court decision. This option remains in the current regime.[149] This is different from any case where there has been a factual error, an imprecision at the time of birth as to the diagnosis of sex; this would be corrected by a simple rectification of records at the Civil Registry.

106. According to the new regime, however, the application must no longer be grounded on a medical report, produced by a multidisciplinary team with sexology skills, from any public or private, national or foreign, institution. Formalities are but an application submitted to a civil registry office to change the mention of the gender and first name.[150] A new request, however, can only be made with previous judicial authorization.[151]

107. The previous marital status is not an obstacle to these changes, probably also due to the recent admissibility of same-sex marriages in Portugal;[152] but the annotation of the new sex in the civil registry can only be made upon consent of the other spouse,[153] in order to preserve the right of intimacy of private and family life.

The pre-existence of children is not an obstacle as well.

Gender self-determination in these conditions is granted to under 18 years of age through their legal representatives and to any intersex person from the moment he or she demonstrates his or her gender identity.[154] Surgeries on the intersex minor before he or she had expressed his or her gender identity are forbidden.[155]

Instead of a long-term proceeding, the new proceeding will take eight days. It is only demanded that the applicants have fulfilled the aforementioned legal requirements and it cannot be demanded any evidence of sex change medical proceedings.[156]

148. Article 69, No. 1, subpara. n) of the Code of Civil Registry.
149. Article 6, No. 1 of Law No. 38/2018.
150. Article 8 of Law No. 38/2018.
151. Article 6, No. 2 of Law No. 38/2018.
152. Law No. 9/2010 of 31 May.
153. Article 70, No. 1, i) of the Code of Civil Registry.
154. Article 7 of Law No. 38/2018.
155. Article 5 of Law No. 38/2018.
156. Article 9 of Law No. 38/2018.

108. It should also be noted that the legal recognition of sex change should be given *ex nunc* force, and therefore it does not affect any rights and obligations previously obtained.[157]

III. Other Cases of Name Alteration

109. Other cases of name alteration include the following:

- Alterations resulting from rectification of records.[158]
- Alterations by means of the simple insertion of connector particles in surnames.[159]
- Alteration grounded on acknowledgement subsequent to registration in the birth records.[160]
- Alteration/elimination of the mother's husband's surnames, upon application by the son or daughter, two years after achieving majority or emancipation.[161]

157. Article 10 of Law No. 38/2018.
158. Article 104, No. 2, subpara. b) of the Code of Civil Registry.
159. Article 104, No. 2, subpara. c) of the Code of Civil Registry.
160. Article 104, No. 2, subpara. a) of the Code of Civil Registry.
161. Article 1876, No. 2 CC–Art. 104, No. 2, subpara. e) of the Code of Civil Registry.

Chapter 5. Nationality

§1. Nationality as a Concrete Manifestation of Personal Law

110. Within the ambit of private international law, is there any consensus as to the determination of personal law – the law of nationality or domicile? Both express a close connection with the person in question and ensure a continuity of the legal qualities and situations of personal status.

The Portuguese system follows the principle of nationality, as does a vast majority of continental European systems (*see* Articles 25 and 31, No. 1 of the CC): personal law (which regulates matters as important as status and capacity of persons, family relations, succession through death, rights of personality, etc.), except when there is a special provision, is nationality law.

Thus, the presuppositions and requirements of marriage (capacity and 'defects of will') are regulated, for each party, by the respective law of nationality.[162] Even in matters of form of marriage, the rule is *lex loci celebrationis*, although if it is a marriage between two foreigners in Portugal, the form of the national law of either of the spouses may be observed if the marriage is to be celebrated before the respective diplomatic or consular agents, and if the same competency of Portuguese agents is recognized by law.[163]

The Council Regulation (EU) No. 1259/2010 of 20 December 2010 (also known as 'Rome III') regulates the applicable law for divorce or judicial separation. The spouses can agree to designate the applicable law with which they have a special connection (common habitual residence, last common habitual residence or common nationality) or the law of the forum. In the absence of this choice of law, the competent law will be determined by the law of the State of their habitual residence at the time the court is seized, or, failing, where they were last habitually resident, or, failing, common national law or, in last resort, the law where the court is seized.[164]

In matters of succession, Portugal is one of a group of countries which, following Savigny, defended the unity of law applicable to succession, upon the personal law of the testator. The national system thus demands that personal law of the nationality applies, regarding both legal and voluntary succession.[165]

The regulation of the succession of persons who die on or after 17 August 2015 is regulated by the Regulation (EU) No. 650/2012 of the European Parliament and of the Council of 4 July 2012. This new regulation determines that the law shall be the law of the State in which the deceased had his or her habitual residence at the time of death, unless the person chooses the law of the country of his or her nationality.[166]

162. Article 49 of the CC.
163. Article 51 of the CC.
164. Article 8 of the Council Regulation (EU) No. 1259/2010.
165. Article 62 of the CC.
166. Articles 20, 21 and 22 of the Regulation (EU) No. 650/2012.

111. However, it is important that this principle of nationality is applied in a flexible way. There are instances in which the principle of nationality does not apply, such as in the case of displaced persons and political refugees.[167] On the international level, the tendency today is taking into account both aspects: nationality and habitual residence. Finally, in the Portuguese system itself, to avoid the uncertainty and instability of legal situations resulting from a divergence between the law of the countries of nationality and residence, there is a compromise solution sanctioned in Article 31, No. 2 of the CC. This involves recognizing certain legal situations constituted abroad under the law of domicile, while national law, in the light of which the deal is invalid, will be the law with primary competency to regulate the situation. Let us suppose that Portuguese courts were asked to appreciate the validity and provide recognition of a marriage celebrated some years before between two Peruvians in Turkey, where they normally resided. Although in the light of nationality law, Peruvian law, the marriage would be invalid, Portuguese courts would recognize it if it were valid under the legal system of the country of residence.

§2. Restrictions on Non-Portuguese Citizens

112. As a principle, under the terms of Article 15 of the Constitution, foreigners and displaced persons that are or reside in Portugal enjoy the rights and are subject to the same duties of Portuguese citizens. For this reason, they cannot be deprived of that essential nucleus of rights, freedoms and safeguards that under no circumstances may be suspended (right to life, to personal integrity, to personal identity, to citizenship, to freedom of conscience and religion, etc.), as well as of rights, freedoms and safeguards strictly related to the development of human personality (e.g., right to constitute a family and to contract marriage).

However, there are some fundamental rights that belong exclusively to Portuguese citizens: political rights; the exercise of public office, when this is not of a predominantly technical nature; and rights and duties reserved by the Constitution and by law exclusively for Portuguese citizens. For example, foreign citizens may not hold posts in the organs of sovereignty (the position of President of the Republic must be held by a Portuguese citizen of origin and not naturalized), the organs of government in the autonomous regions, the armed forces or in the diplomatic service. There are always material grounds to justify any apparent discrimination. The revision of the Fundamental Law in 1992 extended some political rights to foreigners resident in the country, and under conditions of reciprocity, they may be attributed active and passive electoral capacity for the election of the organs of local government.

113. The distinction between Portuguese and foreign citizens is attenuated with regards to two special communities. The Communities of the Portuguese-Speaking

167. Respectively, Art. 32 of the CC and Art. 12 of the Geneva Convention relative to the Status of Refugees of 1958.

Countries may, in certain conditions, have some rights recognized that are not usually conferred upon foreigners; while citizens of EU Member States may be attributed the right to elect and be elected as Deputies of the European Parliament.

§3. Law of Nationality

I. Acquisition

114. Portuguese nationality may be acquired at birth or be derived (acquired at a later moment in the life of the interested party).

A. Acquisition at Birth

115. The acquisition of the Portuguese nationality at birth may result in law directly from three different circumstances:[168]

(a) the case of a child of a Portuguese parent that is born on Portuguese territory or under Portuguese administration;
(b) the case of a child of a Portuguese parent that is born abroad, if the parent is at the service of the Portuguese State;
(c) the case of a child born on Portuguese territory that does not possess other nationality.

However, the will of the interested parties may be allowed to intervene under certain legal conditions. That is the case of children of a Portuguese father or mother born abroad who declare that they wish to be Portuguese or whose parents register the birth in Portuguese civil records;[169] and the case of a birth in Portugal to parents who are not Portuguese.[170]

The relevance of *ius sanguinis* was reduced with the 2006 statutory change, as it was intended to facilitate the acquisition of Portuguese nationality to the children of immigrants, reinforcing for this purpose the criteria of *jus soli.*

B. Derived Acquisition

116. Derived acquisition, though more fragile than acquisition through birth, may occur, for example, in the case of marriage,[171] and in the case of de facto union.[172] The foreigner that is married for more than three years to a Portuguese national may acquire Portuguese nationality upon providing a declaration on the

168. Article 1, No. 1, subparas a), b), and f) of Law No. 37/8 of 3 October.
169. Article 1, No. 1, subpara. c).
170. Article 1, No. 1, subpara. d).
171. Article 3 of Law No. 37/8 of 3 October.
172. Article 3, No. 3.

constancy of marriage; or upon providing a judicial declaration that they live in a situation of de facto union for more than three years. Similarly, the children of a father or mother that has acquired Portuguese nationality and that are minors or disabled may also acquire it through a declaration – a clear intention to value the principle of family unity.[173] It should be noted that those children that have lost their Portuguese nationality during their minority through parental declaration may reacquire it upon reaching majority, also by means of declaration.[174]

The acquisition of nationality by adoption is also a form of derived acquisition, the effects of which are produced by mere effect of law from the date the adoption is decreed.[175] No prominence has been given to simple adoption in matters of nationality, however. On the contrary, the aim of the legislation was that adoptions that took place before the Law of 81 entered into effect would produce the same result, upon a declaration of will.[176]

C. *Naturalization*

117. Finally, there are the cases of naturalization (Article 6). Here the main fact in the acquisition is a decision by a public authority, which, upon application by the interested parties, may or may not grant Portuguese nationality. The interested party will be required to satisfy a set of conditions (majority or emancipation, years of residence in Portugal, knowledge of the Portuguese language, etc.), which allow them to prove the seriousness of the application and the existence of an effective bond with the national community. The Public Prosecution Service is responsible for checking the seriousness of the application, and may oppose the acquisition of nationality on specific grounds. There is for example the solution found by the STJ in 2002, following a case opposed by the Public Prosecution Service:

> for the acquisition of nationality by a foreign citizen, it is not enough to have married in Brazil, where he resides with a Portuguese woman, to have a tax number, bank account and own an autonomous fraction of a building in Portugal, where he obtained an academic degree, through attendance for a year and through equivalence, and to be a member of Portuguese associations based in Brazil.

In a recent amendment of the law it has been included in the conditions to acquire the Portuguese nationality by naturalization not being involved in terrorist activities[177] and it has recognized the possibility of the descendants of Portuguese Sephardic Jews, by demonstrating the membership of a Sephardic community of

173. Article 2.
174. Article 4.
175. Article 5.
176. Article 29.
177. Article 6. subpara. e) *in fine*.

Portuguese origin tradition, based on proven objective requirements of connection to Portugal, including nicknames, familiar language, direct or collateral descent.[178]

II. Loss

118. Anyone who is a national of another State and who declares that they no longer wish to be Portuguese loses their Portuguese nationality. This simple system contrasts with previous legislation, which stipulated various grounds for loss of nationality. There existed automatic causes for the loss, such as the marriage of a Portuguese woman with a foreigner or the voluntary acquisition of a foreign nationality and others that constituted a kind of sanction against 'deviant' behaviour on the part of individuals. This system came to be seen as inappropriate, particularly since the 1960s with the emigration movements. The Constitution of 1976 removed the possibility of loss of nationality for political reasons.

At present, nationality may only be lost in cases of dual nationality and upon the will of the individual concerned. Thus, Portuguese citizens who acquire another nationality may maintain their Portuguese nationality or, if they wish, declare that they no longer wish to be Portuguese. Declarations concerning the attribution, acquisition or loss of Portuguese nationality should be recorded in the Central Nationality Registry Office and annotated in the birth records of the interested party.

178. Article 6. para. 7.

Chapter 6. Domicile and Residence

§1. Practical Importance

119. The Portuguese legal system gives relevance, for various effects, to the notion of domicile as the point of connection between the person and a particular place. The domicile (in rules on the conflict of laws, Portuguese law almost always relies on the formula of habitual residence which corresponds to the notion of general residence) is the element which, according to private international law, determines the law that is applicable; this is despite the fact that Portuguese rules on the conflict of laws give greater importance to the criterion of nationality, as has already been mentioned. Habitual residence is therefore an important residual criterion for the establishment of the law regulating personal and patrimonial relations between spouses, parents and children, and for the constitution of adoptive kinship.[179] The aim of the legislation was to subject these matters to a law that is common to both spouses, which, in the absence of a national common law, will be the law of the country with which the family life is most closely connected, the law of habitual common residence.

Second, residence is important for matters of territorial jurisdiction of Portuguese judicial courts. Actions of divorce and judicial separation are heard by the court of the applicant's area of domicile;[180] for the appreciation of facts and the application of protective measures for children and young people in danger, it is the court of the child/young person's area of domicile that has jurisdiction.[181] The court of the defendant's area of domicile is the general forum or residual court competent to try any kind of suit.[182]

Finally, the reading of the will takes place at the last domicile of the testator.[183] It is also at a person's residence that any inquiries are carried out and to which notifications should be addressed in order to inform them of a fact. If the recipient of a notification or inquiry is not at the domicile and is not contactable, this does not mean that those acts will not be produced. The person's presence at the place of domicile is presumed.

§2. Domicile

120. As a rule, the establishment of a domicile, and its term, is a voluntary act. It is the so-called general voluntary domicile that normally coincides with the notion of habitual residence. A person may have two or more domiciles, if they have two or more habitual abodes.

179. Articles 53, 57 and 60 of the CC.
180. Article 72 of the Code of Civil Procedure.
181. Article 31 of the Educational Tutelary Law.
182. Article 80, No. 1 of the Code of Civil Procedure.
183. Article 2031 of the CC.

On the side of voluntary domicile, the law recognizes professional residence (relevant for professional relations and located at the place where the profession is practiced) and an elective domicile (particularly stipulated in writing for certain businesses). In the case of minors and persons under judicial incapacitation, the domicile is established by law, that is to say, it is independent of will. The domicile of children is in the family residence; if that does not exist, their domicile is at the residence of the parent who has custody. If, as a result of a judicial decision, the child is entrusted to a third party or to an educational establishment or welfare service, the child's domicile is that of the person who exercises parental responsibilities.

121. In accordance with the principle of equality between spouses, the family residence should be chosen by both in common agreement, taking into account issues such as professional life, children's interests and the safeguarding of family life. The family habitual residence is where the duty of cohabitation is fulfilled. When the family habitual residence has been chosen, both spouses are obliged to live there, except when there are ponderous reasons to the contrary (e.g., professional demands, ill treatment). This type of distancing should not, therefore, be used to apply for divorce on the grounds of a de facto separation, if both spouses intend to re-establish a life in common when it becomes possible. The agreement on the habitual residence cannot be revoked or altered unilaterally by either of the spouses. In the absence of an agreement, the law exceptionally allows the intervention of the court for the solution of the conflict.

Portuguese legislation has followed a policy of protection of the family home that is felt at different moments in the marital relationship through various provisions. It is a matter of defending the stability of the family residence in the interests of the spouses and eventually of the children, throughout married life. There are Article 1682-A, No. 2 and 1682-B of the CC to begin with. The first one ensures that the sale, mortgage or renting of the family house depends upon the consent of both spouses. The second one establishes that any act that modifies or extinguishes the legal position of the lessee whose object is the family house also requires the agreement of both spouses. Also, in the event of the death of one of the spouses, under the terms of Article 2103-A of the CC, the surviving spouse has preferential right of residence in the family home and of use of the respective contents.

Finally, there is the question of the protection of the family house in the case of divorce or separation. When the family house is the community property of the couple, it belongs to both spouses in a system of joint ownership or belongs exclusively to one of them. Article 1793 of the CC enables the court to give the house to be rented to either of the spouses, upon application, considering factors such as the needs of each of the spouses and the interests of the children. It is a process of voluntary jurisdiction regulated in Article 990 of the Code of Civil Procedure. This should not be confused with the establishment of a provisional regime of use of the family abode during the process of a divorce without the consent of one of the spouses, laid out in Article 931, No. 7 of the Code of Civil Procedure, since this does not involve any attribution of the house.

When the spouses live in a rented house, the law anticipates the possibility of the spouses agreeing on the attribution of the legal position of lessee, following a divorce or separation; similarly, in the absence of agreement, the judge will decide, taking into account the patrimonial situation of the spouses, the interests of the children, the age and state of health of the spouses, the proximity to place of work, etc.

In the case of separation or divorce by mutual consent, the spouses themselves should agree about the allocation of the family home.[184] This is the condition for the agreement on divorce when divorce takes place in the Civil Registry Office.

Two pertinent issues are discussed in Portuguese courts. When can we say that a house is de-characterized as a family home? Are decisions concerning the allocation of the family home susceptible to be modified in the event of supervening circumstances?

122. The domicile should not be confused with mere residence – the place where the person is living with some permanence. The habitual abode, where a person usually lives and to where they return to after shorter or longer absences, is the criterion for domicile. However, the residence may also be occasional, temporary or accidental. This does not make it into a domicile, although in the absence of a habitual residence, it usually functions as the equivalent.

184. Article 994, No. 1, subpara. f) of the Code of Civil Procedure.

Chapter 7. Adults with Diminished Capacity

123. Portuguese law has abandoned the dualistic system of legal protection of adults with diminished capacity, which prescribed two types of incapacitation and protective measures – guardianship and curatorship. The current regime has been introduced by Law No. 49/2018, of August 14. It establishes a single protective measure – custodianship (*acompanhamento*).

124. The regime of custodianship shall apply to adult persons who by reasons of health, disability or because of their behaviour cannot fully exercise their rights or fulfil their duties in a personal and conscious way.[185]

125. The application may be made by the beneficiary of custodianship or, depending on their authorization, by the spouse, the cohabitee, by any inheriting relative or, regardless of authorization, by the Public Prosecution Service. The required authorization may be given by the court, considering the mental state of the beneficiary of custodianship or other relevant ground.[186]

126. The CC offers a list of possible custodians. The first rank is occupied by the person chosen by the beneficiary of custodianship and appointed by the court. In the absence of such choice, it should be appointed the person who is best suited to take care of the interests of the person under custodianship, namely: the *spouse*, unless in case of legal or de facto separation; cohabitee; either parent; the person appointed by the parent(s) who have exercised parental responsibilities; adult children; either grandparent; the person appointed by the institution that cares for the person under custodianship; the attorney nominated by the person under custodianship; another trustworthy person.[187] There is the possibility to appoint more than one custodian. In such case, it has to be determined which custodian is entrusted with which group of tasks.[188]

127. The protective measure of custodianship is limited by a principle of necessity.[189] It includes those activities that are necessary to attend to the affairs of the person under custodianship and therefore the court may determine, regardless of the petition, the following duties: (a) exercise or parental responsibilities; (b) general or special representation; (c) general or partial administration of assets; (d) authorization for the person under custodianship to act; (e) other specified interventions.

128. As a rule, the person under custodianship is capable of entering into contract deemed to be an everyday transaction. The exceptions may be created by law or by court decision.[190]

185. Article 138 of the CC.
186. Article 141 of the CC.
187. Article 143, No. 2 of the CC.
188. Article 143 No. 2 of the CC.
189. Article 145, No. 1 of the CC.
190. Article 147 of the CC.

129. Regarding personal acts, the same rule applies – the person under custodianship is capable of exercising 'personal rights'. The law has deemed necessary to exemplify this category, including the right of entering into marriage or de facto union, to procreate, to acknowledge or to adopt a child, to take care and raise one's child, to choose the profession, to move across the country and abroad, to determine domicile or residence, to relate with other persons or to draw up a will.[191] However, for instance, the court decision may determine lack of capacity to marry,[192] the 'restriction of personal rights' in the decision that places under custodianship implies lack of capacity to recognize a child.[193]

130. In the particular case of confinement of the person under custodianship, it must be issued an express court authorization.[194]

131. Custodians must attend to the affairs of the persons under custodianship 'with the diligence of a *bonus pater familiae*' and keep personal contact with them, visiting them monthly.[195] In case of conflict of interests with the person under custodianship, the custodian must abstain to act and to require the court the necessary measures on that account.[196]

132. Placement under custodianship does not necessarily imply becoming legally incapacitated, since capacity may be tailored by the court decision. Therefore, acts performed by a person under custodianship are voidable just insofar they are not in accordance with the custodianship decision and are performed (i) after the decision has been registered; (ii) after the legal procedure has been announced, but only after the final decision has been pronounced and in case they prove to be harmful to the person under custodianship.[197] As for those acts performed before the beginning of the legal procedure, they may only be voidable depending on the fulfilment of some legal requirements: (i) the declaration of intent is made in a state of mental disturbance, which prevents either the ability to understand it or the free exercise of will; (ii) as long as that situation is notorious or known by the other party. This is the regime of temporary mental disturbance, to which the custodianship regime refers to.[198]

133. In addition to the regime of custodianship, there are other protection mechanisms to take into account. The new regime has created the 'mandate for custodianship purposes'.[199] Such mandate may encompass representation of the person under custodianship or not. This contract is subject to the general rules of mandate

191. Article 143, No. 2 of the CC.
192. Article 1601, b) of the CC.
193. Article 1850, No. 1 of the CC.
194. Article 148 of the CC.
195. Article 146 of the CC.
196. Article 150 of the CC.
197. Article 154, No. 1 of the CC.
198. Article 154, No. 3 of the CC.
199. Article 156 of the CC.

and it can be freely revoked,[200] but the rights and duties involved, the sphere of representation as well as other elements may be tailored. The court has to take into account the mandate (partially or as a whole) when determining the custodianship and appointing the custodian.[201] The court may also terminate the mandate whenever there is a reasonable presumption that this would be according to the person's wishes.[202]

134. Besides this mandate, in 2012, Law No. 25/2012, 16 July, had already introduced advanced directives in the Portuguese legal system and thus the possibility to plan one's future incapacity in the health care field. This can be done either by declaring one's options in the event of lack of capacity (living wills) or by nominating an representative that will act on the behalf of the person (health care durable powers of attorney).

135. Custodianship is revised by the court within the periodicity defined by the custodianship decision or, at least, every five year.[203] The custodianship is to be cancelled or altered if its requirements cease to be satisfied or have modified. The cancellation or alteration of custodianship may be required by those who may apply for custodianship as well as by the custodian.[204]

136. The custodianship measure may only be established through a legal court procedure, of urgent nature.[205] The kind of public announcement of such procedure is tailored by the court according to each case.[206] In this procedure, the personal hearing of the person by the judge is mandatory so as to evaluate the adequacy of the measure.[207] The court decision establishes not only the concrete measure of custodianship, but also the existence of living wills or health care durable powers of attorney.[208]

137. Article 71 of the Portuguese Constitution stresses that 'physically or mentally disabled citizens enjoy full rights and are subject to duties laid down in the Constitution'; the only exception accepted by the Constitution to this general rule regards the situations of 'incapacitation'. Therefore, according to the Constitution, the State has the duty to create the conditions for their free development. This last dimension configures a true social right. Finally, No. 3 of Article 71 establishes that 'the State supports associations of disabled people'. Subparagraphs g) and h) of Article 74 of the Constitution, that refer to the 'right to education', hold the State responsible for promoting the special education of people with disabilities and the

200. Article 156, No. 2 of the CC.
201. Article 156, No. 3 of the CC.
202. Article 156, No 2 of the CC.
203. Article 155 of the CC.
204. Article 149 of the CC.
205. Article 891 of the Civil Procedure Code.
206. Article 893 of the Civil Procedure Code.
207. Article 898 of the Civil Procedure Code.
208. Article 900, No. 1 and 3 of the Civil Procedure Code.

protection and appreciation of Portuguese sign language as a cultural means of expression and way of providing access to education.

138. Portuguese legislation protects and promotes the rights of people with disabilities on various levels. The Law on the Prevention, Habilitation, Rehabilitation and Participation of Disabled People[209] outlines the principles of the development of global and sectorial policies of rehabilitation. Law No. 36/98 of 24 July establishes the policy on mental health. A special social benefit for the inclusion of persons with disabilities was created by Decree Law No. 126-A/2017 of 6 October. Other special benefits may be found, regarding, for instance, special education.[210] The rights of the worker with disabilities are specially protected by the Labour Code[211] together with a cluster of rules promoting the inclusion of persons with disabilities into the labour market.[212]

209. Law No. 38/2004, 18 August.
210. Decree 3/2016, 23 August.
211. Articles 85 ff. of the Labour Code.
212. Decree Law No. 290/2009 of 12 October, for instance.

Part II. Family Law

Chapter 1. Marriage

§1. The Nature of Marriage

I. The Unity of the Institution of Marriage

139. According to Article 1625 of the CC and Article 16, No. 1 of the Concordat of 2004, the causes relating to the nullity of Catholic marriage are judged by the ecclesiastical courts. Does this mean that civil marriage and Catholic marriage are different *institutions*, governed by different legal rules? In the first case, the unity of marriage will be preserved, and the matter can be explained by abstracting, in principle, from the Catholic-civil duality; only when we are concerned with the *form* of solemnization of the act we would have to distinguish between the civil and the religious form. In the second case, however, two different institutions are designated by the term 'marriage', which have to be dealt with separately.

Before the Constitution of 1976, there was no doubt that civil and Catholic marriages were different institutions. But, in the light of Article 36, No. 2 of the CRP, which enables civil law to regulate the *conditions* of Catholic marriage, the constitutionality of Article 1625 of the CC and of Article 16, No. 1 of the Concordat of 2004, may be thrown open to doubt, since in the hierarchy of sources, the Concordat cannot be given supra-constitutional or even constitutional value. However, the idea that the Constitution revoked Article 1625 is not supported by doctrine or by the dominant jurisprudence, neither does it have any support in the history of law.

Given this situation, it would seem advisable to assume that the causes relating to the nullity of Catholic marriage fall under the domain of the ecclesiastical courts, although this competence is no longer exclusive, and that the two kinds of marriage are governed to a large extent by different legal rules.

II. General Notion of Marriage

140. There is no universal concept of marriage, but it is possible to arrive to an idea common to the legal systems that are culturally similar to our own, namely the idea of marriage as *an agreement between two persons, entered into in accordance with the determinations of law and directed towards the establishment of full conjugal living between them.* Considering marriage as a *state*, we add that this conjugal living is *exclusive*, that is to say, that neither spouse may make a similar agreement with a third party while the first is still in force, and that it is *not freely dissoluble*.

A. *Concept of Civil Marriage*

141. Article 1577 of the CC defines marriage as 'the contract celebrated between two people who intend to constitute a family, with full conjugal living, under the terms of the provisions of this Code'.

It is a full conjugal living when the spouses are reciprocally bound by duties of respect, fidelity, cohabitation, cooperation and maintenance,[213] in a relationship that is exclusive[214] and which is intended or presumed to be lifelong (Article 1773). It is also important to note that procreation, while being a normal or natural end, is not absolutely essential for civil marriage, and therefore should not be part of its definition.

B. *Concept of Catholic Marriage*

142. Catholic marriage, as regulated by canon law, also corresponds fundamentally to the general notion of marriage described above. Canon Law 1057, §2, defines marriage (marriage *in fieri*) as an 'act of will, by means of which a man and woman, through irrevocable pact, mutually give of themselves and receive the other with the purpose of constituting matrimony' (*actus voluntatis, quo vir et mulier foedere irrevocabili sese mutuo tradunt et accipiunt ad constituendum matrimonium*).

It should be noted that the 1917 Code of Canon Law considered the *primary* aim of marriage to be 'procreatio atque educatio prolis', with the 'mutuum adjutorium' and 'remedium concupiscentiae' only as a *secondary* aim,[215] although it does admit that marriage might pursue the secondary aim if, and only if, the primary one is impossible to achieve. This is not maintained in the 1983 Code,[216] which defines marriage (marriage *in facto esse*) as 'an intimate communion for the entire life, ordered by its natural character for the good of the spouses and for procreation and the raising of progeny' (*consortium totius vitae, indole sua naturali ad bonum coniugum atque ad prolis generationem et educationem ordinatum*) – a definition in which 'the good of the spouses' and 'the procreation and education of progeny' are placed side by side as purposes of marriage, with the 'good of the spouses' mentioned in first place.

In any case, consummation continues to have an importance in Catholic marriage that it does not have in civil marriage. It is not that the accomplishment of the act

213. Article 1672 of the CC.
214. Subpara. c) of Art. 1601.
215. Canon Law 1013, s. 1.
216. Canon Law 1055, s. 1.

is necessary (as the so-called *copulatheoria* claimed) since canonical marriage is a *consensual* contract. But as it is consummation that makes the act more stable, it is therefore only after consummation that a Catholic marriage becomes absolutely indissoluble.

143. If we understood marriage not as an act but as a state (marriage *in facto esse*), Catholic marriage clearly displays the same general characteristics of marriage that were described above, and which are its 'essential properties', namely unity or exclusivity, and also indissolubility.[217] According to this last aspect, the lifelong nature of Catholic marriage is much stronger than that of civil marriage, since only in extremely rare cases, laid out in Canon Law 1141–1150, is the dissolution of the matrimonial bond permitted.

III. Description of the Portuguese System

144. The matrimonial system codified in our law is an *optional system of civil marriage*.

145. Up to 2007, civil marriage was an option *for Catholics*, and only for them; for Evangelicals, Jews, Muslims, etc. civil marriage was compulsory since the law did not recognize their respective religious ceremonies.

According to Decree Law No. 324/2007, following the Law of Religious Freedom No. 16/2001, civil marriage became an option not only for Catholics but also for members of other churches or religious communities that could be considered 'based in the country', under the terms of Article 37. All have now the option of choosing between civil marriage and marriage celebrated religiously before a minister of worship.

The fact that civil marriage is available to members of all religions reveals that the system employed in Portuguese law does not make civil marriage a subsidiary form. Civil marriage is not *subsidiary* of any religious marriage, nor, in the event of conflict between the two systems, does our law recognize any principle of *priority* of religious marriage over civil, or vice versa. They are two kinds of marriage, both equally admissible and equally valid.

146. As for the question of whether Catholic marriage is admitted as *another form* of solemnization under Portuguese law, or if it is more than this, a different institution, regulated as to *form* and *substance* by different rules from those that govern civil marriage, this isn't an issue anymore. In fact, if it is the ecclesiastical court that is to judge the validity or nullity of a Catholic marriage (according to the rules of canon law, naturally), it is Canon Law that will decide on matters such as whether a marriage may be declared null and void on the grounds of mistake or other defect of consent, if a sham marriage is valid or null. The State thus gives civil effects to Catholic marriage *as such*, and recognizes or *admits* not only the rules of canon law

---

217. Canon Law 1056.

that govern the matrimonial act, but also the fact that those rules shall be applied by the jurisdictional organs of the Church itself.

There are no such provisions for other religious marriages; therefore, a marriage celebrated according to the rites of any other confession will be a religious marriage as to the form and a civil marriage as to the substance.

147. After the Law of Religious Freedom,[218] Decree Law No. 324/2007 regulated the civil effects of marriages celebrated religiously before a minister of any church or religious community based in the country. This qualification (that the church or religious community should be 'based in the country') shall be *certified* by the Minister of Justice, taking into account the number of members and the history of that church or religious community in the country, and after hearing the Committee for Religious Freedom. Application may only be made for such certification after the church or religious community has had thirty years of organized social presence in the country, unless it was founded abroad more than sixty years before, which thereby constitutes a guarantee of its duration;[219] once the church or religious community appears on the register of legal religious persons, referred to in Article 33, a register created by Decree Law No. 134/2003 of 28 June, a note of the certification is made in the entry of the church or religious community in that register.[220]

148. Despite its acceptance of civil and Catholic marriage as two different institutions and not merely two different forms of celebrating marriage, Portuguese law has sought to avoid inconveniences of the system on some important points.

First, with a view to narrowing the gap between the two systems of impediments, Article 1596 demands *civil capacity* for the solemnization of a Catholic marriage, thus applying in principle the whole system of impediments of civil marriage to Catholic marriage. All impediments to civil marriage are thus also obstacles to a Catholic marriage. Moreover, to give practical value to the principle, the law prohibits the priest, under threat of severe sanctions[221] to celebrate a Catholic marriage without having been presented with a *certificate*, issued by the Civil Registrar, declaring that the intended spouses are free to contract marriage.[222] Of course it has not been possible, even with this measure, to completely unify the two systems of impediments, since Catholic marriage is also, and primarily, subject to the system of impediments laid down by Canon Law. There continues to be marriages that can be celebrated with a civil service and not in the Catholic Church. But, in principle, all marriages that can be celebrated in the Catholic Church may also be celebrated according to State Law.

Second, in order to unify the marriage register, the Code of Civil Registry obliges the priest, under threat of sanctions laid out in Article 296, subparagraph c) of No. 1, to send a copy of the parish record to the relevant civil registry office, so that it

218. Law No. 16/2001 of 22 June.
219. Article 37, Nos 1 and 2 of Law No. 16/2001 of 22 June.
220. Article 37, No. 2, 2nd para. of Law No. 16/2001 and Art. 6 of Decree Law No. 134/2003.
221. Article 296, subpara. a) of No. 1, Code of Civil Registry.
222. Articles 1598, No. 1, CC and 146 and 151 Code of Civil Registry.

may be transcribed into the book of marriages.[223] The *transcription* of the copy of the parish record in the civil registers is now the *legal condition for the marriage to have civil effects*, and the State does not allow a marriage to be *invoked*[224] until the respective entry has been made.

Finally, the third aspect in which Portuguese law avoids the inconvenience of a dual marriage system concerns *divorce*, since Decree Law No. 261/75 of 27 May. Prior to this, civil courts could only decree divorce in the case of civil marriages, or Catholic marriages celebrated before 1 August 1940, under Articles XXIV of the Concordat and 1790 of the CC; Catholic marriages celebrated after this date could not be dissolved by divorce. This strange duality of systems disappeared with Decree Law No. 261/75, and now both civil and Catholic marriages may be dissolved by divorce, in civil courts, with the same grounds and on the same terms.

149. Although similar to civil marriages in these three aspects, Catholic marriage continues nevertheless to be different from civil marriage and governed by other legal rules. However, to describe the Portuguese matrimonial system accurately, it is necessary to know *with which rules (those of civil or canon law) each aspect of Catholic marriage is regulated.* This is ultimately what we are seeking to determine.

Thus, regarding *engagement*, it is clear that Articles 1591 onwards apply to engagements for both civil marriages and Catholic ones, and also to possible situations in which a couple, having agreed to marry, have not yet decided upon the form of marriage to celebrate.[225]

As to the *basic conditions* for a Catholic marriage, there is a distinction to be made. The various problems concerned with *consent* (intentional and unintentional discrepancies between intention and declaration, defects of consent, marriage under condition or constraint, etc.) are decided by canon law, according to the guidelines described above. In fact, these are requirements for the act to be valid, and we know that civil courts cannot yet pronounce on the validity or nullity of the Catholic marriage.[226] It is a matter currently reserved for the ecclesiastical courts, which naturally only apply their own law. As to *capacity*, that is, as to the *matrimonial impediments*, the two legal systems apply, as we have seen. Catholic marriage is of course subject first and foremost to the system of impediments of canon law, but it is also subject to those of civil law, under Article 1596, mentioned above.

The *form* of the marriage is governed, in general, by civil law and by canon law. Thus, as to the *preliminary formalities*, there are both religious formalities (the priest must proclaim the banns in church, etc.) and civil formalities to be observed. The so-called preliminary process (publication of the banns) takes place in the civil registry office and is meticulously regulated by law.[227] Regarding the *solemnization*

223. Articles 1655, No. 1, CC and 169 Code of Civil Registry.

224. According to the general principle of Art. 1669 of the CC.

225. Under the terms of Art. 1591 of the CC, the contract through which two people of different sex promise to contract matrimony, by means of an engagement, betrothal, etc., *does not give the right to demand the solemnisation of marriage, nor to claim compensation, if it is not fulfilled, other than that laid out in Art. 1594, even when resulting from a penalty clause.*

226. Articles XXV of the Concordat and 1625 of the CC.

227. Arts 134–148 of the Code of Civil Registry.

of a Catholic marriage, there are no civil formalities to be observed. As to the *registration* of the marriage, though, both civil law[228] and canon law intervene. We have seen how the Code of Civil Registry regulates even the way in which the priest draws up the parish records,[229] which is understandable, since the copy of the record must be transcribed in the registry office,[230] and it is that transcription which determines the recognition of the civil effects of the Catholic wedding.

As to the causes of *nullity* of marriage and the procedural system of the respective suits, we have already seen that canon law and the ecclesiastical courts are competent.[231] But once a Catholic marriage has been declared null and void by the ecclesiastical court, it is up to civil law to regulate the effects of that nullity, and eventually apply to the case the institution of *putative marriage*. Then, Articles 1647–1648 of the CC will apply and not the corresponding rules of canon law.

As to the *effects of marriage*, both personal and patrimonial, it is civil law that applies. The application of civil law to the *patrimonial* effects of marriage, including here the *simple legal separation of assets*, has never raised any difficulties. These are questions that canon law does not regulate, since the Church has always conveyed the '*mere civiles*' effects of matrimony to secular legislation.

The provisions of civil law relative to the *separation of persons and estate* are also applicable to Catholic marriages.

Finally, regarding the *dissolution* of Catholic marriage, the two legal systems apply. The regulation of dissolution through *death* or *divorce* falls exclusively to civil law, under the terms of Article 36, No. 2 of the CRP, but Catholic marriage also admits a cause of dissolution that is specific to it, namely the *dispensation of an unconsummated marriage*, to which Article 1625 refers and which we will discuss later.

§2. The Capacity to Marry

I. Different Sex

150. According to Law No. 9/2010 of 31 May, difference in sex is no longer demanded for the purpose of matrimony. The definition of marriage has been changed by suppressing the words 'of different sex' and the previous Article 1628, e), establishing the non-existence of same-sex marriages has been erased.

Up to 2010, the satisfaction of the claims of same-sex couples on these matters did not go further than attributing some of the effects of de facto union of different sex couples to same-sex couples[232] or beyond *new forms of shared living*, such as 'living together with shared resources', regulated by Law No. 6/2001 of 11 May.

228. Arts 167–179 of the Code of Civil Registry.
229. Article 167 of the Code of Civil Registry.
230. Article 172 of the Code of Civil Registry.
231. Articles XXV of the Concordat and 1625 of the CC.
232. Law No. 7/2001 of 11 May.

II. Consanguinity and Affinity

151. Amongst the related diriment impediments, the Code mentions in first place *kinship in the direct line* (grandparents, parents and children)[233] *and in the second degree in the collateral line* (siblings),[234] and also *affinity in the direct line* (parents-in-law and children-in-law, stepparents and stepchildren).[235]

These are the only family bonds that constitute *diriment* impediments. It should be taken into account that the impediment of kin also includes, in the case of adoption, the relationships between adopter and adoptee, between the descendants of the adopter and the adoptee, and between the ascendants of the adopter and the adoptee,[236] and between the adoptee and other children of the adopter, if they exist,[237] given the principle expressed in Article 1986.

It will not be necessary to make the *reasons* for the impediments of consanguinity and affinity explicit, or the interests or values that they protect. As to *kin* (with the exception of adoption relations, of course), this essentially involves protecting the prohibition against *incest*; regarding the impediments of *affinity* and *adoption*, we can say that, while eugenic considerations obviously do not apply, the decisive reasons are questions of family morality, as well as the respect due to social conventions, which strongly censures marriages between people covered by these impediments.

152. It should be noted that impediments of consanguinity and affinity operate even if maternity and paternity have not been *established.*[238] The law admits that the respective proofs are made in the process of impending marriage, under the terms of Articles 245 onwards of the Code of Civil Registry, or, if the marriage has already been celebrated, in a suit to declare the nullity or annulment of the marriage.

In any case, the recognition of consanguinity *does not produce any effect* and does not count as the beginning of proof in a suit to investigate maternity or paternity, as laid down in Article 1603, No. 1, which constitutes a clear exception to the rule of the *indivisibility* of the status; the law admits that a person may be taken as the daughter of another *only for the effect of not being able to marry such a person*, given the important reasons that justify the impediment in question.

153. A marriage celebrated with the impediment of consanguinity in the direct line or to the second degree in the collateral line, or of affinity in the direct line, is *voidable*,[239] and the annulment suit may be filed by the spouses or by their relatives

233. Article 1602, subpara. a) of the CC.
234. Article 1602, subpara. b).
235. Article 1602, subpara. c).
236. Article 1602, subpara. a).
237. Article 1602, subpara. b).
238. Article 1603 of the CC.
239. Article 1631, subpara. a) of the CC.

in the direct line or up to the fourth degree in the collateral line, by heirs or adoptees of the spouses or by the Public Prosecution Service,[240] up to *six months after the dissolution of the marriage.*[241]

III. Marriageable Age

154. Being under age is the first of the absolute diriment impediments mentioned in law. The marriage is annullable if one of the parties has not yet reached *marriageable age*, that is, the *minimum* age required to ensure the physical and psychological maturity that the law demands for the celebration of a valid marriage.

According to Article 1601, subparagraph a), being 'less than sixteen years of age' constitutes an absolute diriment impediment, for both sexes.

155. As regards legitimacy for the annulment suit and the respective terms, these are covered by Articles 1639 and 1643. A suit may be filed or continued by the spouses or any relative of theirs in the direct line or to the fourth degree of the collateral line, heirs or adoptees of the spouses and the Public Prosecution Service;[242] the guardian of a minor may also bring an annulment suit or continue one.[243]

As to the *terms*, the law distinguishes between a suit filed by the minor himself/herself or by others: in the first case, the minor should apply within *six months* of reaching majority; in the second case, the annulment should be applied for within *three years* of the celebration of the marriage, but never after the party concerned has reached majority.[244]

It should be noted, however, that annulability is considered remedied and the *validity* of the marriage is re-established from the date of celebration, if, before the annulment sentence transits in *rem judicatam*, the minor confirms the marriage before an official of the registry office and two witnesses, after having reached majority.[245]

IV. Prior Marriage

156. The impediment of *a bond*, referred to in subparagraph c) of Article 1601, is one of those that has the most practical interest. Under the terms of these provisions, a *prior undissolved marriage*, Catholic or civil, constitutes an absolute diriment impediment, even if the respective records have not been entered in the registry office.

The law aims with this impediment to avoid *bigamy*, ensuring civil protection of matrimonial unity, which as we have seen constitutes one of the essential characteristics of marriage as a state.

---

240. Article 1639, No. 1 of the CC.
241. Article 1643, No. 1, subpara. c) of the CC.
242. Article 1639, No. 1 of the CC.
243. Article 1639, No. 2 of the CC.
244. Article 1643, No. 1, subpara. a) of the CC.
245. Article 1633, No. 1, subpara. a) of the CC.

Whosoever is married cannot therefore enter into marriage without the former marriage being *dissolved, declared null* or *annulled*. The cause of dissolution does not play a role: the former marriage may be dissolved by death, divorce or, in the case of a Catholic marriage, dispensation of unconsummated marriage.

157. It is of no importance if the record of the previous marriage has not been filed in the marriage records, as stated in Article 1601, subparagraph c), this provision is aimed particularly at marriages celebrated abroad and Catholic marriages that remain untranscribed.

158. A problem that has been raised is that of knowing whether a prior matrimonial bond constitutes an impediment between spouses that wish to remarry one another. This question, which is apparently meaningless, may be of interest in the case of a marriage that has been celebrated abroad and where there have been delays or difficulties in obtaining the documents necessary for the transcription: in cases like this, the celebration of a second marriage between the spouses might appear the most practical expedient to use. There do not appear to be any reasons for not doing so, excluding of course bigamy that the *obstaclum ligaminis* seeks to avoid.

159. The annulment suit grounded in the impediment of a bond may be filed by the spouses or by any relative of theirs in the direct line or to the fourth degree in the collateral line, by heirs or adoptees of the spouses and by the Public Prosecution Service,[246] and also by the first spouse in the bigamy,[247] up to *six months after the dissolution of the marriage*.[248] However, it cannot be filed or continued while a suit for the declaration of nullity or annulment of the first bigamous marriage is pending,[249] since, if the first marriage is effectively declared null and void or annulled, the validity of the second would be re-established.[250]

V. Insanity

160. Under the terms of Article 1601, subparagraph b), 'notorious insanity, even during lucid moments, and the custodianship, when declared by court decision' constitute absolute diriment impediments to marriage.

It is important to bear in mind that the legal concept of insanity does not coincide with the psychiatric one: in civil law, insanity is simply the same as mental or psychological disorder. It is not the same, therefore, as what is called 'insanity' in the domain of psychiatry, but any disorder, both of intelligence or of will, that prevents the individual from properly managing their own person and property.

This impediment covers both 'insanity' *in law*, derived from the measure of custodianship, decided by a Court, and simple de facto insanity.

246. Article 1639, No. 1 of the CC.
247. Article 1639, No. 2 of the CC.
248. Article 1643, No. 1, subpara. c) of the CC.
249. Article 1643, No. 3 of the CC.
250. Article 1633, No. 1, subpara. c) of the CC.

161. In the case of de facto 'insanity', the law also requires the 'insanity' to be *notorious*, and doubts may arise as to the meaning of this term. What is important in law is that the insanity exists, that it is *certain, unequivocal, not doubtful*, and this is the meaning that tends to be given to the notion of 'notoriety' demanded in Article 1601, subparagraph c) of the CC.

162. The matter of lucid intervals, which was debated in legislation prior to the Code, is today expressly resolved in law,[251] in the sense that insanity constitutes an impediment to marriage *even during those intervals*. This is one of the points on which civil and canon law diverge, since the latter does not recognize the impediment of insanity but rather includes it in the issue of *consent*; consequently, it considers valid a marriage that took place during the lucid intervals, provided that this can be proven.

163. An annulment suit grounded on the impediment of 'insanity' or custodianship declared by court may be filed or continued by either spouse or by their relatives in the direct line or up to the fourth degree in the collateral line (siblings, uncles and nephews, cousins), heirs and adoptees of the spouses or by the Public Prosecution Service,[252] and also by the custodian.[253]

Regarding the *terms* in which a suit may be filed, the law distinguishes between two possibilities: if the suit is filed by the person suffering from insanity, it should be filed up to *six months* after the lifting of the judicial disability or incapacity, or if the insanity has ceased; if the action is filed by other people, it should be within *three years* of the marriage ceremony, but never after the lifting of the custodianship measure on that account.[254]

The law admits, however, the *revalidation* of marriage if, before the transit in *rem judicatam* of the annulment sentence, the marriage is confirmed by the insane person, before the official of the registry office and two witnesses, after the custodianship measure on that account has been lifted, or, in the case of notorious insanity, after the state of mental health has been legally verified.[255]

VI. Conviction for Murder

164. Another diriment impediment is 'the prior conviction of one of the parties for the murder, or for being accomplice to the murder, of the other's spouse, even when the crime has not actually been committed'[256]; the obstacle is valid in the case of an 'unconsummated' murder, and therefore, even in the case of an *attempt*. Condemnation for *involuntary murder* does not constitute an impediment, resulting from both the letter and the spirit of the law.

251. Article 1601, subpara. c) of the CC.
252. Article 1639, No. 1 of the CC.
253. Article 1639, No. 2 of the CC.
254. Article 1643, No. 1, subpara. a) of the CC.
255. Article 1633, No. 1, subpara. b) of the CC.
256. Article 1602, subpara. d) of the CC.

This is a *sanction* imposed upon the perpetrator or accomplice of a murder (even when this has not actually been committed), which the law *suspects* has been committed with the intention of enabling the perpetrator to marry the victim's spouse. However, it should be noted that the law only demands that the murder be voluntary; it does not require it actually to have been performed with that intention.

165. In accordance with Article 1602, subparagraph d), the impediment of conviction for murder only exists from the date of the transit in *rem judicatam* of the respective *sentence*. As it would frustrate the aim of the law if the sentence were to be delayed long enough for the interested parties to contract marriage, the 1966 Code admitted the *obstructing* impediment of *indictment* for murder, under the terms of Article 1604, subparagraph f), giving practical value to a prohibition which, otherwise could easily be evaded.

166. The annulment suit grounded on the impediment of conviction for murder may be filed by the spouses or by any relative of theirs in the direct line or up to the fourth degree in the collateral line, by heirs and adoptees of the spouses and by the Public Prosecution Service,[257] within *three years* of the marriage ceremony.[258]

VII. Previous Exercise of Parental Responsibilities

167. Law No. 137/2015 of 7 September added a new diriment impediment to marriage grounded in a previous relationship of parental responsibilities over a child of one of the adults living in a married couple or in a de facto union. The law regulates the possible end of the marriage or the de facto union and the eventual intention of marriage between one former partner and the other's child. The annulment lawsuit follows the rules established for the diriment impediment of consanguinity or affinity.

§3. The Consent to Marry

I. Marriage by Proxy

168. Consent should be *personal*, that is, expressed by the intended spouses themselves, personally, during the marriage ceremony. As laid out in Article 1619, 'the desire to contract marriage is strictly personal in relation to each member of the couple'.

The law does admit, however, the so-called marriage by proxy. The power of attorney for the marriage should be drawn up by public deed or by written document and signed by the person represented with recognition *in praesentia* of the handwriting and signature;[259] only one member of the couple may be represented in

257. Article 1639, No. 1 of the CC.
258. Article 1643, No. 1, subpara. b).
259. Article 43, No. 2 of the Code of Civil Registry.

this way by proxy.[260] Finally, there is also the matter of representation in which special powers are conferred for the act, the person of the other partner is individualized and the kind of marriage is indicated.[261]

II. Defects of Consent

A. *Sham Marriage*

169. The question of sham marriage has never been raised in Portuguese courts; but it is debated in doctrine and seems to have recently gained a certain interest.

Marriages may be simulated in order to achieve particular purposes that are alien to true marriage. However, if a marriage is determined by one of these motives, but the couple is nevertheless prepared to undertake a life together in reality, then there is no simulation and the marriage is valid.

170. The sham marriage may be annulled.[262]

Annulment may be applied for by the spouses themselves and by any person who may have been prejudiced by the marriage,[263] within three years from the ceremony, or if the applicant did not know of the marriage, within six months following the date when he/she learned of it.[264]

Since the Law No. 23/2007 of 4 July (Immigration Law), sham marriage in order to get permission to enter the country or to get Portuguese nationality is a crime punished with a penalty from one to four years of imprisonment. The mere attempt is punishable, as well, and the repeated or organized promotion of sham marriages is punishable with a penalty from two to five years of imprisonment.

B. *Mistake*

171. Mistake is covered by the terms of Article 1636. It falls to the person to whom the marriage has been contracted and concerns an essential quality of that person. The *restrictive* system of defects of consent, in matters of marriage, is reflected in the case of mistake in two important limitations. First, of all the possible forms that the mistake might take, only one is relevant: a mistake about the person of the other party, and about that person's qualities; second, not any quality may be taken into account for this effect, but only essential ones.

172. These are the *specific* conditions governing the relevance of mistake, to which the *general* conditions are added, in accordance with the orientation already described.

260. Articles 1620, No. 1, CC and 44, No. 1, Code of Civil Registry.
261. Articles 1620, No. 2, CC and 44, No. 2, Code of Civil Registry.
262. Article 1635, subpara. d) of the CC.
263. Article 1640, No. 1 of the CC.
264. Article 1644 of the CC.

Taking all these conditions together, it may be said that the relevance of mistake in a marriage depends upon the following presuppositions: *it is necessary that the mistake was made about the essential quality of the person of the other spouse, that this be a proper mistake, that it be pardonable and that the circumstances under which the mistake was made played an essential role in determining the desire to contract marriage, both subjectively and objectively.*

First, the mistake is only relevant if it concerns the *essential* quality of the person of the other spouse; it may not deal with *non-essential* qualities. As a general rule, it can be said that essential qualities are those that are particularly significant, those that *in the abstract* are fundamental for determining consent. These include: the marital or religious status of the other spouse; nationality; the committing of an ignominious crime; dishonourable lifestyle or habits; impotence; serious physical deformity; incurable disease or disease that is hereditary or contagious.

Second, the mistake must be *a proper mistake*, or rather, it cannot hinge upon some legal requirement or concern the validity of the marriage. Thus, if one of the spouses wrongly supposes that the other is of marriageable age, or that the other is divorced when he/she is still married, the mistake is not personal. The marriage is annullable, though not strictly speaking for mistake, but rather, *irrespective of the mistake made*, concerning the absence of the legal conditions to which the mistake refers.

The mistake should also be *pardonable*. This is a requirement not usually made for most legal transactions, but it results expressly from Article 1636. The unpardonable or gross mistake, which could not have happened to a normal person during the circumstances of the case, may not therefore be invoked as a motive to invalidate the marriage.

Finally, the mistake must concern a circumstance that was fundamental in determining the decision, in such a way that, if the mistake had not been made, and the person had had full knowledge of that circumstance, he/she would not have wished to enter into marriage. The demand that the circumstance upon which the mistake is made is a *determining factor*, should however be made in particular terms. It is not enough that the mistake was *subjectively* determining, as in most legal transactions;[265] nor is it enough that the circumstance under which the mistake was made was essential *for the party concerned* in determining their desire to contract marriage. This subjective essentiality has to be supplemented with an *objective* essentiality; that is to say, it has to be *reasonable given the circumstances of the case and in the light of the dominant social conceptions*, so that, in making the decision to marry, the circumstance about which the mistake was made was decisive. The conditions of annulability through mistake are the same as those for duress.

C. Duress

173. Marriage may also be annulled on the grounds of *duress*, under the terms of Article 1638 of the CC.

265. Cf. Arts 247 and 251 of the CC.

Duress, as a defect of consent, applies when there has been *fear or apprehension caused by the threat of some harm towards their own person, honour or property, or towards a third person.* The fear that the threat will ultimately be consummated is what makes duress case of lack of consent. It is of interest also to refer that the harm that is feared has to be threatened precisely with the intent of extorting consent for the transaction in question,[266] the transaction that is said to have been celebrated under duress.

174. Duress must be *essential* or must have *determined* the decision; there has to have been *intention* to *extort the declaration*; finally, the threats must also be *unfair* and illicit, a condition that is not easy to define precisely.

Under the terms of Article 1638, No. 1, a marriage celebrated under moral duress is voidable, providing that the harm with which the party was illicitly threatened was *serious* and *justified* the fear of its consummation.

Duress is relevant even when the threat is against property interests, and when it is directed at a third party, whatever the relationship (family or otherwise) between that party and the coerced declarant. It is enough that the threat of the harm to be caused to the third party, given that relationship, has determined the will of the declarant, as if it had been directed at him/her.

175. When consent has been given through mistake or duress, and if the respective conditions of relevance are in place, then the marriage is *voidable.*[267]

The annulment suit may only be *filed* by the spouse that was mistaken or has been coerced, within six months of the cessation of the defect,[268] or rather, six months after the date when he/she learned of the circumstance of the mistake or on which the duress ceased; but it may be *continued* by other blood relatives, relatives by affinity in the direct line, heirs or adoptees if the person died while the suit was pending.[269] In addition, annulability may be remedied by *confirmation*, which may be express or tacit, as legal transactions in general, under the general terms of Article 288.[270]

266. Cf. Art. 255, No. 1 of the CC.
267. Article 1631, subpara. b) of the CC.
268. Article 1645 of the CC.
269. Article 1641 of the CC.
270. Article 288, No. 3 of the CC.

§4. Formalities of Marriage

I. Civil Marriages

A. *Preliminary Formalities*

176. There are various formalities to be observed before the celebration, and these constitute a series of acts, a 'process' – the so-called *marriage process* or *preliminary process of* marriage, regulated in Articles 134–177 of the Code of Civil Registry, vastly changed by Decree Law No. 324/2007.

Under the terms of Article 134, the organization of the preliminary process falls to any registry office, regardless of the area in which the couple lives or has established residence.

The first step in the preliminary process is the *declaration of the intention to marry*. Whosoever intends to contract marriage should declare it before the official of the registry office, personally or through a suitable proxy, or electronically, and apply for the institution of proceedings.[271] The declaration should contain the following information: the kind of marriage (civil or Catholic); the registry office or parish where the couple wishes the ceremony to take place; and whether or not there will be a prenuptial agreement (except in situations where the property system is mandatory).

The *notice of intended marriage* used to be affixed to the notice board of the registry office for eight consecutive days, during which time anyone who knew of any lawful impediment to the marriage was invited to declare it at the registry office.[272] Decree Law No. 324/2007 of 28 September abolished this kind of publicity; now, publicity is granted by allowing anyone to ask for a copy of the initial notice of intended marriage.

The registrar needs to verify both the identity and the matrimonial capacity of the couple, and for these purposes he/she may need to do some research, questioning people, including the applicants, or searching for documents.

Closing the proceedings, the registrar should issue the *final order* authorizing the marriage or closing the proceedings.[273] If the order does not allow the marriage to take place, the couple will be notified, and they may appeal against it within eight days of the notification, under the terms of Article 292.[274]

177. It may be necessary to obtain *dispensation* from the obstructing impediments which, under the terms of civil law, may be given dispensation.[275] Dispensation is applied for in the registry office chosen for the organization of the publication process. The interested parties should address their claim to the registrar, explaining their reasons; when the process has been organized and the particulars prepared, the registrar issues a decision, with grounds, on whether the

271. Article 135 of the Code of Civil Registry.
272. Article 140, No. 1 of the Code of Civil Registry.
273. Article 144, No. 1 of the Code of Civil Registry.
274. Article 144, No. 4 of the Code of Civil Registry.
275. Article 1609 of the CC.

dispensation is granted or refused. The interested parties are notified of the decision and are entitled to appeal to the district court.

178. Impediments to the marriage may be pointed out, and this is the most important aspect of the preliminary process.

When the existence of an impediment has been declared, the registrar must summon the couple to impugn the impediment within twenty days, or risk this being taken as confessed.[276] If it is not impugned within the period or is confessed, the registrar issues an order granting the impediment and ordering the marriage proceedings to be closed.[277]

B. Ceremony

179. If the final order is favourable, the marriage may take place within the following ninety days.[278]

The couple may choose the registry office where the marriage ceremony will take place, but the day and the time are agreed between the couple and the registrar.[279] Both parties must be present during the ceremony, or one of them and the proxy of the other, and the registrar. It is also compulsory for two witnesses to be present, when the identity of either of the parties or of the proxy cannot be verified in one of the ways laid out in subparagraphs a), b) and c) of No. 3 of Article 154.

The ceremony, which is public, is regulated by Article 155 of the Code of Civil Registry. The registrar announces that the marriage ceremony is to take place and reads, from the initial declaration, information concerning the identification of the parties and their intention to marry, the final order or, if the ceremony is taking place in a different registry office to the one where the process took place, the parts of the certificate relating to the identification of the parties and to the authorization for marriage.[280] The people present are called upon to declare if they know of any lawful impediment to the marriage[281] and, if none is declared, after referring to the rights and duties of the spouses laid out in Article 1672 of the CC, the registrar asks each in turn if they accept the other as consort,[282] to which each will clearly respond, in turn: 'It is my free will to marry F ... '(indicating the complete name of the other party) (subparagraph e)). When consent has been declared, the marriage is considered celebrated, which the official will proclaim, declaring aloud: 'In the name of the Law and of the Republic of Portugal, I hereby declare F. and F. (indicating the complete names of the spouses) united in marriage.'[283]

This is followed by the registration of the marriage.

---

276. Article 247, No. 1, of the Code of Civil Registry.
277. Article 248 of the Code of Civil Registry.
278. Article 1614 of the CC.
279. Article 153 of the Code of Civil Registry.
280. Article 153, subpara. a) of the Code of Civil Registry.
281. Article 153, subpara. c) of the Code of Civil Registry.
282. Article 153, subpara. d) of the Code of Civil Registry.
283. Article 155, No. 2 of the Code of Civil Registry.

C. Registration

180. The registration of the marriage is compulsory and is very important, since the marriage can only be *proven*[284] by means of access to the register or certificates extracted from it.[285] In reality, the register does not affirm the existence of the marriage, neither, strictly speaking, its validity nor even the force of the act, but it is merely its proof. The register is simply *the only legally admitted proof of marriage*, and a marriage that is unregistered, cannot be *invoked* (meaning that it is as if everything that has taken place is without effect), for the people directly concerned, their heirs or representatives, and for third parties.[286]

The record of the marriage may be entered by *inscription*[287] or by *transcription*;[288] consideration must also be made of the case, laid out in Article 179, of the Catholic marriage celebrated between spouses already bound by a prior civil marriage that has not been dissolved and which is *annotated* in this one's records. As regards civil marriage, that is unique at the moment concerned, the record is entered by being inscribed in the respective register.

The marriage record should be *entered, read and signed* immediately after the solemnities;[289] and, in addition to the general requisites, should also contain *mentions* to Article 181 of the Code of Civil Registry.

181. The *omission* of the marriage record may only be remedied upon the decision of the registrar in a special procedure.[290] In addition, the marriage record, like any other, may also be declared *non-existent* or *null and void*, particularly in the case of *falsity*, and may be *cancelled*; for any of these situations, the general rules of registration described above apply.

182. The effects of marriage are not only produced *ex nunc*, from the date of registration, but *ex tunc*, from the date of the ceremony. The principle of retroactivity is expressed in Articles 1670, No. 1 of the CC and 188, No. 1 of the Code of Civil Registry, according to which, once the record has entered, and even if it is subsequently lost, the civil effects of marriage are retroactive to the date of its celebration.

However, if we take the principle of retroactivity to its logical end, the interests of third parties who had expectations of entering into marriage with one of the spouses on the basis of the marriage being non-existent will be left unprotected. For this reason, No. 2 of Article 1670, in the wording of Article 61 of Law No. 16/2001 of 22 June, safeguards the rights of *third parties*, compatible with the personal rights and duties of the spouses and their children, that had been acquired prior to the registration, unless, in the case of registration by transcription, this has been done

284. Article 211 of the Code of Civil Registry.
285. Articles 212 onwards of the Code of Civil Registry.
286. Article 1669 of the CC and 2 of the Code of Civil Registry.
287. Article 52, subpara. e) of the Code of Civil Registry.
288. Article 53, No. 1, subparas c), d) and e) of the Code of Civil Registry.
289. Article 180 of the Code of Civil Registry.
290. Article 83, No. 1, subpara. a) of the Code of Civil Registry.

within *seven days* of the marriage ceremony; the record has retroactive effects in this case, even in relation to third parties.

D. Urgent Marriages

183. When there is a justified fear that one of the parties might die in the near future, even if this is derived from external circumstances, or when there is an imminent birth, marriage may be celebrated without the preliminary process and without the intervention of the official.[291] Marriages celebrated under these circumstances are called *urgent* marriages, and their form is very simple.

The *preliminary formalities* are reduced to the proclamation referred to in subparagraph a) of Article 156 – an oral or written proclamation made at the door of the house where the couple is found, by the official of the registry office or, in his/her absence, by any of the people present. The prior publication of notice is therefore not required, nor is the intervention of the registrar.

The *celebration* of the marriage is referred to in subparagraph b) of Article 156. It requires the express declaration of consent from each of the parties before four witnesses, two of whom should not be inheriting relatives of the parties.

Finally, the *celebration* of urgent marriages also has important particularities. Under the terms of subparagraph c) of Article 156, a record of the marriage should be drawn up, following the celebration, on regular paper and without special formalities, signed by all intervening parties that know how to write, if it is not possible to immediately enter a provisional record in the proper book.

If the preliminary process has been organized and completed, the registrar issues a final order within a period of three days counting from the date of the record of the marriage or the last inquiry made in the procedure, unless there is a reason for that period not to be observed;[292] if the preliminary process has not taken place, the official should organize this officiously, so that it may be concluded within thirty days of the provisional record, and declare, in the final order, if he/she *ratifies* the marriage or not.[293]

184. Causes for the non-ratification of the marriage are referred to in Articles 1624 of the CC and 160 of the Code of Civil Registry. The marriage should not be ratified if the legal conditions, laid out in Article 156, and which permit the marriage to be celebrated urgently, have not been met: if the formalities prescribed in Articles 156 and 157 have not been observed; if there are serious indications that those conditions or formalities are false or hypothetical; if the marriage has been contracted with some *diriment* impediment; or, finally, if the marriage has been considered as a Catholic one by the church authorities and is transcribed as such.

185. The urgent marriage that is not ratified is legally *non-existent.*[294]

291. Articles 1622, No. 1 of the CC and 156 of the Code of Civil Registry.
292. Article 159, No. 2, of the Code of Civil Registry.
293. Articles 1623, No. 2 of the CC and 159, Nos 1, 4 and 5 of the Code of Civil Registry.
294. Article 1628, subpara. b), of the CC.

The ratification order establishes the elements that should appear on the record, which should be entered in the period of two days counting from the date of that order.[295]

186. Urgent marriages are always considered to be celebrated under the matrimonial property system of *separation of assets*;[296] it can be said that this is the only substantial specificity of this system.

E. Marriages of Portuguese People Abroad and of Foreigners in Portugal

187. Article 161 of the Code of Civil Registry admits that *marriages contracted abroad between two Portuguese people or between a Portuguese person and a foreigner* may be celebrated in three ways: (a) before a minister of the Catholic Church; (b) before Portuguese diplomatic or consular agents abroad, in a form established in civil law; (c) or before local authorities with the required jurisdiction, in a form laid down in the law of the country where the marriage will take place. In all cases, the marriage should be preceded by the publication process, organized under the terms of Articles 134 onwards, except in those cases in which the law allows it to be celebrated with dispensation of the process.[297] The organization of the preliminary process falls to the Portuguese diplomatic or consular agents or to the registry office competent for that effect. A Portuguese citizen, resident in Portugal, who wishes to marry abroad may apply to any registry office for recognition of their matrimonial capacity and for the issue of the respective *certificate*, following the organization of the preliminary process of publication.[298] In the case of a Portuguese citizen resident abroad who wishes to marry before the local authorities, his/her matrimonial capacity is recognized by any registry office or by the diplomatic or consular agents responsible for organizing the process of publication; the duplicate of the certificate should in this case be sent as well to the registry office responsible for drawing up the marriage records.[299]

The Catholic marriage contracted abroad between Portuguese citizens or between a Portuguese citizen and a foreigner that is taken as a Catholic, should be transcribed based on the parish records.[300] The transcription is the responsibility of the registry office.[301] Articles 184 onwards of the Code of Civil Registry are applicable, and the transcription may be refused under the same terms, laid out in Article 174, as may the transcription of a Catholic marriage celebrated in Portugal.[302]

295. Article 182 of the Code of Civil Registry.
296. Article 1720, No. 1, subpara. a) of the CC.
297. Article 162 of the Code of Civil Registry.
298. Article 163, Nos 1–2 of the Code of Civil Registry.
299. Article 163, No. 3 of the Code of Civil Registry.
300. Article 178, No. 1, of the Code of Civil Registry.
301. Article 10, subpara. a) do No. 2 of the Code of Civil Registry.
302. Article 178, No. 2 of the Code of Civil Registry.

The record of a marriage celebrated abroad before our diplomatic or consular agents is entered by *inscription* in the proper book of the consulate,[303] and the consul should send a copy of the marriage record to the relevant registry office,[304] so that it may be *included*, under the terms of Article 54, No. 3, in the book of consular records in the registry office.[305] As to determining which registry office is competent for this matter, which may be a civil registry office or the Central Registry Office, Rules Nos 2–6 of Article 186 apply.

Finally, if the marriage is celebrated in a form laid down by the law of the place of solemnization before the proper local authorities, it should be registered by *transcribing*, in the proper book of the consulate, the document proving marriage, issued in accordance with the same law,[306] or directly in the relevant registry office, with any of the documents referred to in subparagraphs a) and b) of No. 1 of Article 187 In either case, the transcription may only be made upon prior organization of the preliminary process,[307] and should be refused if there is any *diriment* impediment to the celebration of marriage.[308]

188. Regarding the *marriage of foreigners in Portugal*, it is regulated by Articles 165 and 166 of the Code of Civil Registry. The marriage may be celebrated according to the form and under the terms laid down in the national law of either of the parties, before the respective diplomatic or consular agents, provided that the same competence is recognized of Portuguese diplomatic and consular agents,[309] or by any of the forms covered in the Code of Civil Registry. In this case, the party concerned should file the preliminary process with a *certificate of matrimonial capacity*, issued by the competent authority of the country of which he/she is a national, or given the conditions laid down in Article 166, No. 2, obtain the declaration that, according to his/her personal law, there is no impediment to the celebration of marriage.

F. Civil Marriages Celebrated in a Religious Form

189. Article 19 of the Law of Religious Freedom[310] regulates the formalities of marriage celebrated in a religious form before a minister of a church or religious community based in the country. This minister should be of Portuguese nationality or be a national of one of the Member States of the EU, or, if not, have authorization for permanent or temporary residence in Portugal.

Anyone who wishes to marry in this way should declare so, personally or by proxy, at the competent civil registry office, that is, in the registry office of the area in which one of the couple is domiciled or has established residence for at least

303. Articles 52, subpara. e), and 184, Nos 1 and 2, first part of the Code of Civil Registry.
304. Articles 54, No. 1 and 186, No. 1 of the Code of Civil Registry.
305. Articles 10, No. 3, and 11, No. 2 of the Code of Civil Registry.
306. Article 184, No. 2, 2nd part of the Code of Civil Registry.
307. Articles 185 of the Code of Civil Registry.
308. Articles 185, No. 3 of the Code of Civil Registry.
309. Articles 51, No. 1 of the CC and 165 of the Code of Civil Registry.
310. Law No. 16/2001 of 22 June.

thirty days prior to the date of the declaration. In the declaration of intention to marriage, the parties should indicate the minister of worship qualified for the act. In a similar process to that which takes place in the case of Catholic marriages,[311] Article 19, No. 2 of Law No. 16/2001 allows the declaration of intention to marry also to be made before a minister of worship, in a formal petition signed by him/her.

Following the preliminary process of publication, if no impediments have been declared, or if any impediments declared have been dismissed, the registrar draws up the final order authorizing the couple to celebrate marriage and issues the respective certificate, under the terms laid out in Articles 146 and 147 of the Code of Civil Registry. The certificate should make mention that the parties have knowledge of the provisions of Articles 1577, 1600, 1671 and 1672 of the CC and also mention the name and credentials of the minister of worship that will celebrate the marriage, to whom the registrar will send the certificate officiously. If any supervening impediment is declared, the registrar should communicate that fact to the minister of worship.[312]

Article 19, No. 4 regulates the solemnization of marriage, in which the following presences are mandatory: the couple, or one of the members and the other's representative, the minister of worship and also two witnesses.

After the solemnities, the minister should enter the record in duplicate in the register of the church or religious community, and send a copy to the competent registry office within a period of three days, for it to be transcribed into the book of marriage records; the registrar should carry out the transcription within a further two days and communicate this fact to the minister before the end of the following day.[313]

II. Catholic Marriage

190. If the couple opts for a Catholic marriage, they have to observe the conditions laid out in the Code of Canon Law. In addition to this, the Portuguese legal system demands that they also prove their *capacity under civil law.*[314]

In fact, the impediments to marriage under civil law are also impediments to a Catholic marriage, and this may only be celebrated if the priest is presented with a *certificate* issued by the registrar declaring that there are no civil impediments known to prevent the celebration of the Catholic marriage.[315]

191. However, if a Catholic marriage is celebrated without complying with this rule, and there are impediments under civil law, *quid iuris?*

We know that a Catholic marriage may not be annulled in the civil courts;[316] the marriage should not have been celebrated if there are civil impediments, but if it

311. Article 135, No. 2 of the Code of Civil Registry.
312. Article 19, No. 3 of the Law of Religious Freedom (Law No. 16/2001 of 22 June).
313. Article 19, No. 5 and 6 of the Law of Religious Freedom.
314. Article 1596 of the CC.
315. Article 1598 of the CC.
316. Article 1625 of the CC.

was, the civil courts cannot pronounce on its validity. The problem that is raised for the State is only of knowing *if it should or should not allow the transcription of the marriage.*

It has been conceived that the transcription must be refused in any case. It might be thought that, since civil impediments prevent the Catholic marriage from being celebrated, they would also prevent the transcription into the civil registry books once the marriage has been celebrated.

But the legal system is not this strict, as we shall see.

If the rules that establish matrimonial impediments all aim at protecting public interests, the truth is that *the celebration of a Catholic marriage causes a new public interest to arise*, namely the interest that the Catholic marriage, which should not have been celebrated but was, produces civil effects, for which reason there are no unions that are legitimate in the eyes of the Church and illegitimate in the eyes of the State.

Attempting to reconcile these two interests in the best way possible, the law authorizes or not the transcription on the basis of the kind of impediment in question. Impediments that are less essential are sacrificed (obstructing impediments), since these are based upon public interests of a second order, which should give way before the new public interest to which we refer; but it does not sacrifice *diriment* impediments, which are based upon fundamental public interests.

All this applies to *common* marriages.

192. If the Catholic marriage is *urgent*, then it may be legally celebrated even without the preliminary process or the issue of the certificate, and the legal solution is different. In this case, even the diriment impediments are sacrificed, with the exception of the three of them in which the two systems of impediments – civil and canonical – diverge the most: lack of marital age; notorious insanity and, when declared by court decision, custodianship; and prior undissolved civil marriage, since, in any of these cases, the impediment still persists. Only in these cases may the registrar refuse to transcribe the Catholic marriage. This is what is laid out in subparagraphs d) and e) of No. 1 of Article 1657 of the CC and in Article 174, No. 1 of the Code of Civil Registry.

A. *Preliminary Formalities*

193. The preliminary process of a Catholic marriage takes place in the civil registry office just like a civil marriage. It follows basically the same terms. There are only two new aspects to highlight:

> The first is that the declaration for marriage may also be made in this case in the form of a signed application by the priest responsible for organizing the ecclesiastical process, before whom it is naturally presumed that the couple has expressed their intention to marry.[317]

317. Article 135, No. 2, of the Code of Civil Registry.

In addition, we have already seen that the Catholic marriage may not be celebrated without the presentation to the priest of the *certificate* issued by the registrar, in which it is declared that the couple may contract marriage.[318] Only in the case of urgent marriages it does not work this way,[319] as we shall see. A priest that officiates at a wedding without having been presented with the certificate may incur a penalty of qualified disobedience,[320] as laid out in subparagraph a) of No. 1 of Article 296 of the Code of Civil Registry.

B. Celebration

194. As regards the *celebration* of the Catholic marriage itself, there are no civil formalities.

C. Registration

195. Immediately after the celebration of the Catholic marriage, the respective *parish records* should be entered in duplicate,[321] containing the indications given in No. 1 of that Article. The record and the duplicate should be signed by the spouses, witnesses and priest that entered them.[322]

The priest should send the copy of the record to the civil registry office within three days to be transcribed in the register of marriages;[323] the copy should be sent to the registry office that issued the certificate, or, in the absence of a certificate, to the registry office of the place where the marriage was celebrated.[324]

The registrar should carry out the *transcription* of the copy or certificate of the parish records within one day.

§5. Effects of Marriage

I. Equality Between Spouses and Joint Orientation of the Family

196. Article 1671 of the CC lays down two fundamental principles regulating the effects of marriage: the principle of equality of rights and duties between spouses[325] and, in correlation, the principle of joint orientation of the family.[326]

318. Articles 146 and 151 of the Code of Civil Registry.
319. Article 151, No. 2 of the Code of Civil Registry.
320. Article 348, No. 2 of the Criminal Code.
321. Article 167 of the Code of Civil Registry.
322. Article 168, No. 1 of the Code of Civil Registry.
323. Articles 1655, No. 1, CC and 169, No. 1 of the Code of Civil Registry.
324. Article 171, No. 1 of the Code of Civil Registry.
325. *Ibid.*
326. Article 171, No. 2 of the Code of Civil Registry.

197. Equality between spouses is one of the constitutional principles of family law. Stipulating that 'spouses have equal rights and duties as to their civil and political capacity and as regards the maintenance and upbringing of the children', Article 36, No. 3 of the CRP uses a reduced formulation, but this does not prevent the principle from being applied to other aspects that are not covered by the text of the provision (liability for debts, administration of children's property, etc.). Indeed, Article 36, No. 3 is a mere corollary of the general principle of Article 13, No. 2, which prohibits any kind of discrimination on the basis of sex. Men and women are equal before the law,[327] and do not cease to be for being married to one another; this is the essence of Article 36, No. 3.

Article 36, No. 3 of the CRP (1976) had immediate application,[328] making unconstitutional numerous legal provisions reflecting the supremacy of the husband. Regarding civil legislation, the 1977 Reform made a *rigorous* application of the principle of equality between spouses, thus eliminating all the inequalities admitted by the 1966 Code, although these inequalities had already come to an end when the Constitution came into force. Examples of this are: Article 1674, in its former wording, according to which the husband, as head of the family, would decide upon all the acts of the conjugal life; Article 1677, former wording, which conveyed the keeping of the house to the wife; Article 117 of the 'law of the contract of employment',[329] which gave the husband the right to oppose any contracts of employment that his wife wished to enter into, for important reasons to be examined by the judge. All of these came to an end on 25 April 1976, and not only on 1 April 1978, when the 1977 Reform came into force. The only inequalities that naturally remained (and which are obviously not removed on the account of the Constitution) are those that are grounded on the 'biological' nature of woman. That is the case, for example, of the *larger* inter-nuptial period demanded of her in Article 1605, No. 1 and of the special maternity rights recognized for working mothers.

198. The principle of *joint orientation of the family*[330] is thus a corollary of the principle of equality of the spouses. If the spouses are equal, then the orientation of the family should belong to both and not exclusively to one of them. But the comprehensiveness of the principle and of the terms under which it is presented in the Code requires a certain clarification and development.

First, we should observe that this is a *mandatory* precept. The orientation of the family falls to both spouses, which would render null and void any contract in which the parties agreed that orientation would belong to only one of them, or any contract in which decisions concerning all acts of conjugal life would be the responsibility of just one of the spouses, who would nevertheless have to hear the other with regards to certain acts.

Second, it should be noted that the law imposes upon spouses the *duty* to 'agree upon the orientation of their conjugal life, taking into account the good of the family and the interests of both'. The duty to agree on the orientation of their conjugal

327. Article 13, No. 2 of the Portuguese Constitution.
328. Article 18 of the Portuguese Constitution.
329. Decree Law No. 49 408 of 24 Nov. 1969.
330. Article 1671, No. 2 of the CC.

life is thus a personal duty of the spouses, to be added to the five duties laid out in Article 1672. Of course, spouses may not arrive at an agreement about a particular act or matter in their conjugal life, but they should be prepared to try to reach an agreement. The spouse who wishes to decide all matters of matrimonial life alone violates this duty, deliberately refusing to come to an agreement with the other.

199. The third point to consider is the *object* of the agreement. This should only concern the *orientation* of their conjugal life (as the law stipulates), and the notion that the power to put into practice what has been agreed upon naturally belongs to either of the spouses. It should also be remembered that the law only obliges the spouses to agree on the orientation of their *conjugal life*; the personal or private lives of husband and wife thus remain outside. Marriage does not limit the rights of personality of the spouses, except the right to sexual freedom, since each owes the other the 'marital debt' (spouse's sexual commitment to one another) as well as to refrain to have sexual relations with third parties. Article 1677-D, according to which each spouse may exercise any profession or activity without the consent of the other, falls within this framework.

200. Equality has its price, considering that spouses may disagree about the orientation of family life and, since the decision does not fall to either party, they have to know how to resolve their differences. The question that arises is that of knowing if the court should intervene and under what terms. In principle, our law denies judicial intervention. In the ambit of personal relations between spouses,[331] there are only three cases in which the Code admits that a conflict should be decided in court: in cases of disagreement about the establishment or alteration of the family home;[332] about the given name or surnames of the children;[333] and about matters of particular importance to do with the exercise of parental responsibilities[334] These are cases in which it is especially necessary or urgent to find a solution to the conflict. It is necessary to establish the family home in order to know where the duty of cohabitation is to be fulfilled. The children must have a name; conflicts about the exercise of parental responsibilities in matters of particular importance (such as the opportunity for a child of the couple to have surgery) may require a rapid solution. Apart from these cases, the disagreement should be resolved by the family, between the spouses themselves. The law refuses to intervene and appeals to the couple's sense of responsibility and to their capacity to regulate the family on their own.

331. Unlike in property relations, where intervention is largely admitted: cf. Art. 1684, No. 3 of the CC.
332. Article 1673, No. 3 of the CC.
333. Article 1875, No. 2 of the CC.
334. Article 1901, No. 2 of the CC.

II. Taking of Name in Marriage

201. The effects of marriage as to the *patronymic name*, that is, the *surnames* of the spouses, are regulated in Articles 1677–1677-C, which, in accordance with the new principle of equality, introduced substantial alterations to the system established by the 1966 Code.

The fundamental rule is that of Article 1677, according to which spouses retain their own surnames but may add surnames of the other, to a maximum of two.

Thus, traditional practices are retained in our law, such as the fact that marriage does not cause either spouse to *lose* their original family name, nor to be under any *obligation* to take surnames of the other spouse; indeed, spouses may at any moment renounce surnames adopted.[335] But the possibility of adding one's spouse's surnames to one's own was also extended to the husband, a possibility which prior legislation had only granted to the wife, which did not seem to conform to the principle of equality, expressed in Articles 13 and 36, No. 3 of the CRP. This option is usually exercised on the occasion of marriage, but the law does not prevent it from happening later. Application to do so should be made to the official of the registry office where the spouse's birth records are held, where the alteration to the surname will be annotated.[336]

202. The spouse that has adopted the other's surnames will retain them in the event of being *widowed*, and even upon *remarrying*, if the intention to do so is declared before the second marriage is celebrated,[337] though in this case it is not possible to add surnames of the second spouse.[338] If the declaration is not made before the date of remarriage, then the widow or widower loses any surnames that he/she might have adopted from the first spouse,[339] and may then add surnames of the second one, under the general terms of Article 1677, No. 1.

203. The case of *separation* is laid out in the 1st part of No. 1 of Article 1677-B, according to which, when separation has been decreed, each spouse may retain any surnames that they may have adopted from the other, as in the case of widowhood. However, nothing prevents them from renouncing their spouse's surnames, under the general terms of Article 104, No. 2, subparagraph d) of the Code of Civil Registry.

204. A different system operates in the case of *divorce*, in which, in principle, each spouse will lose any surnames that they have adopted from the other; under the terms of Article 1677-B, No. 1, second part, they may however retain them if the ex-spouse gives his/her consent, in any of the ways laid down in No. 2 of the precept, or if they have been authorized to use them taking into account the reasons

335. Article 104, No. 2, subpara. d), of the Code of Civil Registry.
336. Article 69, No. 1, subpara. j) of the Code of Civil Registry.
337. Article 1677-A of the CC.
338. Article 1677, No. 2 of the CC.
339. Article 1677-A, 2nd part, *a contr.* of the CC.

invoked. If they retain their former spouse's surnames, and go on to remarry, they may not add the surnames of the new spouse.[340]

Application for the authorization to use the surnames of the former spouse may be made during the divorce process; but it can also be done through a special suit, even after the divorce has been decreed.[341]

205. Finally, it should be pointed out that, in the event of the death of the one of the spouses or of a separation order, the spouse that retains the other's surnames may be *deprived* of the right to use them when that use seriously harms the moral interests of that spouse or of his/her family.[342] Petition may be made to deprive the former spouse of the use of the name, which follows the terms referred to in 'proceedings tending to the formation of agreement between the parties',[343] in the case of divorce or separation, without the consent of one of the spouses or by mutual consent, by the other spouse or ex-spouse and, in the case of widowhood, by descendants, ascendants or siblings of the deceased spouse.[344]

III. Duty of Consortium

206. Under the terms of Article 1672 of the CC, spouses are reciprocally bound by the duties of respect, fidelity, cohabitation, cooperation and maintenance. These are reciprocal duties, as demanded by the principle of equality between spouses. There are no longer specific duties, namely according to the gender of the spouses.

207. The question of knowing whether the list in Article 1672 is exhaustive, or, as sometimes is said, alongside the *explicit* conjugal duties in that precept there are also *implicit* ones, is sometimes raised in doctrine. The positive solution may be based upon 'full conjugal living'[345] which constitutes, in short, the content of the conjugal relationship. But it is not easy to think of duties that are not covered by one or another of the *explicit* duties laid out in Article 1672. Thus, the duty of *sincerity* falls under the duty of respect; the duty of each spouse to *inform* the other about their property, particularly so that they contribute towards the expenses of family life, may also fall under the duty of respect, or perhaps more accurately, of cooperation, etc.

208. The legal strength of these duties is quite different nowadays, since divorce cannot be grounded on the fault of the spouses upon infringing one of these duties. CC keeps these duties as included in the normal content of a matrimony but their violation, as a rule, has no longer legal consequences. These rules on matrimonial duties are what ancient Roman lawyers called *leges imperfectae*.

340. Article 1677, No. 2 of the CC of the CC.
341. Article 1677-B, No. 3 of the CC.
342. Article 1677-C, No. 1 of the CC.
343. Article 5, No. 1, subpara. c) of Decree Law No. 272/2001.
344. Article 1677-C, No. 2 of the CC.
345. Article 1577 of the CC.

IV. Duty of Cohabitation

209. This word has a more technical and broader meaning in matrimonial law. To 'cohabit' does not merely mean living together, in the same house or merely sharing resources, but also the full sharing of bed and board (*tori, mensae et habitationis*).

In this aspect, marriage binds spouses to the so-called marital debt. Marriage implies a legal limitation of the right to sexual freedom, in the double sense that the married person is sexually committed to his/her spouse and has to abstain from having sexual relations with third parties.

The refusal to consummate the marriage or to have sexual relations with the other spouse constitutes a violation of the duty of cohabitation. Motives related to the health of one of the spouses may justify not only the failure of the ill party to have sexual relations with the other but also vice versa; indeed, the imposition of sexual relations upon a sick spouse by the other may even constitute a violation of the duty of respect.

The community of *ménage*, the sharing of resources, is the second aspect into which the duty of cohabitation may be broken down.

In accordance with the principle of equality between spouses, it is they who should agree together (expressly or tacitly) upon the *family home*, or rather, upon the place where they will live; under the terms of the law, the spouses should give attention particularly to the demands of their professional lives, the interests of the children and the need to safeguard the family unity.[346] Other factors to be taken into account are: the place of work of the spouse or spouses; the location of real estate that one or the other wishes to exploit or manage; the location of schools, if they have children of school age, etc.

210. The family home is the *place of fulfilment* of the duty of cohabitation; once the family residence has been chosen, both spouses have an *obligation* to live there, except when there are important reasons to the contrary.[347] Demands of professional life, particularly, may justify one spouse leaving the family residence for a shorter or longer period. This does not constitute a de facto separation of spouses, for the effects laid down in Article 1781, subparagraphs a) and b), if both have the intention of re-establishing conjugal living when this becomes possible.[348] Another important reason why one of the spouses may not reside in the family home is when conjugal life has become intolerable, due to ill treatment or injury inflicted by the other.

211. The agreement about the family home may not be unilaterally revoked by either spouse; *alteration* of residence also requires the agreement of both.[349]

In the absence of an agreement about the location or alteration of the family home, the law permits, exceptionally, that either spouse applies to the court to

346. Article 1673, No. 1 of the CC.
347. Article 1673, No. 2 of the CC.
348. Article 1782, No. 1 of the CC.
349. Article 1673, No. 3 of the CC.

resolve the problem. The legal solution thus understands that desertion of the family home constitutes a violation of the duty of cohabitation and, as such, is a cause for divorce; there is, therefore, a need to establish the respective place, in order to know if one of the spouses, and which one, has infringed that duty.

212. The law seems to presuppose that there is always a family home, chosen by the spouses or by the court upon petition by one of them; but there may be no family home, if there does not exist an effective cohabitation between the spouses. Let us suppose that the spouses are two young people who study, he in Lisbon and she in Coimbra, each of them living in bed and breakfast accommodation or in rented rooms. This is of course a different scenario to that in which one of the spouses, for months or years, does not reside in the family home because of professional demands. In that case, there does not cease to be a family home, where the other should fulfil the duty of cohabitation and he/she himself/herself should fulfil it, as soon as the reasons that justify failure to do so come to an end.

V. Duty of Fidelity

213. This is a purely *negative* duty, since the so-called marital debt (i.e., the sexual commitment of the spouses) is not part of the duty of fidelity but of cohabitation, one of the duties (sharing of bed) into which that duty may be broken down. The duty of fidelity obliges each of the spouses, first and foremost, not to commit *adultery*, that is, not to have consummated sexual relations with a person that is not their spouse. When we speak of consummated sexual relations, we include not only copulation but also anal and oral sex, since these three situations should be considered here as equivalent, as they are in the Criminal Code for various effects.

Finally, it should be noted that, in addition to the *objective* element constituted by the existence of consummated sexual relations, adultery also supposes a *subjective* element, the intention, or at least the awareness of the violation of the duty of fidelity.

214. However, it is not only adultery that constitutes a violation of the duty of fidelity. An attempt at adultery constitutes a violation of the same duty, even though sexual relations may not have been consummated. And, irrespective of whether the sexual relations are consummated or attempted, licentious or dissolute conduct on the part of one spouse in relation to a third party, or a sentimental attachment and amorous correspondence or virtual relationship maintained with that person, are also violations of the duty of fidelity. It should be noted that these facts are themselves relevant as violations of the duty of fidelity, even when, under the circumstances of the case and according to the judge's appreciation, they do not count as presumptions of adultery.

VI. Duty of Cooperation

215. Article 1672 mentions the duty of *cooperation*, which obliges spouses to mutually support and assist each other, and to assume joint responsibility for the family life that they have founded.[350] The first one obliges spouses to support each other mutually throughout good and bad times, during happiness as well as during trying times; while the second one, which is an innovation of the 1977 Reform, obliges them to assume together all the responsibilities intrinsic to family life. This is not a question of helping each other. It is rather the notion that the family is a joint task and both should shoulder joint responsibility. Thus, the spouse that reveals complete lack of interest in the health and education of the children does not only infringe a duty in relation to them but also in relation to the other spouse, the duty of assuming together with him/her the responsibilities inherent to family life.

VII. Duty of Respect

216. The duty of *respect* is naturally a *residual* duty. Of course, adultery, the desertion of the family home and failure to contribute to the family expenses also constitute a lack of respect, but those are autonomous violations of the duties of fidelity, cohabitation and maintenance respectively. Thus, violations of the duty of respect are only those acts or behaviours that do not constitute direct violations of any of the other duties mentioned in Article 1672.

217. The duty of respect is a duty that is simultaneously negative and positive. As a *negative* duty, it is first and foremost the duty that demands of each spouse not to offend the physical or moral integrity of the other. 'Moral integrity' is understood to encompass all the assets or values of personality, the violation of which constitutes 'injury' in the eyes of the 1910 divorce law: honour, social esteem, self-respect, sensitivity and even personal susceptibility. The spouse who mistreats or offends the other infringes the duty of respect; the spouse who repeatedly ridicules the other's religion or the political system to which he/she has pledged his/her allegiance; the spouse who, without the consent of the other, introduces into the family home a child conceived outside matrimony;[351] the wife who, without the consent of her husband, resorts to techniques of assisted procreation with a sperm donor, or being pregnant with the couple's child, voluntarily terminates the pregnancy; the spouse who donates his/her gametes without the consent of the other, etc. The voluntary sterilization of one of the spouses, unless for therapeutic purposes, also constitutes a violation of the duty of respect, if it is done without the consent of the other.

But the duty of respect as a duty of *non facere* is also, in second place, the duty of each spouse to refrain from conducting themselves in an unworthy or dishonourable fashion, in a way that is undeserved of public respect. In the current divorce law, our doctrine speaks of 'indirect injury'. Although it may not be addressed to

350. Article 1674 of the CC.
351. Cf. Article 1883 of the CC.

the other spouse, the relevance of this notion of injury is grounded on the notion that the couple is a moral unit (as is held in some jurisprudence), so that the dignity, honour and reputation of one of the spouses is at the same time the dignity, honour and reputation of the other. Transposing these ideas into current law, it could be said that the duty of respect as a negative duty is also the duty to refrain from practicing acts or adopting behaviours that constitute 'indirect injuries'. If one of the spouses frequently gets drunk or takes drugs, or commits a notorious crime, he/she is violating the duty of respect to the other spouse.

218. The duty of respect is, however, also a *positive* duty. It is not the duty of each spouse to love the other, since the law does not and cannot impose feelings. The '*marriage de raison*' is in conformity with law, just as the '*marriage d'amour*'. However, the spouse that does not talk to the other, that does not show the smallest amount of interest in the family that he/she constituted, that does not maintain any kind of spiritual contact with the other, does not respect the personality of the other spouse and infringes the corresponding duty.

VIII. Duty of Maintenance

219. Finally, Article 1672 refers to the duty of maintenance, which includes the obligation to provide maintenance and to contribute to the expenses of family life.

The obligation to maintain only arises in situations when spouses are separated, whether legally or even only de facto. If they live together, the 'duty to maintain' becomes the 'duty to contribute to the expenses of family life'. In the case of judicial or administrative separation, and simple de facto separation, no family life exists, and therefore it makes no sense to speak of a contribution to the expenses of that; however, under certain conditions, the law admits a duty of each spouse to provide maintenance for the other.

220. The duty of contributing to the expenses of family life falls to both spouses *under the same terms* (in accordance with the principle of equality between the spouses, there is no stereotyping of functions of spouses according to gender) and may be fulfilled by either of them in two ways: by directing their resources (income and profits) to those expenses or by means of work done in the home or in the maintenance and upbringing of the children. Each spouse may therefore fulfil the obligation to contribute to the burdens of family life in one of the ways referred to in Article 1676, No. 1 in the other or in both. It is certainly possible for one of the spouses to fulfil the obligation in one way and the other in a different way; but it is also possible that both fulfil it in both ways. All depends upon what has been agreed between them.

Article 1676 was introduced by the 1977 Reform and is of great significance. But the legislation was trying to affirm that the work performed by one of the spouses in keeping the house and raising the children has the same economic value as professional work. No. 2 entitles one spouse to a compensation credit whenever he or she has contributed with much more than he or she was expected to during marriage, resulting in a clear considerable economic disadvantage; whenever one spouse misses the duty to financially contribute to house's expenses, No. 5 entitles the other spouse to get part of the debtor's wages directly from his or her employer.

§6. Void and Voidable Marriages

I. Civil Marriage

221. Civil marriages may be non-existent or voidable; there are no *ipso iure* null civil marriages.

Instances that are non-existent are laid out in Article 1628: marriages celebrated before a person that does not have functional competence for the act;[352] marriages were there has been no formal declaration of consent by the couple or by one of them.[353]

However, a marriage celebrated before a de facto official is not considered non-existent, nor even voidable.[354]

Law No. 9/2010 of 31 May abolished the third case of non-existence: same-sex marriages.

222. Voidable cases are exclusively those laid out in Article 1631 of the CC.

The following marriages are voidable:

(a) Those that have been contracted with some diriment impediment (under age, insanity, custodianship, when declared in the court decision, an undissolved former marriage, kinship in the direct line, kinship in the second degree in the collateral line, affinity in the direct line and conviction of murder).
(b) Those celebrated without a declaration of consent on the part of one or both of the partners (temporary mental disturbance or another cause that determines lack of awareness of the act, mistake concerning the physical identity of the other party, physical duress and simulation).
(c) When there has been a legally relevant defect of will (mistake and moral duress).
(d) Marriages celebrated without the presence of the witnesses required by law.

The system of voidability is described above, with regards to each of these cases.

223. Generally speaking, voidability does not operate *ipso iure*, and may not be invoked for any legal or extra-legal effect until it has been recognized by a judgment passed in special proceedings brought specifically for this purpose.[355] In addition, the annulment suit may only be brought by certain people[356] and within certain

352. Article 1631, subparas a) and b) of the CC.
353. Article 1631, subparas c) and d) of the CC.
354. Article 1629 of the CC.
355. Article 1632 of the CC.
356. Articles 1639–1642 of the Civil Code.

periods;[357] in some situations, the voidability may even be considered cured and the marriage valid.[358] This system is not the same as the standard nullity of the CC (which explains why, in legal terminology, there are no 'null' marriages but only 'voidable' ones), since the standard nullity in CC is invocable at any moment, by any interested party, and may be declared officiously in court.[359] The difference is explained by the fact that marriage, and family relations generally, have a particular need for certainty and security.

There is, however, not one but *various* systems of voidability, as we have seen. The circle of people that may file an annulment suit varies greatly, from case to case, as does the period in which they are permitted to do so, and the possibility of the voidability being cured is admitted by law in some cases but not in others.

224. Whether the marriage is declared void or annulled, the effects already produced may be maintained up to the date of the declaration of nullity or annulment, when certain requirements are met. This is what is called a *putative marriage*.

This institution is regulated in Articles 1647–1648 of the CC, and its justification is clear.

Indeed, given the principle of retroactivity of the declaration of nullity or annulment,[360] no effects should be attributed to a marriage declared void or annulled. The conjugal arrangement will be taken as de facto union, and, upon the death of one of the spouses, if the marriage has been declared void or annulled, the surviving spouse may only seek the protection of Article 2020 and the other benefits attributed in the event of the death of one of the partners. Children of the marriage will be taken as having been born out of wedlock, and so the presumption of paternity of Article 1826, No. 1 will not apply. Prenuptial agreements and gifts *si nuptiae sequuntur* made by the spouses or by third parties will also cease to be valid. Neither spouse may invoke majority[361] or nationality acquired through the marriage and so on. All consequences are detrimental, for the spouses themselves, their children and even for third parties.

The institution of putative marriage seeks to avoid these inconveniences.

When society has interests in putting an end to a marriage, all that matters is that it *ceases*; it is not necessary to wipe out the legal effects produced in the past, since it will certainly not be possible to extinguish the de facto effects already produced.

The production of putative effects depends upon three legal requirements.

First, it is necessary for the marriage to actually *exist*. If the marriage is non-existent, due to one of the situations stipulated out in Article 1628, it does not have putative effects.[362]

Second, it is necessary for the marriage to have been *declared void* or *annulled*:[363] invalidity of the marriage does not operate *ipso iure*[364] and, until this

357. Articles 1643–1646 of the CC.
358. Article 1633 of the CC.
359. Article 286 of the CC.
360. Article 289 of the CC.
361. Article 132 of the CC.
362. Article 1630, No. 1 of the CC.
363. Article 1647, Nos 1 and 3 of the CC.
364. Article 1632 of the CC.

has been recognized by judgment, in a suit especially brought for that purpose, the marriage continues to produce all its effects.

The third requirement is the *good faith* of the spouses or of one of them. This is necessary for the marriage to produce effects in relation to the spouses or to the spouse that had acted in good faith, and reflexively, produces effects in relation to third parties. The putative efficacy in relation to offspring does not, however, depend on the good faith of the spouses; as a result of Article 1827, this efficacy is produced even when both have contracted the marriage in bad faith.

The law *presumes* the good faith of the spouses,[365] which, in principle, consists of excusable *ignorance* of the defect causing the nullity or voidability.[366] It is a subjective notion, but the law extends it a little, also considering the spouse whose consent was extracted through duress to have acted in good faith: the notion of good faith here is *objective* and *moral.*

II. Catholic Marriage

225. Unlike civil marriage, Catholic marriage may be null *ipso iure.*

But, as a result of Article XXV of the Concordat between Portugal and the Holy See, the civil court does not have the jurisdiction regarding the assessment the validity or nullity of a Catholic marriage; this is a matter reserved for the competent ecclesiastical courts.[367]

Under the terms of Article 1626, the decisions of these courts, when definitive, pass to the higher competent ecclesiastic authority for verification and, upon request of any of the interested parties, after further review or confirmation by the competent state court, and are annotated in the civil register.

The state Appeal Court verifies that the ecclesiastic decision is in accordance with the requisites established in Article 980 of the Portuguese Civil Procedure Code. The judgment of the ecclesiastical court acquires full civil efficacy, with respect to everyone and everything, as if it were a judgment pronounced by a Portuguese court.

226. Canon law admits, however, validation (*convalidatio*) of a Catholic marriage, by means of which the invalid marriage becomes valid. This may take two forms: simple validation and retroactive validation (*sanatio in radice*), referred to in Canon Law 1156–1160 and 1161–1165 respectively. *Simple validation* is the ordinary form of validation of a Catholic marriage. More than being just a ratification, it consists of a *renovation* of the marriage, by means of a new declaration of consent, of a *novus voluntatis actus in matrimonium,*[368] which only has *ex nunc* effects from the moment of the validation itself. Simple validation naturally supposes that the spouses may now contract a valid marriage, since the reasons for its invalidity have ceased (e.g., a diriment impediment of a temporary nature). *Sanatio in radice,*

365. Article 1648, No. 3 of the CC.
366. Article 1648, No. 1 of the CC.
367. Article 1625 of the CC.
368. Canon Law 1157.

which is an extraordinary form of validation, is the one that truly implies a ratification (*sanatio*) of the invalid marriage. It is distinguished from simple validation because now the renewal of consent is dispensed with, and instead, the consent already given for the invalid marriage is used. The validation of the marriage is not done here through a *novus voluntatis actus in matrimonium*, but results from a concession by a competent authority, a concession that makes the marriage valid (valid *ex tunc*, and not only *ex nunc*, as in the case of simple validation).

Chapter 2. Divorce

§1. Grounds

I. Divorce by Mutual Consent

227. Divorce by mutual consent is the divorce that is applied for by both spouses, in joint agreement.

Law No. 47/98 of 10 August suppressed the demand for a minimum period of marriage, allowing couples to apply for divorce by mutual consent 'at any time', including immediately after the wedding.

228. Up to 2008, the only presupposition required for divorce by mutual consent in addition to the joint intention of both spouses, was that they agreed about maintenance obligations to the spouse that would require them, about the exercise of parental responsibilities over children, and on the allocation of the family home.[369]

The granting of a divorce by mutual consent was dependent upon the ratification of the spouses' agreements concerning these three sequels to divorce, which should adequately protect the interests of the spouses themselves and of their children. If one of these agreements was not ratified because those interests were not sufficiently protected, then the divorce was not granted.[370]

From 2008 on, the ratification of these agreements are mere requisites to divorce at the Civil Registry Office; the lack of any ratification implies that the proceedings are transferred to the court were the judge will decide the issue that the couple has not been able to solve by agreement. In the end, there will be a divorce by mutual consent, although the court has decided one or some of the relevant issues. The rationale has been to underline the agreement for divorce, without any other issue being an impediment for a more peaceful dissolution.

229. In the 1977 reform of family law, the possibility of obliging the spouses to decide in advance about the distribution of their joint property was discussed. However, this idea was abandoned, since it was felt that the exercise of the divorce law should not be made even more difficult in cases (so common in practice) in which the distribution of property raises complex problems that the couple is not in a condition to resolve on the occasion.

II. Divorce Without the Consent of One of the Spouses

230. A divorce without the consent of one of the spouses is one that is petitioned by one of the spouses against the other, grounded in a particular cause. Divorce has been made easier, but it is not a unilateral divorce.

Divorce without the consent of one of the spouses is always judicial.

369. Article 1775, No. 2 of the CC before 2008.
370. Article 1778 before 2008.

The grounds for divorce without the consent of one of the spouses used to be the fault of the spouse or the spouses who had violated conjugal duties or the breakdown of conjugal living.[371] Law No. 61/2008 of 31 October suppressed the first ground for divorce and, therefore, Portuguese system became purely no-fault.

Divorce based upon a breakdown of conjugal living may be grounded on four 'objective' situations: on de facto separation for one consecutive year; on the alteration of the mental faculties of one of the spouses that has lasted for more than one year, if this is so severe as to make it difficult to sustain conjugal life; on absence without notice, provided that a period of one year has elapsed since the date of the last news; on any other reason that shows a marriage definite breakdown.

Law No. 61/2007 changed the duration of the relevant periods from three years to one year; and added the fourth broad ground for divorce, broad enough to encompass mainly facts of domestic violence that may ground a petition without forcing the victim to wait for any period of time.

§2. Procedure

I. Divorce by Mutual Consent

231. The procedure of divorce by mutual consent is usually the responsibility of the Civil Registrar, at the Civil Registry Office. Exceptionally, the procedure is filed at the court when the spouses cannot agree on any of the relevant issues from the beginning;[372] it is sent to the Court when the spouses have agreed on all relevant issues but the Civil Registrar does not ratify any of the agreements;[373] it is of the full responsibility of the Court when, in the case of a divorce without the consent of one of the spouses, during an attempt at reconciliation or in any other moment of the procedure, the spouses agree to divorce by mutual consent.[374]

The procedure is filed at any Civil Registry Office, upon signed *application* by both spouses or by their representatives; the application is filed together with the documents mentioned in Article 1775, No. 1 of the CC and also with the agreement about the exercise of parental responsibilities if there are children who are minors and this has not already been judicially regulated.[375]

The Civil Registrar should summon the spouses for a *meeting*. This meeting used to be aimed, in the first place, to reconcile the applicants. However, it appeared that the Civil Registrars' efforts were as limited as the results; therefore, Law No. 61/2008 suppressed the reconciliation issue and, in its turn, made an invitation to mediation, for the first time in CC. Nevertheless mediation means are modest up to now, and we may say that the invitation to mediation was not more than a cautious way to promote mediation among lawyers and society in general.

371. Articles 1779 and 1781 of the CC before 2008.
372. Article 1778-A of the CC.
373. Article 1778 of the CC.
374. Cf. Art. 931, Nos 2 and 3 of the Code of Civil Procedure.
375. Article 1775, No. 1 of the CC.

In this meeting, the Civil Registrar checks that all the 'legal requirements' of divorce are in place, and examines the agreements on maintenance provisions to the spouse that requires them; the allocation of the family home; the exercise of parental responsibilities over children, when there are minor children, and if there is no prior regulation; the allocation of pets, if they exist. Additionally it is also demanded a document, the description of the common property, whose technical relevance is far from clear in the legal doctrine and in the courts.[376]

The agreement about parental responsibilities must have been previously examined by the Public Prosecution Service in a court of law; for this effect, the registrar of the civil registry office, before arranging a date for the meeting in which he/she will try to reconcile the spouses, must send the divorce process to the Public Prosecution Service, so that it may pronounce upon the agreement between the spouses on the exercise of parental responsibilities within a period of thirty days.[377]

Under the terms of Articles 1776-A and 1778-A of the CC, the registrar must, during the meeting, ratify the agreements that will count during the suit, and may alter them, having heard the spouses, if the interests of the children so demand; he/she will also examine the agreements that will be valid after the divorce is decreed, inviting the spouses to alter them if the interests of either one or of their children are not adequately protected.

If the spouses do not alter the agreements, or after having done so, the interests of one of the spouses or of the children are still not adequately protected, the registrar may refuse to ratify them and may send the proceedings to court.[378]

II. Divorce Without the Consent of One of the Spouses

232. The divorce suit must be filed in the family and juvenile court,[379] when it exists, or if there is no family and juvenile court, in the district court of the area of residence of the plaintiff.[380]

After the initial petition has been presented, in which the plaintiff formulates the application[381] and indicates the cause for the petition, and if the petition is in a condition to be granted, the judge must arrange a date for a reconciliation attempt, and the plaintiff will be notified and the defendant summoned to appear.[382] With both spouses present, the judge must attempt to reconcile them, and, if this is not possible, attempt to obtain their agreement for a divorce by mutual consent.[383]

376. Article 1776, No. 1 of the CC.
377. Article 14, No. 4 of Decree Law No. 272/2001.
378. Article 1778 of the CC.
379. Article 81 of the Law of Organization and Functioning of Judicial Courts – Law No. 3/99 of 13 January.
380. Article 72 of the Code of Civil Procedure.
381. Article 552, No. 1, subpara. e) of the Code of Civil Procedure.
382. Article 931, No. 1 of the Code of Civil Procedure.
383. Article 931, No. 2 of the Code of Civil Procedure.

If, in the reconciliation attempt, the judge is unable to reconcile the spouses but obtains an agreement for a divorce by mutual consent, the process will go ahead under the terms of Articles 931 onwards, with any necessary adaptations.[384]

If, in the reconciliation attempt, the judge does not manage to reconcile the spouses nor obtain their agreement for a divorce by mutual consent, he/she should try to get them to reach an agreement as to maintenance provisions and as to the exercise of parental responsibilities over children that are minors, and also as to the use of the family home during the hearings.[385] It should be noted that, if it is not possible to obtain the agreement of the spouses on these points, this does not mean that the case will not go ahead, since it is not dependent upon the obtention of this agreement. However, at any other moment of the process, the judge may, on his/her own initiative or upon request by one of the parties, if he/she deems it convenient, establish a provisional system regarding the three sequels of the divorce, so that the law may carry out the necessary inquiries.[386]

233. Up to 2008, when divorce petition was grounded on marital fault, only the innocent spouse was supposed to fill the petition; on the contrary, when divorce was grounded on marriage breakdown, any of the spouses could make the application. That ground has been erased in 2008; nowadays, any of the spouses may ask for divorce without the consent of one of the spouses.

234. Up to 2008, the sentence that granted the petition in a divorce without the consent of one of the spouses' suit was not always limited to decreeing the divorce.

Thus, in first place, it should declare if one or both of the spouses was guilty, and, if so, which party bore most of the fault, if the fault of one was considerably superior to that of the other.[387] This declaration served as the basis for the application of sanctions of patrimonial nature upon the guilty party or the one bearing most of the fault. The 'declaration of conjugal fault' expressed the result of an overall judgment about the marital crisis, as to knowing if the divorce was imputable *equally* to both spouses or *exclusively or predominantly* to one of them. This judgment had patrimonial consequences.

Law No. 61/2008 eliminated divorce on the grounds of marital fault, and that declaration has no sense anymore.

235. As we will see in the next paragraph, divorce may also imply the allocation of the family home; the duty to provide maintenance for the other[388] or compensate him/her for the non-patrimonial damage caused by the dissolution of the marriage;[389] the authorization to retain the surnames adopted by the other spouse;[390] and the establishment of the date upon which the cohabitation of the

384. Article 931, No. 4 of the Code of Civil Procedure.
385. Article 931, No. 2 of the Code of Civil Procedure.
386. Article 931, No. 7 of the Code of Civil Procedure.
387. Article 1787 of the CC before 2008.
388. Articles 2016 of the CC and 555, No. 2 of the Code of Civil Procedure.
389. Article 1792, No. 2 of the CC, in favour of a mentally ill spouse.
390. Article 1677-B of the CC.

spouses ceased, for the effects laid out in Articles 1789, No. 2 and 1829, No. 2, subparagraph b), if the proofs produced in the process so allow.

§3. Effects of Divorce

I. Introduction

236. The effects of divorce are generally produced from the transit in *rem judicatam* of the court decision.[391]

There are, however, exceptions to this principle, laid down in the second part of No. 1 and No. 2 of Article 1789 of the CC, introduced by the 1977 Reform.

In the first place, the effects of divorce are retroactive to the date the suit was proposed, regarding the patrimonial relations between the spouses. It should be noted that the exception operates only in the ambit of *property relations*, and that personal relations remain apart. Thus, for example, if the property regime governing the marriage is that of universal community of property and one of them comes into an inheritance during the divorce proceedings, the property inherited will not become joint property to the other spouse, since the spouse that inherits, in accordance with the principle of retroactivity in Article 1789, No. 1, 2nd part, and if the divorce is in fact decreed, it is understood that he/she divorced for this effect, from the date the suit is initiated.

237. In the second place, if the de facto separation is proven in the process, any of the spouses may apply for the establishment of the date upon which separation formally began, and the patrimonial effects of the divorce will be retroactive to that date. This is what is laid down in Article 1789, No. 2. Proof that separation began on a particular day can be made when the petition for divorce without the consent of one of the spouses is grounded on the de facto separation of the spouses.[392] This may happen, for example, if a spouse applies for divorce against the other, in a suit or cross action, on the grounds that the spouse has deserted the family home. The law allows to apply for a decision that establishes the date when the family home was abandoned and which makes the effects of the divorce retroactive to that date; this means that, if they were married under the property regime of universal community of property, any property she may have inherited through legal or testate succession, does not pass to the spouse who abandoned the home during the period of their separation.

II. Distribution of Property

238. With the dissolution of marriage, patrimonial relations between spouses cease[393] and the distribution of property may proceed. This is generally done in

391. Article 1789, No. 1, first part of the CC.
392. Article 1781, subpara. a) of the CC.
393. Article 1688 of the CC.

accordance with the stipulated property regime (or, that which, in the absence of any stipulation, operates *in lieu*), with each spouse receiving their own property and half of the joint property.[394] This may be done by inventory in the Public Notary Office.

Since 2008, in any case of dissolution by divorce, none of the spouses may receive in the distribution of property more than he/she would receive if the marriage had been celebrated under the property regime of community of acquisitions.[395]

III. Allocation of the Family Home

239. We have seen that, in a divorce by mutual consent, the spouses may agree on the 'allocation of the family home',[396] and also upon 'its use during the pending suit' (No. 3); this is one of the complementary agreements that the registrar of the civil registry or the judge should ratify for the divorce to be decreed.[397]

240. Regarding divorce without the consent of one of the spouses, the law in this case does not demand that the allocation of the family home is established in the divorce order. Neither does it establish a period in which the spouse that is interested in the attribution of the renting rights may apply for this. The matter is regulated in Articles 1793 and 1105 of the CC, depending upon whether the case deals with the couple's 'own' home (one that has not been rented) or with a rented property.

When the family home is the property of the couple, that is, it belongs to both spouses as a community assets, under a regime of joint ownership as a joint asset or exclusively to one of them, Article 1793 of the CC enables the court to grant renting rights of the family home to either of the spouses, upon application, taking into account the needs of each one and the interests of the couple's children.

It will be up to the court to define the conditions of the contract, though hearing the couple, as stipulated in Article 1793, No. 1; when there is no contract, the general rules for lease will apply. Above all, the court will have to define conditions relating to the duration of the contract and to the amount of rent to be paid.

The fact that the court has granted rental rights of the family home to one of the spouses and the value of the rent will be taken into account in the establishment of maintenance provisions, if these are applied for. When the value of the rent has been established, the spouse or ex-spouse that has benefited from the right to rent will pay this amount to the other, if the house belongs exclusively to him/her; if the house is community property of the couple or is jointly owned by them, he/she will pay the other spouse or ex-spouse half of that amount. In this case, if in a future distribution of community property, the house is attributed to the lessee, the rent arrangement will naturally be extinguished; if it is attributed to the spouse or to the ex-spouse that is the owner, he/she will go on to receive the total value of the rent.

394. Article 1689 of the CC.
395. Article 1790 of the CC.
396. Article 1775 of the CC.
397. Articles 1778 and 1778-A of the CC.

The renting of the family home, constituted under the terms of Article 1793, No. 1, may however be *resolved* by the court, upon application by the owner, when supervening circumstances justify.[398]

241. The possibility that the spouses live in rented accommodation is covered in Article 1105 of the CC, according to which 'once the divorce or judicial separation has been obtained, the spouses may agree on whether the position of lessee will belong to one of them' (No. 1). In the absence of an agreement, it is up to the court to decide, taking into account the interests of the children, the interests of the ex-spouses, and all relevant factors. Basically, the right to rent the family house should be attributed to the spouse or ex-spouse *that most needs it*. In fact, in allowing the judge to decide whether to maintain the entitlement to rent with the spouse that is the lessee or transfer it to the other spouse, the law is designed to *protect the spouse or ex-spouse that will be most affected by the divorce or separation, regarding the stability of the family home* – the spouse or ex-spouse, therefore, that will be awarded most of the custody of the children.

242. In the case of both divorce by mutual consent and divorce without consent of one of the spouses, 'the owner of a house should be officiously notified of any agreement ratified by the judge or by the Civil Registrar, according to the case, or by judicial decision, involving the transfer of the right to rent to the spouse of the lessee'.[399]

243. Whether the agreement about the allocation of the family home has been established in a process of divorce or separation without the consent of one of the spouses or whether it has been in a process of divorce or separation by mutual consent, the controversial question is that of knowing whether the agreement might be *altered*, after it has been ratified by the court or by the registrar of the civil registry office, upon application by one of the spouses or ex-spouses, on the grounds that there had been an alteration in the circumstances upon which the original decision has been based. Courts have understood that this was not possible, since there was no law that allowed it, although alterations to the agreement on maintenance provisions[400] and on the exercise of parental responsibilities[401] were expressly admitted. Since 2008, Article 1793, No. 3 expressly admits alterations according the rules of voluntary jurisdiction. Voluntary jurisdiction allows resolutions to be altered on the basis of supervening circumstances, gives sufficient grounds for the application to alter the agreement about the allocation of the family home, when supervening circumstances are alleged and proven, in the face of which, in the case of divorce or separation by mutual consent, the agreement would not *now* be ratified for not duly protecting the interests of one of the spouses or of the children.

398. Article 1793, No. 2, 2nd part of the CC.
399. Article 1105, No. 3 of the CC.
400. Article 2012 of the CC.
401. Article 42, No. 1, of the General Regime of Civil Tutelage.

IV. Loss of Succession Rights

244. The succession rights of the spouse, in intestate succession (intestate in favour of forced heirs, intestate in favour of legal heirs), also cease with the divorce. As laid out in Article 2133, No. 3, the spouse will not inherit if, on the date of the death he/she is divorced and the sentence has transited in *rem judicatam* or will do so, or if the divorce was decreed after that date, under the terms of No. 3 of Article 1785.

A similar system operates in the case of testate succession. The institution of heir and legatee is forfeited if it falls to the spouse of the testator and on the date of death he/she was divorced by a sentence that had transited in *rem judicatam* or would do so, or if the divorce had been decreed after that date.[402]

V. Loss of Benefits

245. Another effect of divorce is that laid out in Article 1791, according to which any of the spouses loses all benefits received or that are to be received from the spouse or from a third party in view of the marriage or in consideration of their marital status, whether they were stipulated before or after marriage. The rationale is not to take marriage as a mean to acquire property. Marriage has been the cause of benefits; and the marriage has ended, therefore benefits must be lost since they have lost their cause.

246. On the subject of 'benefits', the law here intends to refer to *gifts* received or to be received by any of the spouses. Article 1791 thus covers: gifts between intended spouses, while alive or upon death, made to one spouse by the other spouse, in view of their future marriage, and the gifts made by third parties in view of the marriage to the intended spouse;[403] gifts between spouses,[404] even when these are simple indirect gifts, made to one spouse by the other spouse; gifts made to both spouses by a relative of one of them in consideration of the marital status of the beneficiary; and testamentary bequests, in the form of the institution of heir or legatee, with which one spouse has benefited the other.

247. The donor may decide the benefit to be transferred to the children of the marriage, instead of being cancelled.[405]

402. Article 2317, subpara. d) of the CC.
403. Cf. Art. 1760, No. 1, subpara. b) of the CC.
404. Cf. Art. 1766, No. 1, subpara. c) of the CC.
405. Article 1791, No. 2 of the CC.

VI. Maintenance Obligations

248. The first rule is that each spouse must provide for his/her support after divorce. This main rule is in accordance with the growing autonomy of ex-spouses; nevertheless, there are still claims for maintenance in courts.

249. Spouses that intend to divorce, or ex-spouses, have the right to come to an agreement about the provision of maintenance, under the general terms of Article 2014, within the general freedom of transaction. Upon close inspection, this is revealed to be the same thing that spouses do when they are involved in a process of divorce by mutual consent and satisfy the legal requirement of presenting the judge with an agreement about maintenance provisions.[406] However, spouses that intend to divorce, and ex-spouses, do not always manage to reach an agreement on this matter.

Before the divorce law reform of 2008, it made sense to ask who had the right to apply for maintenance. *Either of the former spouses* had this right if they had divorced by mutual consent or if, having divorced litigiously, both were found equally guilty or neither of them was. Therefore, if there was only one guilty party or if one person's fault had been considered to be manifestly superior to the other's, only the *innocent* or *less guilty* party had the right to apply for maintenance. In the special case of divorce decreed on the basis of an alteration of mental faculties, the right belonged expressly to the defendant.[407]

After Law No. 61/2008, any of the spouses has the right to apply for maintenance, regardless of the type of divorce.

250. The court may exceptionally, 'for reasons of equity', not grant maintenance to any of the spouses. We can imagine that these conditions are satisfied by a spouse who is filling a petition for maintenance, though for many years did not fulfil his/her legal matrimonial obligations, did not contribute to any family expenses and suddenly, after divorce, finds himself/herself in a situation of unexpected need to which the ex-spouse could only help with a considerable sacrifice.

251. What measure of maintenance should be provided to the ex-spouse that wishes to exercise a right to maintenance has been debated.

According to a strict interpretation, the amount of maintenance that may be expected results from the general rules on maintenance obligations; that is, the ex-spouse may claim that which is *indispensable* for his/her survival, for clothing and board (Article 2003, No. 1) and also for health and travelling expenses. Whether the couple had previously lived much above this minimum standard is of little importance.

According to another interpretation, the maintenance granted should be greater. It is a question of maintaining the ex-spouse (who has become poorer) at *the level of the standard of living enjoyed* during marriage. Above all, in systems like the Portuguese one before 2008, in which the innocent, or less guilty spouse, had the right

406. Article 1775, No. 2 of the CC.
407. Article 1791, No. 2 of the CC.

to apply for maintenance in a divorce suit, it might be considered fair to ensure that the ex-spouse did not at least lose their standard of living – he/she who lost their marriage through the guilt of the other.

There has also been an intermediary position conceived for maintenance obligations: the ex-spouse may aspire to a level of support that puts him/her in a *reasonable situation* – above the survival threshold, but probably below the standard of living that the couple previously enjoyed.

Article 2016-A, No. 3 of the CC, after 2008, states that the petitioner does not have the right to expect to be maintained at the level he/she has enjoyed during marriage.

252. Article 2012 of the CC expressly determines the possibility of *altering the maintenance obligations* established.

VII. Obligation to Pay an Indemnity

253. Up to 2008, Article 1792 obliged the spouse whose fault had been (exclusively or mainly) declared in the divorce procedure, and also the spouse who had applied for divorce on the grounds of alteration of the mental faculties of the other, to repair the non-patrimonial damages caused to the other spouse by the dissolution of the marriage.

Law No. 61/2008 of 31 October totally changed the way the Portuguese legal system dealt with indemnifications following divorce. No spouse has the right to get indemnity for damages caused by the dissolution of the marriage, with the exception mentioned in the next paragraph.

According to the new main rule, any spouse may, as any other person and holder of personality and fundamental rights, ask for indemnity for damages caused by violations of those rights, regardless of the marital status and of the divorce, in appropriate civil courts, according to the general rules of tort liability and not family law rules.

254. A mentally ill spouse, against whom divorce has been filled, may ask for indemnification for non-patrimonial damage caused by the dissolution of the marriage. The petition is obligatorily filed *during the divorce suit itself*;[408] despite the fact that it deals with *future* damages, which the spouse has not yet suffered when applying for the divorce suit, they are *predictable* damages.

VIII. Effects Relating to the Children

255. The exercise of parental responsibilities may have been judicially regulated before the divorce is applied for during the de facto separation of the

408. Article 1792, No. 2 of the CC.

spouses.[409,410] In this case, the simple divorce decree has no effects upon the regulation of the exercise of parental responsibilities in force, though this may be the object of new regulation, under general terms.

256. When, however, the exercise of parental responsibilities has not yet been judicially regulated, spouses that intend to divorce by mutual consent at the Civil Registry Office should previously come to an agreement on this matter; as we have seen, this is one of the three complementary agreements that need to be ratified for the divorce to be decreed by the Civil Registrar. Otherwise, spouses may divorce by mutual consent but in court.

In the case of divorce without the consent of one of the spouses, the exercise of parental responsibilities over children that are minors is regulated by agreement between the parents, subject to ratification by the court.[411] In the absence of an agreement or if court ratification is refused on the grounds that the agreement fails to adequately protect the interests of the minor, including his/her interests in maintaining a close relationship with the parent that is not given custody, the judge will decide, under the terms of Article 1906.

IX. Effects Relating to Third Parties

257. Divorce is the object of civil registry,[412] and the patrimonial effects of divorce that we have examined may only be argued against third parties, as laid out in Article 1789, No. 3 of the CC, from the date that the sentence is annotated in the birth records[413] and in the marriage records.[414] Although the record of divorce has, in principle, retroactive effects to the date of the transit in *rem judicatam* of the sentence, as can be concluded from the general principles and from the analogical application of Article 1670, No. 1 of the CC, the law protects the confidence of third parties who have entered into contracts with the spouses unaware that they have divorced, just as it does in relation to marriage.[415]

409. Article 1909 of the CC.
410. Article 1912 of the CC.
411. Articles 1905, No. 1 of the CC and 34 of the General Regime of Civil Tutelage.
412. Article 1, No. 1, subparas d) and l) of the Code of Civil Registry.
413. Article 69, No. 1, subparas a) of the Code of Civil Registry.
414. Article 70, No. 1, subparas b) of the Code of Civil Registry.
415. Article 1670, No. 2 of the CC.

Chapter 3. De facto Union

§1. Definition

258. Law No. 7/2001 of 11 May describes the situation designated by de facto union as 'the legal situation of two persons, regardless of their sex, who live together under conditions similar to those of spouses for more than two years'. The couple shares bed and board (*tori, mensae et habitationis*), as if they were married, although they are not bound by the formal bond of marriage. The circumstance of living *as if they were married* creates an external appearance of marriage, in which third parties can rely, which explains some of the effects attributed to de facto union. Sexual relationships that are casual, temporary or occasional do not therefore count as de facto union. It is distinguished also from long-term concubinage, however long-lasting it may be, for although there may be shared bed, there is not shared board. Finally, it refers to the unity or exclusivity of de facto union, which is demanded by the experience of living 'under conditions similar to those of spouses'. A person may only cohabit with one other person, not with two or more. It is clear, however, that de facto union does not cease to exist because one of the partners in the relationship is unfaithful to the other, and has sexual relations with another or with other persons.

Up to 2001, this notion of de facto union covered only relationships *between persons of different sex*, who lived together as husband and wife. Law No. 7/2001 gave legal relevance to cohabitation *between people of the same-sex*, and recognised equal status with de facto union between people of different sex for several legal effects. Law No. 23/2010 of 30 August changed the previous Law, amplified the effects attributed to de facto union and applied them all to same-sex relationships, except for adoption and access to medically assisted reproduction. Subsequently, in 2016, joint adoption by same-sex couples, including those living in de facto union, has been allowed[416] and same-sex couples of women (living in de facto union) have been granted the possibility to resort to Medically Assisted Procreation (MAP) techniques.[417]

§2. Conditions and Proof

259. De facto union only produces effects when certain conditions are met.

Under old Law No. 135/99, the first of these conditions was *heterosexuality*. This is not the case in present law, however, in which the de facto union between people of the same-sex has equal status as de facto union between people of a different sex and enjoys equal protection under the law.[418]

Second, de facto union only produces effects if it has lasted *more than two years*.[419]

416. Law No. 2/2016 of 29 February.
417. Article 6 of Law No. 32/2006 of 26 July, as amended by Law No. 17/2016 of 20 June.
418. Article 3, No. 3 of Law No. 7/2001.
419. Article 1 of Law No. 7/2001.

Finally, there cannot exist any *diriment* impediment to the marriage of people who have been cohabiting outside marriage.

260. The proof of de facto union may be made by any legally admissible means; there is not, generally, a pre-constituted proof.

According to Article 2-A of Law 7/2001, revised in 2010, a document issued by the parish council of the area of residence of the interested parties testifying that a person cohabits or has cohabited with another may be admitted. Considering that this is normally a matter of fact attested on the basis of the declarations made to authorities responsible for providing documentation, the fact is that[420] the document does not provide full proof, and it may be proved that the de facto union is not real, since cohabitation did not exist or has not existed for a particular period.

False declarations are punishable according to the Criminal Code.[421]

§3. Effects of De Facto Union

I. Effects on the Persons

261. Not having taken any vows, cohabiting partners are not bound by any of the personal duties that are imposed upon spouses by Article 1672 of the CC. Neither of them may add the surnames of the other to their own.[422]

The law does not however neglect the *personal relationship* that connects cohabiting partners to each other. Law No. 7/2001 validates this personal relationship, particularly in allowing the couple to adopt, under the terms laid out for spouses in Article 1979 of the CC,[423] that is to say, if the relationship has lasted more than four years and both partners are over 25 years of age. There are many other relevant legal provisions that deal with this kind of personal relationship. For example, whosoever cohabits or has cohabited with one of the parties in a court case may refuse to testify;[424] people who have lived in de facto union for more than two years[425] and work in the same company have the right to take holidays at the same time, unless this seriously prejudices the employer;[426] and people who have lived in de facto union for more than two years have priority for the booking of holidays at the same time when they work for the same public institution[427].

According to the new version of the Law No. 37/81 of 3 October the de facto union for three years is a ground for acquisition of Portuguese nationality.[428]

420. Article 371, No. 1 of the CC.
421. Article 2-A, No. 5 of Law 7/2001.
422. Cf. Art. 1677 of the CC.
423. Article 7 of the CC.
424. Article 497, No. 1, subpara. d) of the Code of Civil Procedure.
425. Articles 1, Nos 1 and 3, subpara. c) of Law No. 7/2001.
426. Article 217, No. 5 of the Labour Code, approved by Law No. 99/2003 of 27 August.
427. Article 5, No. 9 of Decree Law No. 100/99 of 31 March, which contains the legal system of absences, holidays and leave for employees and agents of public administration.
428. Article 3 on 'Law of Nationality'– Law No. 37/81 of 3 October, revised in 2006.

262. As far as children are concerned, there is a presumption of paternity that functions within the context of establishing paternity outside marriage, when the mother and claimed father have lived together as if they were married for an extended period that includes the 'legal period of conception'.[429] If the parents live together conjugally, the exercise of parental responsibilities belongs to both; in this case, the provisions that regulate parental responsibilities within marriage will apply,[430] as will those relating to the regulation of the exercise of parental responsibilities in the case of divorce, separation and declaration of nullity or annulment of marriage,[431] as laid down in Article 1911. Finally, it should be noted that children born to cohabiting parents, like other children born out of wedlock, are equal under law to those born within it, by force of No. 4 of Article 36 of the Constitution.

II. Effects on Property

263. The partners of a de facto union are, in terms of the general patrimonial effects, considered as 'common strangers'. Therefore, general rules of the law of obligations and property rights apply. According to the rules of common law, each one may sell movable or immovable property, let or rent property, and contract debts. They may also make contracts between themselves; enter into contracts for purchase and sale, labour, hiring, bailment, loan and loan for use, etc.

264. This being the general principle, the matter however requires further explanation.

The so-called sharing of board, or sharing of resources, is one of the important aspects of a de facto union. This may continue for many years, during which time the partners may acquire property, incur debts, hold bank accounts in the name of one of them or both, etc., all of which will interfere with their respective estate. The question that is raised is that of knowing whether partners may themselves regulate, by means of a notarial document, the patrimonial aspects of the relationship that they have established or will establish, by, for example: making an inventory of the assets that belong to the couple; establishing presumptions about the ownership of movable property or bank accounts; regulating the contribution that each one will make towards household expenses, the payment of debts and the distribution of assets that they may acquire during their life together. In some countries, the validity of these 'cohabitation agreements' is not in doubt; but in other countries the issue is not clear, and in Portugal it has not been raised.

The project of law that initiated the amendment of the Law 7/2001, in 2010, clearly proposed the admissibility of a 'cohabitation agreement', but the rule has not been received in the final document.

The recognition of cohabitation agreements is the recognition of the partners' private autonomy (Article 405 of the Portuguese CC) and, therefore, such agreements

429. Article 1871, No. 1, subpara. c) of the CC.
430. Articles 1901–1904 of the CC.
431. Articles 1905–1907 of the CC.

may be valid as long as they respect the limits of the latter principle as well as the principle of equality between partners, which derives from the general principle of equality (Article 13 of the Portuguese Constitution). In a final analysis, the matter should be examined case by case, clause by clause.

265. A cohabiting couple shares bed and board, *as if they were married.* Hence a de facto union may appear to creditors as an actual marriage, and therefore they could rely on the application of matrimonial rules. It thus would seem reasonable to propose that the rule of joint responsibility of spouses for debts concerning the living expenses of the family (Article 1691(1)(b) of the Portuguese CC) would or should also apply to the de facto union.[432] This regime has been proposed in the project of law that initiated the amendment of the Law No. 7/2001, in 2010, but the rule does not appear in the final document.

266. As has already been mentioned, Article 3, subparagraph d) of Law No. 7/2001 makes the income tax laws (IRS) applicable to partners under the same conditions as married persons that are not separated.

§4. Termination of De Facto Union

I. Introduction

267. De facto union may be extinguished, either by breakdown of the relationship, by mutual consent, upon the initiative of one of the members or as a result of the death of one of them.

Once the relationship is terminated, it is necessary to proceed to the liquidation and distribution of the couple's property, which may cause problems, especially when their common life has lasted a long time; there will often be assets acquired by the partners, debts incurred by one of them or both, bank accounts in joint names, confusion as to the ownership of movable assets, etc.

The project of law that initiated the amendment of the Law No. 7/2001, in 2010, intended to help solving the difficulty of distribution of jointly owned movables assets. The proposal was to consider both parts as equal, whenever it was impossible to ascertain the value of the contribution of each member to the acquisition. However, the rule does not appear in the final document.

As Articles 1688 and 1689 of the CC are only applicable to marriage, the rules that apply are those that have been agreed upon in any 'cohabitation agreement' that may have been celebrated, and, in the absence of such agreement, those of the general law of contracts and property rights. It may be argued that the couple's property may be liquidated according to the principles of de facto companies, as long as its demands are fulfilled.

432. Article 1695, No. 1 of the CC.

II. Separation

268. Since partners do not exchange vows, each may break off the relationship whenever they want, freely and without formalities, without the other being able to apply for any indemnity. This is the solution that results from general principles, since neither of them has the *right* to demand that the maintenance of the relationship, and their *interest* in maintaining it is not protected by any legal provision.[433] Portuguese Courts have so far decided this way. However, it is possible that the end of the de facto union in particular circumstances is deemed as a particularly unfair situation, in which the limits of good faith or *boni moris* may have been exceeded, so that the breaking off the relationship is deemed to be abusive.[434]

269. An issue of great practical interest is the allocation of the family home in the event of a breakdown of the relationship. A distinction has to be made between the home that is owned (property that is jointly owned or by one of the partners in the relationship) and one that is rented.

In the case of *owned home*, Article 4 of Law No. 7/2001 makes applicable Article 1793 of the CC. Thus, if the family home belongs jointly to both partners, either of them may apply to the court for the right to rent the house, under the conditions and terms prescribed in that Article; similarly, if the house is the property of one of the members of the relationship, the other may make a similar application.

If the cohabiting partners live in *rented accommodation*, the two may come to an agreement that the role of lessee belongs to either one of them;[435] in the absence of any agreement, it is up to the court to decide, taking into account the circumstances mentioned in Article 1105 of the CC, for which applies Article 4 of Law No. 7/2001, duly adapted to the case.

270. Particularly with regard to the rights granted in Article 4 of Law No. 7/2001, it is important to bear in mind the provisions of Article 8, No. 2 according to which the dissolution of de facto union on the will of one of the partners has to be judicially declared when they intend to exercise rights that are dependent upon this.

III. Death

271. The surviving partner of a de facto union that had lasted for more than two years has the right to claim *maintenance* from the inheritance of the deceased partner. This is what is laid down in Article 2020 of the CC, as amended in 2010. According to the old version of Article 2020, the surviving partner ought to try to get maintenance from his/her relatives in the first place, and the claim against the inheritance would only be admitted but showing if proven that he/she had not

433. Article 483 of the CC.
434. Article 334 of the CC.
435. Articles 4 of Law No. 7/2001 and 1105 of the CC.

obtained it from those relatives. In the 2010 version of Article 2020, the surviving partner is allowed to choose freely against who to claim for maintenance.

It has been understood that the value of the maintenance does not necessarily aim to maintain the same standard of living that the couple previously enjoyed.

272. Law No. 7/2001 also grants the surviving partner the right of *residence of the family home and the use of its contents* for a minimum period of five years, or more, to the extent of a time equal to the total duration of the de facto union.[436]

Exceptionally, this right of residence may be extended, on grounds of equity, considering the exceptional value of previous contributions of the surviving partner, mainly in favour of the deceased or his/her relatives, and any severe actual need he/she is actually going through.

Once those periods of time exercising the right of occupation having elapsed the surviving partner may remain in the house as a lessee, unless any other person is entitled by law to occupy the house.

If the partners jointly owned the family home, the surviving partner may benefit from those rights with exclusion of any other co-owner.

273. The law also gives the surviving partner the *right of priority in the sale of the house* for the time he/she is using it upon any legal title. This means that the house must be sold to the surviving partner as long as he/she pays the price anyone else is willing to pay.

274. In the event of death of the partner who is the tenant of the family home, there is also a special regime. The lease does not expire if the de facto union has lasted for more than one year and the surviving partner has lived in the leased home for more than one year.[437]

275. If damage is suffered as a result of the death of one of the cohabiting partners, can the surviving partner demand *indemnity* for the damage suffered? When it is a case of patrimonial damage, the claim may be grounded on No. 3 of Article 495 of the CC, if the deceased made maintenance provisions to the survivor, and if this provision, though it is not possible to legally claim it, corresponds under the circumstances to a duty of justice and therefore to a fulfilment of a 'natural obligation'.[438] If it was a case of non-patrimonial damage, the matter used to be debatable: while on the one hand Article 496, No. 2 limited the circle of persons that might apply for indemnity for the death of the victim, and did not take into consideration the person with whom he/she cohabited, on the other hand, the Constitutional Court, in 2002, judged this rule unconstitutional, because of the difference in treatment between the spouse and the person with whom the victim lived in a de facto union; later decisions, however, reversed the previous one.

436. Article 5, Nos 1 and 2 of Law No. 7/2001.
437. Article 5, No. 10 of Law No. 7/2001 and Art. 1106, No. 1, c) of the CC.
438. Article 402 of the CC.

The revision of the Law, in 2010, expressly included the surviving partner in the number of possible beneficiaries. The surviving member and the descendants of the deceased person are entitled to indemnity.

276. The law also gives the surviving partner the *right to a death grant and survivor's pension*, if the deceased was an employee or agent of public administration or of regional or local administration.

For a long time, courts did not recognize the right to the pension unless the claimant proved that he/she was in a needy situation and couldn't get maintenance from his/her relatives or from the inheritance of the deceased partner. This issue has been dealt with as an important one to keep de facto union and marriage really different, as a surviving spouse could ask for the pension by simply showing the death of the other spouse. There have been several decisions of the Constitutional Court most of them supporting the mainstream solution, keeping the difference clear between de facto union and marriage.

The reform of Law No. 7/2001, in 2010, however, changed the legal regime by letting the surviving partner get the pension in the same terms as the surviving spouse.

277. Law No. 7/2001 also grants to the person who cohabited with the deceased the right to benefits for a death resulting from a work accident or professional illness[439] and to field-allowances and pensions for exceptional and relevant services to the country.[440]

278. Finally, we should refer to Article 227, No. 2 of the Labour Code, which allows the worker *to be absent* from work for five consecutive days following the death of the person with whom he/she cohabited, provided that the de facto union lasted for more than two years (as a result of Article 1, Nos 1 and 3, subparagraph c) of Law No. 7/2001, the 'special legislation' to which that provision refers).

439. Article 3, subpara. f); cf. Arts 20–22 of Law No. 100/97 of 13 September.
440. Article 3, subpara. g); cf. Arts 5, 6 and 8 of Decree Law No. 466/99 of 6 November.

Chapter 4. Filiation

§1. Maternity

I. At the Civil Registry Office

279. Maternity 'results from the fact of birth',[441] without the subsequent need for an acknowledgement of maternity by the mother, for both the children of married women and the children of single women.

We should bear in mind, however, that:

(a) within lesbian couples (married or living in a de facto union), it is now allowed[442] for one of the women to register biological maternity, and to for the other to register maternity based both on the consent to use MAP techniques within the relationship, and on the will to assume the status of the legal mother; in this case, official inquiry for paternity is not applied;

(b) surrogate motherhood has been recognised by Law No. 25/2016 of 22 August, but only in extreme circumstances: in cases of absence of uterus, lesion or disease of the uterus which absolutely or definitively prevents pregnancy, or other clinical situations which justify it. This would allow to establish *legal maternity* regarding a woman who is not able to bear a child and who had benefited from a free surrogacy provided by another woman, setting aside the general rules. However, the legal regime of surrogacy enclosed in Law No. 25/2016 raised several constitutional issues and the Constitutional Court was requested to review the constitutionality of its rules. The Constitutional Court considered that: (i) according to the law, the right of the pregnant woman to revoke consent is very limited in time and, for this reason, it breaches the fundamental right of the pregnant woman to develop her personality; the court held that the period for revocation should be extended up until the moment she is fulfilling the essential obligation to hand over the child; (ii) the law is very unclear as to the possibility for the parties to agree clauses other than those included in the standard contract, specifically as regards imposing 'lifestyles' on the pregnant woman. Thus, the CNPMA (National Council on Medically Assisted Procreation) guidelines for authorizing and supervising the agreement are uncertain and eventually arbitrary and do not comply with the constitutional demands. The regulations of Law No. 25/2016 of 22 August that were endorsed in this decision have now become inapplicable, and with them other important aspects of law.

Subsequent paragraphs explain the cases considered normal up to now. In 2007, Law No. 28/2007 of 28 August set a scheme of taking notice of the birth at the health unit where the birth takes place. The formal notice of the birth is then transmitted to the competent social security office and to the competent local general

441. Article 1796, No. 1 of the CC.
442. Article 20, No. 1 of Law No. 17/2016 of 20 June.

practitioner centre. The newborn ends up registered automatically at the most important public services devoted to citizen's protection. This new scheme is being spread throughout the country.

280. The maternity is established upon the occasion of the registration of birth. The person who makes the declaration of birth must *identify* the mother, and this identification is sufficient for the registration official to *mention* the mother's name in the entry of birth.[443] If the birth occurred less than a year before, the maternity mentioned is deemed established, and the mother will have to be notified of that fact, in case it was not her or her husband who made the declaration.[444] If the declared birth occurred a year or more before, the abnormality of the situation justifies some measures of precaution, unless the mother is the one to make the declaration, is present at the act or is represented by an attorney; in this case, the mother is in a situation that allows her to corroborate the establishing of the relationship. If, on the contrary, the mother is not in a situation that enables her to control the establishing of maternity, the legislator avoids the automatic establishing of maternity, opting for the person indicated as the mother to be notified so as to grant her the opportunity to oppose it; her silence, however, will be equivalent to agreeing to it. If the woman indicated as the mother denies the maternity, or if she has not been notified, the reference to maternity will not be converted into the establishing of maternity and will produce no effect.[445]

281. In another type of case, though an exceptional one, maternity may be established after the registration of birth; the registration has already been made, but it is incomplete regarding maternity. The technical means to set the establishing of maternity in motion is now the *declaration of maternity* made by the mother herself;[446] or the reference to or identification of the mother made by somebody else.[447] The maternity declared by the mother or the maternity indicated by a third party are mentioned in the registration document, and thereby maternity is established; however, if maternity is referred to by a third party and if the birth occurred a year or over a year before, the caution system prescribed by Article 1805 of the CC comes into effect: the mother must be personally notified so that she may confirm or deny the maternity, 'under the sanction of the child being deemed to be hers'. It should be added that if, as a rule, the declaration of maternity is made before the registry official, it is equally true that the declaration may be made by will or deed;[448] these ways are substantially equivalent to one another, and they only involve different registration techniques: while the declaration before the official leads to a record by means of an entry, the declaration made by other means leads to a registration added by transcription to the birth entry.

---

443. Article 1803 of the CC.
444. Article 1804 of the CC.
445. Article 1805 of the CC.
446. Article 1806, No. 1, first part of the CC.
447. Article 1806, No. 2 of the CC.
448. Article 157 of the Code of Civil Registry.

282. In very special cases, the law prohibits the late registration of the mother's name, either by declaration of maternity or by indication by a third party.[449] Those cases are the ones in which the birth registration is made lacking the mother's name but involving acknowledgement of paternity, and where the mother is married to a man other than the one who acknowledged the child. In such situations, the establishing of maternity has to be achieved through a lawsuit.[450] The reason for this difference of system does not lie in any particular difficulty as to the establishing of maternity; in fact, if maternity results from the fact of birth, it makes no difference whether the woman who gives birth to a child is married or single, nor does the situation of there being an acknowledgement of the child by a man other than the husband make it more difficult for the mother's identity to reach the registry. In other words, the establishing of maternity on its own would not require any deviation in such cases. The reason for the different rule lies in the problem that the establishing of maternity may cause to the establishing of the child's paternity. In fact, on establishing maternity, if the mother is found to be married, paternity would have to be established automatically through the presumption of the husband's paternity; but, in such cases, paternity has already been established by a third party through acknowledgement. Thus, at the moment maternity entered registration, a conflict between the paternity previously registered and the paternity of the husband, required by the legal presumption of Article 1826 of the CC, would emerge. And to ensure that the conflict is resolved before paternity is established and that the registration expresses the 'biological truth' from the very start, there is no alternative but to settle the matter through a lawsuit, which is the right means to file an ordinary proceeding, to contest and present the adequate evidence. This is the reason why the mother must request the declaration of maternity from the court rather than make a declaration of maternity at the civil registry.[451] This lawsuit creates the possibility to impugn the husband's paternity,[452] which, if successful, does not alter the filiations previously registered.

283. The veracity of the established maternity is subject to later control through the suit that impugns maternity.[453] This is a means of challenging established maternity, regardless of the defects that may have affected the means used to take maternity to the registry and that may be the foundation for an autonomous suit of invalidation. False maternity is impugned; the declaration made before the official, the will, or the deed may be invalidated, as they are legal acts.

The right to impugn does not become forfeit. The public interest in the coincidence between legal truth and biological truth, which recommends no time limits for the claim, overrides the demands of security and stability of established family relationships.

449. Article 1806, No. 1, 2nd part of the CC.
450. Article 1824 of the CC.
451. *Ibid.*
452. Articles 1823 and 1824, No. 2 of the CC.
453. Article 1807 of the CC of the CC.

II. Official Inquiry: Remission

284. Official inquiry is a procedure common to both maternity and paternity. It is regulated by Articles 1808–1813 of the CC regarding maternity and Articles 1864 and 1865 of the CC regarding paternity.

The purpose of the official inquiry, as we will see, is to seek the parents who were not part of the birth entry at the right time; and, although there are unknown mothers – namely in the cases of registration of abandoned children – there is an incomparably greater number of parents who are not known at the moment of birth. Hence, the rules will be explained further below, within the establishing of paternity.

III. Lawsuit

A. Ordinary Suit

285. Under Article 1814 of the CC, the establishing of maternity may result from 'a suit especially filed by the child to that effect'.

This suit will be filed by the Public Prosecution Service, within the officious activity; or by the child, on his/her own behalf, if they have legal capacity, or by the child represented by the 'general representative of the incompetent persons' – the Public Prosecution Service.

286. The plaintiff has to demonstrate that the child 'was born of the alleged mother'.[454]

Common doctrine claims that evidence of maternity results from proof of the *parturition* and of the *identity* of the child. That is to say that the plaintiff has to demonstrate that the alleged mother gave birth to a child, and that the child is the individual born of that parturition.

As may be readily seen, the proof of birth is fairly easy to produce, since it is usually an event witnessed by qualified staff or neighbours, although there may be cases, increasingly rarer, when labour took place at home, perhaps unassisted, and where evidence may be difficult to produce as time goes by.

Evidence of the identity is more difficult to produce since it is not always possible to witness the growing up of the alleged son or daughter in such a way that one may guarantee that the teenager or the adult of today is the child born, many years before, of the parturition given as proved. However there being no special legal requirements regarding this proof, the court may resort to presumptions and signs that will help it come to a firm belief, as with any other suit.

It is also possible to ascertain the biological relationship through scientific tests, namely Deoxyribonucleic Acid (DNA) tests which, in addition to the proof of the birth and other attempts to demonstrate the identity of the alleged son or daughter, may convince the court of the existence or non-existence of the maternity relationship. In fact, the traditional evidence of birth and identity was mandatory because

454. Article 1816, No. 1 of the CC.

there were no alternatives – no scientific means were available to demonstrate what was required. Today, however, there is no reason for that evidence to be regarded as necessary, provided that maternity may be ascertained through direct scientific tests.

So as to make it easier for the plaintiff to produce evidence, Article 1816, No. 2 has regulated two cases where maternity is presumed. Hence, if the plaintiff is capable of demonstrating that he/she lived as his/her son (*posse de estado*) or daughter (paragraph a)), or if he/she produces a written document in which the alleged mother claims the maternity (paragraph b)), the plaintiff will not be required to prove the maternity relationship; it will be presumed by law.

The presumption established in Article 1816, No. 2 may be refuted by the defendant by demonstrating facts that raise 'serious doubts' in court.[455]

B. Special Suit

287. The suit for the investigation of maternity assumes a special character due to the fact that the child was born or conceived in wedlock, or because the child was acknowledged by a person other than the mother's husband. These norms prescribe certain specificities when compared with the ordinary suit that translate into differences in terms of who may file the suit or against whom the suit must be filed and into the possibility of requesting the impugnment of the husband's paternity.

The alleged mother's husband may file the suit during the child's minority. The interest that the alleged mother's husband may have in taking the initiative to clarify the filiation in legal terms is thus protected, a clarification that might be neglected by others.

The mother herself may file a special suit for the establishing of maternity.[456] The legislator tried to avoid a situation in which the mother might, by means of a simple declaration of maternity before the registry official, automatically set in motion the presumption of conjugal paternity, and lead to the officious rectification of the reference to the paternity by a third party. The possibility of the establishing of maternity being tardy, and the existence of filiation by somebody other than the husband, suggest the need to ascertain the truth and give rise to doubts about the justice of automatically and preferentially attributing paternity to the mother's husband. Hence, the need for a suit in which the people involved are summoned so that the paternity conflict between the husband and the man who acknowledged the child is resolved.

The Public Prosecution Service may file the suit as well, the official inquiry taking place under Article 1808 and subsequent ones.[457]

Concerning the possibility of the husband's paternity being impugned within this special suit to investigate maternity, its purpose has already been referred to: the aim is to avoid the need for a posterior and autonomous suit to impugn paternity when the husband was not the father, a situation that would occur with the establishing of maternity of a married woman and the inevitable establishing of paternity of the

455. Article 1816, No. 3 of the CC.
456. Article 1806, No. 1 of the CC.
457. Article 1810 of the CC.

husband through the legal presumption. In addition, if a voluntary acknowledgement of the child by the biological father had previously taken place, it would have to be deleted from the registry, despite its possible reinstatement if the husband's paternity were to be successfully impugned.

§2. Paternity

I. Children Born in Wedlock

288. Under Article 1826, 'the child born or conceived in wedlock is presumed to have the mother's husband as father'.

The presumption of paternity applies not only to the child conceived and born during the marriage, but also to the child conceived before the marriage and born during the marriage; it applies to the child conceived during the marriage and born after it has been dissolved.

289. Articles 1828, 1829 and 1832 deal with the cases in which the law does not prescribe the presumption of paternity of the mother's husband, even though the conception or the birth have occurred within the formal duration of the marriage. The legislator assumes that conception took place before the marriage was celebrated, at a time when the mother was not yet subject to the duty of cohabitation with the current husband,[458] or at a moment when conjugal life has ended either because the couple is formalizing the legal rupture of the relationship,[459] or because there was no news of the husband,[460] or because the spouses are actually separated and nothing appears to connect the child with the mother's husband.[461] Under the circumstances defined by the legislator, the possibility of the mother's husband being the child's father is rather remote; so much so, that it seems more reasonable to exclude the legal presumption, from the very start, and to allow its re-establishment, on the initiative of the interested parties, when special circumstances have been proven.[462] Article 1832 prescribes another way for ceasing the *pater is est* … rule, possibly inspired by the French law of 1972; it was devised for the cases in which the married woman, actually separated from her husband, had a child out of wedlock. Under the general rules, and according to the *pater is est* … rule, the establishing of maternity of this child would entail the automatic establishing of the husband's paternity, and under the traditional Latin systems, the posterior impugning of this paternity proved difficult, either because only the disinterested husband was allowed to file the suit or due to the difficulty in proving any of the 'specific grounds' of the suit. Being aware of such consequences, mothers tended to omit their names on the birth registration, thus avoiding the attributing of false

458. Article 1828 of the CC.
459. Article 1829, No. 2, paras a) and b) of the CC.
460. Article 1829, No. 2, para. c) of the CC.
461. Article 1832 of the CC.
462. Article 1831 of the CC.

paternity and favouring the acknowledgement of the child by the biological father. Consequently, the coincidence between law and biological truth was achieved going against the law and by illicit means.

The 1977 Reform recognized the great improbability of the husband being the father of the child in those circumstances, despite the formal subsistence of the marriage. Thus, rather than impose a presumed paternity, the law devised a simple and adequate means to establish the maternity of the married woman without the husband's paternity being mentioned.

According to the initial version of the 1977 precept, the married mother might declare the birth accompanied by a statement indicating that her child was not her husband's. This indication would set aside the presumption of paternity, provided that it was corroborated by a judicial declaration stating that the child had not been, at the time of birth, in possession of such a status relative to both spouses.

Decree Law No. 163/1995 of 13 July, transferred the organizing of that brief proceeding from the court to the registry, whose official is not only in charge of receiving the declaration but of reinforcing its credibility as well, so as to allow the presumption of paternity concerning a child born and conceived in wedlock to be dismissed.

However, Decree Law No. 273/2001 of 13 October, simplified the system: the mere declaration of the mother is sufficient to make the presumption of the husband's paternity cease.[463]

290. When the husband or the child considers the presumption to have been abusively dismissed, they may use the 'renewal of the presumption of paternity' rules, prescribed in Article 1831.[464] While it is highly probable that the conjugal cohabitation ceased at the dates prescribed in Article 1829, No. 2, paragraphs b) and c), it is, nevertheless, recognized that the husband may be the father whenever the whole or part of the 'legal period of conception' occurred between the two mentioned dates and the transiting in *rem judicatam* of the sentences of divorce or separation; in this case, the law foresees the means to re-establish the presumption, under the final part of paragraph 1. For the presumption to be re-established, it is required that the initial appearance is contradicted and overcome by demonstrating the plausibility of paternity, under Article 1831. The so-called renewal of the presumption is not designed to prove that the husband is the father; it only aims to reinforce the probability that grounds the *pater is est* presumption.

291. The presumed paternity may be impugned.

In 1977, the Portuguese law widened the range of people entitled to impugn. In addition to the husband, the law clearly prescribed the active entitlement of the child, of the mother, and of the man who is considered to be the biological father. The latter, however, may only act through the Public Prosecution Service.

Article 1839, No. 3 allows the possibility of an agreement between the spouses designed to allow the wife to resort to MAP with sperm from a donor. In such case, by definition, the husband will not be the biological father and is aware of that. It

463. Cf. the current text of Art. 1832 of the CC.
464. Article 1832, No. 6 of the CC.

would be technically simple to demonstrate that he is not the father by means of an impugnment suit. Nevertheless, Portuguese law does not recognize the claim of the spouses who made such an agreement to impugn.

The above-mentioned restriction does not apply to the child, who still has the right to impugn in general terms.

Under Article 1839, No. 2, the plaintiff must prove that the husband's paternity is *highly improbable*, which means that the plaintiff has to convince the court that the husband is not the father.

292. Under the current system, the husband has the right to impugn within two years, starting 'when he had knowledge of the circumstances from which it may be assumed that he is not the father'. The mother has a time limit of two years beginning at the birth. The child may take action during his/her minority through his/her legal representative and, on his/her own initiative, during the year subsequent to coming of age or being emancipated. However, if he/she only came to the knowledge of the circumstances leading to the presumption of not being the child of their mother's husband later in time, the time limit of one year begins at that time.

293. Concerning the children conceived before the marriage, the mother's husband, or the mother, whose child was born within the 180 days subsequent to the date of the marriage, may impugn the legal ascribing of paternity by means of the simple proof of the dates of the marriage and birth. It is not necessary to demonstrate the non-paternity, its impossibility or improbability.[465]

The legislator, however, considered certain situations regarding the alleged father and husband to be verifiable, situations that preclude this right to impugn under Article 1840, No. 1. They concern the knowledge of pregnancy prior to the marriage; the consent, given in person or by attorney, to the registering of the child as his at the civil registry; and the acknowledgement of the child by any means.

The verification of any of those facts prevents the impugnment from following the course prescribed in Article 1840, but it does not stop paternity from being challenged in general terms, under Article 1839.

II. Children Born Out of Wedlock

A. Recognition by the Father

294. The legal recognition of paternity out of wedlock usually takes place by means of acknowledgement. This consists of a person who comes forward as the father of a child who has no established paternity. This act is registered at the civil registry, and then paternity is considered to be established, retroacting to the date of the child's birth.

The law allows for a number of ways to make the declaration.

Acknowledgement before the Civil Registrar (paragraph a)) is the most common form. If the father is present at the registration of birth, his declaration is registered

465. Article 1840, No. 1 of the CC.

on the birth entry, on the place designed to identify the father of the child to be registered; if the father is not present, his identification may only be introduced in the birth registration by addition, after an autonomous acknowledgement act, recorded on a special entry, has taken place.

Acknowledgement may be made in a will (paragraph a)). This form of acknowledging a child is quite common, since the *mortis causa* efficacy of the will guarantees the secrecy of the acknowledgement up to the time of the progenitor's death, while it serves his interest in doing justice.

Any deed may be used for voluntary acknowledgement (paragraph c)). That will be the case of partition while the father is still alive,[466] if the father donates his property to some acknowledged children and to a child who had not been acknowledged yet; or if he makes a donation or a prenuptial agreement.

The typical case of acknowledgement carried out by means of deed in court (paragraph d)) is the one in which the alleged father confirms his paternity in the course of an official inquiry.[467] But acknowledgement may occur in the context of any legal suit, for example, it may be done by a defendant in the course of a suit for maintenance, or by the defendant in a paternity investigation.

Acknowledgement may take place at any time, even when the child has not yet been born, or has already died.

295. Once the acknowledgement has taken place, it may not be revoked.[468]

296. Nevertheless, acknowledgement may be annulled whenever it was completed by someone who did not have capacity to do it, or whenever it has taken place with mistake or under moral duress.

297. However, under Article 1859, No. 1, 'acknowledgement that does not correspond to the biological truth is impugnable ... '. The aim of the plaintiff is to demonstrate that the acknowledger is not the progenitor of the acknowledged person. The grounds for the request are the lack of conformity between legal truth and biological truth; the plaintiff may use any means of proof to convince the court that the acknowledger is not the biological father. It is obvious that present-day scientific evidence is the kind of evidence suitable for the resolution of the issue.

Article 1859, No. 3 prescribes a special rule: it gives the mother and the child the opportunity to impugn the relationship established without evidence of non-paternity. In fact, it consists of an impugnment 'by mere negation', which reminds one of the traditional system prescribed in Article 1840, referring to the husband's paternity. The aim is to facilitate the elimination of false cases of paternity, which result from acknowledgements made in a spirit of complacency or from purely frivolous and abusive acknowledgements.

The lawsuit for impugnment may be filed 'at any time'; in other words, the suit is not subject to time limits.

466. Article 2029 of the CC.
467. Article 1865, Nos 2 and 3 of the CC.
468. Article 1858 of the CC.

B. Official Inquiry

298. Whenever the birth registration of a minor does not include the father's name, the Civil Registrar must refer the full certificate of that registration to the court, so that the latter orders the father's identity to be investigated ex officio – Articles 1864 of the CC and 121 of the Code of Civil Registry. It is obvious that in order to obtain any reliable clue about the father's identity, it is indispensable, almost a logical necessity, for maternity to have been established, since it is only through established maternity that paternity may be ascertained, when it is possible to ascertain it at all.

Thus, the first measure to be taken by the court should be precisely the hearing of the mother, in an attempt to ascertain to whom she ascribes the paternity of her child.[469] And if the court, by this or any other means, manages to gain knowledge of the alleged father's identity, it will hear him next,[470] the result being one of three possibilities: (a) the alleged father confirms his paternity, and the correspondent term of acknowledgement will be recorded in court;[471] (b) a suit to investigate paternity is initiated by the Public Prosecution Service, whenever the alleged father denies or does not confirm his paternity and, however, after having taking the necessary measures, the court deems the suit to be viable, which means that, given the existence of conclusive evidence (convincing proof in this concrete case) in support of paternity, the suit has a good chance to succeed;[472] (c) or, finally, the reverse situation, the official inquiry will be dismissed for lack of evidence.

Bearing this in mind, it is clear that the official inquiry will not lead us to a third form of acknowledgement of paternity concerning children born or conceived out of wedlock – as we have seen, the official inquiry will lead to voluntary acknowledgement[473] – or to the legal establishing of paternity – judicial recognition,[474] as the case may be.

299. This official commitment to ascertain kinship was introduced in Portugal by the 1966 CC. However, such commitment should cease whenever it may lead to the negation of its fundamental scope – the protection of the child's interests. That might be the probable case of the so-called incestuous children, and for that reason, the court will not publicize such sensitive situations: cf. Article 1866, paragraph a). Thus, there is no place for official inquiry when, on the one hand, the court ascertains that the mother and the alleged father are related by blood in direct line or to the second degree in collateral line;[475] on the other hand, the investigation will no longer be possible in the cases where the birth occurred over two years before,[476] taking into consideration that, most of the time, it would prove difficult for the Public Prosecution Service to gather the required evidence of paternity. Additionally, in

469. Article 1865, No. 1 of the CC.
470. Article 1865, No. 2 of the CC.
471. Articles 1853, para. d), and 1865, No. 3 of the CC.
472. Article 1865, Nos 4 and 5 of the CC.
473. Cf. Art. 1894 of the CC.
474. Article 1847 of the CC.
475. Cf. No. 2 of Art. 149 of the Code of Civil Registry as well.
476. Paragraph b) of above-mentioned Art. 1866 of the CC.

the context of MAP, it is also possible to find other situations in which the purpose to ascertain biological (paternal) kinship is set aside: however only in the case of single women, using MAP techniques, is the official inquiry expressly not to be applied.[477]

C. *Paternity Lawsuit*

300. After the 1977 Reform, the suit, as happened regarding the judicial acknowledgement of maternity under the 1966 CC, is *free* and *permitted*, as a rule. For paternity to be legally established under this new legal system, any means may serve.[478]

The requirements for admissibility under the former law were generally transformed by the Reform into *legal presumptions* of paternity. Thus, far from being a hindrance or a restriction, today they are a means to facilitate the job of the plaintiff in investigation suits. Paternity *is presumed* if the plaintiff produces evidence of any of the circumstances mentioned in paragraphs a), b), c), d) or e) of Article 1871.

Under paragraph a), paternity is presumed when the plaintiff proves the status that entails, *jointly and cumulatively*, the reputation as child of the alleged father, the treatment as child by the alleged father, and public recognition, that is, the requirements known as *nomen*, *tractatus* and *fama* by the classic doctrine.

Paternity is presumed when the plaintiff proves the existence of a letter, or any other document, in which the alleged father unequivocally declares his paternity.

The law makes no special formal requirements here: a simple private writing, even unsigned (for instance, a page from a personal *diary*), will be sufficient; it may even be a photocopy or another reproduction of the original document, whose probative value will be determined by the general rules applicable to documents.[479]

Another basis for the presumption of paternity is the existence, within the legal period of conception, of 'lasting, shared life together in circumstances similar to those of spouses, or lasting concubinage between the mother and the alleged father'.

The transcribed formula encompasses two different situations, which may be differentiated as: *lasting community*, presupposing regular community of bed and table, the same permanent residence and, as a rule, a social pattern of behaviour similar to that of spouses; *lasting concubinage* does not include the above-mentioned type of community, but it presupposes a lasting and stable relationship, not an occasional one, lived in exclusive terms (hence its presumptive strength).

Paragraph d) requires the existence of seduction of the plaintiff's mother. The law enumerates two situations in which seduction is relevant: in the first one, young age and the woman's virginity are essential; in the second one, these factors are unimportant, but there is a mandatory rule about the ways used by the seducer to obtain the mother's consent considered legally relevant – promises of marriage, abuse of confidence or abuse of authority.

477. Article 20 of Law No. 32/2006 of 26 July, as amended by Law No. 17/2016 of 20 June.
478. Namely scientific, under Art. 1801 of the CC.
479. Articles 363 and subsequent ones.

Added in 1998, paragraph e) considers the presumption of paternity to be founded on simple evidence of sexual intercourse between the mother and the alleged father.

301. The presumption will be dismissed if *serious doubts* about the paternity of the person investigated emerge.[480]

Unlike the ordinary *iuris tantum* presumptions that would only be dismissed if proven wrong, these are presumptions – previously qualified as hybrid – which may be disputed by means of counter-evidence that raises '*serious* doubts'. Although *weaker*, this presumption still has the practical effect of *reversing the burden of proof* of paternity.

302. The most common way to conduct a paternity suit is to prove cohabitation between the defendant and the child's mother, adding to this information scientific evidence based on blood tests or DNA profiling.

It is yet under discussion if a claimant may apply for a declaration that a named person is his/her father upon the mere result of a scientific test, without producing any further allegation or evidence.

480. Article 1871, No. 2 of the CC.

Chapter 5. Adoption and *Apadrinhamento Civil*

§1. Introduction

303. Traditionally, Portuguese law admitted two kinds of adoption: *full adoption* and *simple adoption*,[481] and the conditions and effects of adoption varied in accordance with the *kind* of bond that was constituted, although it also allowed simple adoption to be converted into full adoption if the respective conditions were met.[482] Simple adoption had a very limited legal and practical importance, and the recent Law No. 143/2015 of 8 September has abolished it.

304. Application for adoption, may be made by *joint applicants* or by a *sole applicant*, depending upon whether it is undertaken by a couple (by two people that are married or who cohabit) or by a single person, married or single.

Since 2016,[483] adoption by same-sex couples has been allowed. It has thus granted the right of adoption, regardless of their sex, to all those who lived in de facto union[484] or are married.[485]

The same Law took into consideration hypothetical cases in which same-sex couples, married or living in a de facto union, had wished to carry out co-adoption in the past. Co-adoption means the adoption by one member of the same-sex couple of the biological child or adopted child of the partner. Co-adoption was proposed in 2014, but was rejected by Parliament. It is accepted now that same-sex couples can proceed with the process of adoption that they were formerly prohibited by law, even though their de facto union or marriage might have ended.[486] They are now able to proceed with the process if they can prove that when they lived together, or were married, they met all the legal requirements for legal adoption; and if they can now present a co-adoption-agreement approved by the court. The presentation of such an agreement, obviously, does not dispense with the normal development of the entire adoption process.[487]

305. Adoption, which under the terms of Article 1974, No. 1, 'aims to satisfy the superior interests of the child', is only ordered when the general requirements expressed in Articles 1974 and 1975 are fulfilled.

First, under the terms of No. 1 of Article 1974, it is necessary that adoption presents real advantages for the adoptee, that it is grounded in legitimate motives, does not involve unjust sacrifice for the other children of the adopter, and that it is reasonable to suppose that the adopter and adoptee will establish a bond similar to that of parenthood.

481. Article 1977, No. 1 of the CC.
482. Article 1977, No. 2 of the CC.
483. Law No. 2/2016 of 29 February.
484. Article 2 of Law No. 2/2016.
485. Article 3 of Law No. 2/2016.
486. Article 5, No. 1 Law No. 2/2016.
487. Article 5, No. 2 of Law No. 2/2016.

Second, the adoptee should have been in the care of the adopter for a period long enough to enable the suitability of the attachment to be assessed.[488] The law does not establish that period, which depends upon circumstances; but, as we shall see, for adoption to occur, it is necessarily preceded by the *placement* of the child under the care of the future adopter. After the establishment of an administrative placement order or a judicial placement order, a *pre-adoption* period begins, of no more than six months, during which time the child's situation will be monitored by a social security body, which will also carry out an *inquiry*, referred to in No. 4 of Article 50 of the Legal Regime for the Procedure of Adoption (RJPA).[489] Only after this stage may the adoption be applied for.

Finally, and except when the adopters are married to each other (or cohabit, we may now add), the law demands that there is no prior adoption order still in force in relation to the adoptee.[490]

§2. Who May Adopt?

306. The adopter should not be more than 60 years old on the date the child is entrusted to him/her, upon establishment of administrative or a judicial placement.[491] After the age of 50, however, the difference in age between the adopter and adoptee may not be more than 50 years, unless, exceptionally, there are important reasons to justify it, such as the fact of there being siblings involved, when there may be a greater age difference in relation to one or more of the siblings.[492] If the adopters are 57 years old, they cannot therefore adopt a child of one or two years of age, in principle, but they can, if they wish to, adopt a child of eight or nine. These being the principles, they also have to be reconciled with the demand, formulated in Article 1974, No. 1, as one of the general conditions of adoption, that 'it is reasonable to suppose that between the adopter and adoptee, a bond similar to that of parenthood will be established'. Thus, adoption should not be ordered if, although the adopter is not yet 60 years old, the report prepared by the social security body that monitored the minor during the pre-adoption period, under the terms of Article 50 of RJPA, has demonstrated that it is not reasonable to suppose that a bond similar to that of parenthood will be established between adopter and adoptee. Finally, it should be noted that the maximum age limit established in Article 1979, Nos 3–4 does not apply if the adoptee is the child of the adopter's spouse (No. 5).

307. As to the minimum age limit, this varies according to whether the adoption is applied for by joint or sole applicants: those who apply for joint adoption should be over 25 years of age; the sole adopter should be over 30, except if they are adopting their spouse's child or the child of the person with whom they cohabit, when

488. Article 1974, No. 2 of the CC.
489. RJPA is the new set of rules concerning the whole adoption procedure, approved by Law No. 143/2015 of 8 September.
490. Article 1975 of the CC.
491. Article 1979, No. 3, first part of the CC.
492. Article 1979, No. 3, 2nd part, and No. 4 of the CC.

they need only be 25 years of age.[493] In the case of joint adoption, the law also requires the spouses to have been married for at least four years and not to be separated (either legal or de facto separation);[494] the same requirements as to the period of cohabitation applies to persons who live in de facto union, since they may adopt 'under the same conditions as those laid down in Article 1979 of the Civil Code'.

308. The capacity to adopt does not however depend only upon the age of the adopter but also upon his/her application being approved in the *study* carried out by social security[495] and upon the report of the *inquiry* that necessarily precedes the adoption order.[496] The adopter's capacity results from it having been recognized in the study and in the inquiry and, ultimately, in the court's understanding that the adoption is in the interest of the child, since the final stage of the adoption procedure is a matter of voluntary jurisdiction and, in these processes, the court is not subjected to criteria of strict legality.[497]

§3. Consents to Adoption

I. Necessary Consents

309. Adoption presupposes before all else that the *adopter* has given his/her consent to adopt.

Adoption does not however require only the consent of the adopter but also the consent of the people referred to in the various subparagraphs of No. 1 of Article 1981: the adoptee, when he/she is over 12 years of age; the spouse of the adopter that is not separated, in the case of sole adoption; the adoptee's birth parents, when they are minors and even if they do not exercise parental responsibilities, provided that there is no protective measure of placement with a person or institution with a view to future adoption; and the ascendant, collateral relative to the third degree, or guardian that lives with the minor and is responsible for him/her, in the situations covered in subparagraphs c), d) and e) of Article 1978, No. 1.[498]

II. Blank Consent and Prior Consent

310. In order to constitute the adoptive relationship, the law allows those people whose consent is necessary, under the terms of No. 1 of Article 1981, to give a 'blank' consent, irrespective of whether the adoption process has already been set in motion;[499] if, in the period of three years, the minor has not been adopted nor

493. Article 1979, Nos 1 and 2 of the CC.
494. Article 1979, No. 1 of the CC. The time of a previous cohabitation of the applicants, immediately before the actual marriage, is relevant (No. 6).
495. Art. 49 of RJPA.
496. Art. 50 of RJPA.
497. Article 987 of the Code of Civil Procedure.
498. Article 1981, No. 2 of the CC.
499. Article 1982, No. 2 of the CC.

entrusted upon administrative placement order or judicial protective measure of placement with a person or institution with a view to future adoption, the Public Prosecutor shall take all the appropriate measures of protection.[500]

311. 'Prior' consent, preceding the date on which it should be given, may be granted by the birth parents and any other person whose consent is demanded by law (adoptee; spouse of the adopter; ascendant, collateral relative to the third degree or guardian of the adoptee), and whatever the situation of the adoptee is. It may be given in any court that is competent to hear family and juvenile matters, irrespective of the residence of the minor or of the people that should provide it.[501]

The granting of prior consent has great practical interest because it allows the judicial placement order of the minor with a view to future adoption.[502]

III. Dispensation of Consent

312. The consent of the persons referred to in the various subparagraphs of No. 1 of Article 1981 of the CC may however be *dispensed* with by the court, in the adoption process itself, in two cases laid down in No. 3 of the precept.

First, the court may dispense with the need for consent if the persons that should grant it are deprived of the use of their mental faculties or if, for some other reason, there is a serious problem in hearing them.

Finally, the court may dispense with the consent of the birth parents, if they have been deprived from the exercise of parental responsibilities and if eighteen months have passed since the transit in *rem judicatam* of the court decision that has decreed the deprivation.

§4. Discharge

313. Adoption is irrevocable;[503] like the relationship of paternity or maternity that it substitutes, adoption is not at the parties' disposal.

314. An adoption order, however, may be *reviewed*: (a) if the adopter has not given his/her consent or if it was given in mistake concerning the person of the adoptee, or if it was given under moral duress; (b) if the consent of the birth parents was necessary and was not given, was unduly dispensed with or was given under moral duress;(c) if the adoptee's consent was necessary and was not given. In addition, grounds for revision of any res judicata in Civil Procedure Code are relevant.[504]

500. Article 1983, No. 2 of the CC.
501. Article 29, a) of the RJPA.
502. Art. 1978, subpara. b) of No. 1 of the CC.
503. Article 1989 of the CC.
504. Article 1990, No. 1 of the CC.

But even when the grounds for review mentioned above exist, the review will not be granted when the interests of the adoptee may be considerably affected, except if the reasons invoked by the adopter overwhelmingly demand it.[505]

315. When it is grounded on an *ab initio* defect of adoption, the review of the adoption order has retroactive effects. The adoptee thus ceases to be the son/daughter of the adopter, not only *ex nunc* but *ex tunc*, as if they had never been adopted, and, similarly, the relations that were maintained with the family of the adopter are extinguished as if they had never existed. Conversely, the relationships between the adoptee and his/her birth family, which had been severed by the adoption, are re-established as if they had never been interrupted.

316. The adoption is registered by annotation in the birth records of the adoptee.[506] However, the law also allows adoption to be integrated into the text of the birth record that has been annotated, upon verbal petition by the interested parties or their legal representatives, through the drawing up of a new birth record,[507] thus protecting the interests of the adoptive parents by extinguishing from the birth records the past history of the child. It is, in principle, only from this new record, which does not contain information about the birth parents of the adoptee, that certificates may be extracted.[508]

§5. Access to Information and Contact

317. However, there are exceptions to this principle: (a) as matrimonial impediments concerning relationships between the adoptee and his/her birth family, referred to in Article 1602 of the CC[509] are maintained, the natural parentage of the adoptee is always mentioned on certificates designed for marriage processes, and are extracted from the birth record that registers the natural parentage of the adoptee and to which the adoption was annotated; (b) the law admits that the natural parentage of the adoptee is mentioned in narrative certificates extracted from the corresponding birth record if the applicant expressly requests it, except if the birth parents have expressly declared their opposition to their identity being revealed to the adoptee.

Finally, Article 214, No. 2 of the Code of Civil Registry allows the issue of certificates that are complete copies or photocopies of the birth record of the adoptee (which naturally contains mention of their natural parentage) upon petition by the adoptee, his/her descendants or heirs and even ascendants, provided that the adopter has declared that they do not oppose their identity being revealed to the birth parents.

505. Article 1990, No. 3 of the CC.
506. Articles 1, No. 1, subpara. c), and 69, No. 1, subpara. d) of the Code of Civil Registry.
507. Article 123, No. 1 of the Code of Civil Registry.
508. Article 213, No. 2 of the Code of Civil Registry.
509. Article 1986, No. 1, *in fine* of the CC.

The new RJPA allows the adoptee of 16 or more to have access to his/her origins, granting full technical support and counselling from public services; minors, however, need authorization from adoptive parents or other legal representative.[510]

318. It should be noted that the law gives more protection to the secret identity of the adopter than to the secret identity of the natural parents: the identity of the adopter may not be revealed to the birth parents, unless the adopter *declares that he/she does not oppose* this (if the adopter remains silent on this issue, the secret may not be revealed to the natural parents); while the latter is only not revealed to the adopter if the natural parents *declare that they oppose* this (if they remain silent, the secret may be revealed to the adopter).

§6. Foreign Adoption

319. The new RJPA, after some general provisions (Articles 61–75), regulates respectively the placement abroad of minors resident in Portugal with a view to their adoption (Articles 82–89), and the adoption by residents in Portugal of minors resident abroad (Articles 76–81).

320. As to the placement abroad of children resident in Portugal with a view to their adoption, RJPA keeps the careful regulation of the previous law in order to combat the international trafficking in children, which international adoption can propitiate, and to ensure the stability of the adoptive relationship that will be constituted abroad. Thus, in particular, the matter involves the principle of subsidiarity, and it is not permitted, in principle, for a child to be placed abroad for adoption, when adoption in Portugal is a viable option.[511]

§7. *Apadrinhamento Civil*

321. Law No. 103/2009 of 11 September and Decree Law No. 121/2010 of 27 October established the new legal regime of *Apadrinhamento Civil*. As far as we know, there is no similar legal regime abroad. It is inspired in the Catholic relationship between godparents (*padrinhos*) and godchildren (*afilhados*); it is close to guardianship but with a more personal and familial nature. Maybe it is possible to find similarities with UK's Special Guardianship.

It has been designed mainly to find a new family for children placed in institutions. So far, only a few cases have been registered.

322. *Apadrinhamento Civil* results from a compromise made by biological parents, *padrinhos*, the local child protection Commission, social security and the institution where the child is placed. The court accepts the compromise and makes it official. Proceedings have been reduced to the minimum.

510. Article 6 of the RJPA.
511. Articles 62 a) and 82 of RJPA.

323. The child will be living with *padrinhos,* who exercise parental responsibilities; biological parents keep being parents and have the right to be informed about the child's life, and the right to contact and to visit the child. *Apadrinhamento Civil* is a lifelong relationship.

Chapter 6. Kinship and Relationships of Affinity

§1. Kinship

324. Kinship is a blood tie, and for this reason is also called consanguinity: kin are people who descend from one another or who proceed from a common ancestor.[512] The relationship in the first case can be said to be *linear* or in the *direct* line, and in the second case in the *transversal* or *collateral* line.

325. The effects of kin are produced in any degree in the direct line but *only up to the sixth degree* in the collateral line, except where there is legal provision to the contrary; the only one that exists is Article 2042, according to which, in intestate succession, there is always representation in the collateral line to benefit the descendants of the sibling of the deceased, whatever the degree of relationship.

There are, however, many cases in which the law restricts even further the legal relevance of kin, for particular effects. Thus, collateral relatives that are not descendants of siblings, for example, only have succession rights to the fourth degree.[513]

326. Kinship is calculated by means of *lines* and *degrees*. Under the terms of Article 1579, 'each generation forms a degree and the series of degrees constitutes a line of kin'.

327. It is clear that two people may be relatives in both the *paternal* and the *maternal* line at the same time, and that the law sometimes gives relevance to this *double* or *bilateral* relationship. Thus, full brothers or sisters (related in both lines) have generally more rights than half brothers or sisters, whether these be on the father's or the mother's side: Article 2146. The possibility of a *double* relationship is not however restricted to this possibility. If two brothers marry two sisters, the children that are born from these marriages will be relatives (cousins) in the paternal and maternal lines at the same time.

Having defined the lines of relationship, it is also important to know the *degree* of relationship in the respective line. Degrees are calculated according to the rules of Article 1581: in the direct line there are as many degrees as people that form the line of kin, excluding the parent; in the collateral line, the degrees are counted in the same way, ascending by one of the branches and descending by the other, but without counting the common parent. It is easy to see how, according to this process of counting, siblings, or grandparents and grandchildren are related to the second degree, uncles/aunts and nephews/nieces to the third degree, direct cousins to the fourth degree, etc.

328. The main effect of kin is in *succession*: descendants, ascendants, siblings and their descendants, and other relatives in the collateral line up to the fourth degree, constitute respectively the first, second, third and fourth classes of heirs in the legal order of succession established in Article 2133. Although this is thus a

512. Article 1578 of the CC.
513. Article 2133, subpara. d) of No. 1 of the CC.

common effect of the various kinship relations mentioned, we can see that the law establishes a hierarchy between them. This hierarchy is revealed both by the principle of priority of class or heir group, and by the principle of priority by degree of kin within each class of succession, and it is upon these principles that intestate succession depends. It should also be noted that the relatives in the direct line, descending or ascending, who occupy alongside the spouse, the first two classes of beneficiaries of No. 1 of Article 2133, are forced heirs (those entitled to the legitim of the inheritance).[514]

329. Another very important effect of kin is the obligation to provide *maintenance*, which the law imposes upon particular relatives: descendants, ascendants, siblings and uncles/aunts (this last group, of uncles and aunts, during the minority of the creditor), exactly in the indicated order.[515] As there are various relatives involved, they are all liable in proportion to the portions they will receive as legal heirs of the creditor.[516] If any of these is unable to provide maintenance or does not have the economic means to fully assume their responsibilities, the burden will fall on the next in line.[517]

330. It should also be noted that, on the death of a lessee, and in the absence of a surviving spouse, the right to *rent* for the purpose of occupation is transferred to a person with whom they have cohabited for more than one year and, in absence of it, to a person with whom he/she lived in shared economy for more than a year;[518] the right to rural rent passes to relatives in the direct line that lived with that person habitually, with shared board or in a system of shared resources, for more than one consecutive year.[519]

331. The capacity as relative may also lead to the obligation to exercise *guardianship* or to take part in a *family council*, under the terms of Articles 1931, No. 1, and 1952, No. 1, respectively.

332. Mention should also be made of Article 1639, with which the law confers legitimacy to bring an action of annulment of marriage grounded on a diriment impediment, or to continue with it, if the plaintiff has died with the suit pending, upon any relative of the spouses in the direct line or to the fourth degree in the collateral line; in addition, under the terms of Articles 1640, No. 2, and 1641, a marriage annulment suit grounded on absence (apart from sham marriages) or on defect of consent may be filed by any relative of the spouse to whom the law confers legitimacy to do so (the spouse who did not give his/her consent or who was victim of mistake or duress).

514. Article 2157 of the CC.
515. Article 2009 of the CC.
516. Article 2010, No. 1 of the CC.
517. Article 2009, No. 3 of the CC.
518. Article 1106 of the CC.
519. Article 23, Nos 1 and 2 of the Law of Rural Leasing.

333. Finally, there are the effects of kin that become *limitations* or *restrictions* upon legal capacity.

Of interest here are subparagraphs a) and b) of Article 1602, according to which relatives in the direct line may not marry, nor relatives to the second degree in the collateral line (siblings). Relatives to the third degree in the collateral line (uncle and niece, aunt and nephew) are also unable to marry;[520] this is now merely an impediment, and may admit dispensation (Article 1609, No. 1, subparagraph a)). If, when there exists acknowledgement of paternity, the claimed mother and the acknowledger are relatives in the direct line or to the second degree in the collateral line, official inquiry of maternity is not admitted;[521] similarly, official inquiry of paternity is not admitted if the mother and the claimed father are connected by ties of kin.[522] Other effects that the law bestows upon certain ties of kin and which also lead to limitations on capacity are laid down in special legislation.

§2. Affinity

334. Affinity is the bond that links a spouse to the relatives of the other spouse.[523]

The source of affinity, or of the various relationships of affinity, is therefore marriage. As marriage is the cause of affinity, these relationships only begin upon the marriage ceremony. However, does affinity also cease when the marriage that gave rise to it is dissolved? Traditional rule affirmed that affinity did not cease upon the dissolution of marriage. In the case of divorce, this might surely arise reservations. The solution of Article 1585, after Law No. 61/2008 of 31 October, makes affinity to end after dissolution by divorce.

335. Relations of affinity, as those of kin, are numerous and must necessarily be defined and ordered, in order for a *calculation* to be made. However, in this respect, there is no more to add than what has already been said about consanguinity. Affinity is also counted by lines and degrees; it is calculated in the same way. That is to say, a spouse will be related through affinity in the direct line to relatives in the direct line of his/her spouse, and is related through affinity in the collateral line to relatives of his/her spouse in the collateral line; similarly, he/she is related by affinity to the second degree to relatives of his/her spouse to the second degree, related by affinity to the third degree to his/her relatives to the third degree, etc.

336. Compared to the effects of consanguinity, the effects of affinity are less extensive. People related through marriage do not have rights of succession, and, regarding maintenance obligations, the law only establishes such imposition upon the stepfather or stepmother, with relation to stepchildren that are still minors at the

520. Article 1604, subpara. c) of the CC.
521. Article 1809, subpara. a) of the CC.
522. Article 1866, subpara. a) of the CC.
523. Article 1584 of the CC.

death of the spouse, who is responsible for them.[524] People related through affinity in the direct line may also succeed in the law of rural renting[525] in the event of the death of the lessee, but only in the absence of blood relatives. As for the obligation to exercise guardianship or to take part in the family council, this may equally fall upon people related by affinity, under the terms of Articles 1931, No. 1, and 1952, No. 1, mentioned above. Finally, there are also some effects of affinity that lead to restrictions upon capacity and incompatibilities of various kinds. The ones that interest us most are those alluded to above. Article 1602, subparagraph c), considers affinity in the direct line to be a diriment impediment to marriage, and Articles 1809, subparagraph a), and 1866, subparagraph a), already mentioned, prohibit the official inquiry of maternity and paternity respectively, when the claimed mother and the acknowledger, in the first case, or the mother and claimed father in the second case are connected by bonds of affinity in the direct line. The remaining effects of affinity are covered by special legislation.

524. Article 2009, subpara. f) of No. 1 of the CC.
525. Article 23, Nos 1, 2, subpara. b), 3 and 4, Law of Rural Leasing.

Chapter 7. Parental Responsibilities

337. The CRP (1976) established some principles that directly affected the regulation of parent-child relations. These were: *the principle of equality of spouses regarding the maintenance and education of children*[526] – parental responsibilities now belonged to both parents, since the law did not attribute special powers to either one;[527] the *principle of attribution to parents of the right and duty to educate and maintain their children*;[528] and the *principle of inseparability of children from their parents.*[529]

From these constitutional principles, we can deduce that the Fundamental Law of Portugal is proposing a different perspective from the traditional one for the analysis of parent-child relations, and, especially, parental responsibilities. The principles referred to seem to highlight *the relational aspect* of parental responsibilities, and especially, the need to *care for the child's person* through *maintenance and education.* Maternity and paternity are declared 'eminent social values'[530] and are subject to 'the protection of society and the State in fulfilment of their irreplaceable action in relation to their children, namely their *education*'.[531]

338. The law regulating the parent-child relation underwent considerable modifications with the Constitution of the Republic in 1976 and the consequent Reform of the CC of 1977. It became oriented by a different model of family: the model of the 'small family' that is egalitarian and democratic, based upon affection, solidarity, comprehension, respect and mutual support. In accordance with this conception, parent-child relations began to include reciprocal rights and duties; the duties of respect, support and maintenance are now understood to be mutual between parents and children.[532]

The best *interest of the child* was expressly established as a guiding criterion for the exercise of the rights and duties that make up parental responsibilities.[533]

This consideration of the child's interest and the new model of the family were also reflected in the imposition upon parents of a *positive duty to respect the personality of their child.* In accordance with the maturity of the children, parents should take into account their opinions in important family matters and allow them autonomy in the organization of their own lives.[534] The children, however, were still subject to the duty of obedience with regards to their parents.[535]

526. Article 36, No. 3 of the CRP.
527. Article 1901 of the CC.
528. Article 36, No. 5 of the CRP.
529. Article 36, No. 6 of the CRP.
530. Article 68, No. 2 of the CRP.
531. Article 68, No. 1 of the CRP.
532. Article 1874, No. 1 of the CC.
533. Article 1878, No. of the CC.
534. Article 1878, No. 2, 2nd part of the CC.
535. Article 1878, No. first part of the CC.

We should also mention that the Reform, in homage to the principle of equality,[536] abandoned the previous two-part structure regarding paternal power, according to which 'legitimate' and 'illegitimate' children were treated differently; instead, they were different only insomuch as the way paternal power in the two situations was regulated.

339. The alterations to the system of paternal power introduced by the Reform also covered some aspects of property relations. Thus, the Reform eliminated the right of usufruct that parents had over their children's property, and established the possibility of their being able to use income from the property belonging to their minor children to provide support, safety, health and education for that child, and, within reasonable limits, for the rest of the family.[537]

340. The legal nature of parental responsibilities does not present any controversies today. In accordance with the current model of the family and the concept of parent-child relations and the respective position that each one occupies in the family group, parental responsibilities appear now as a *functional power* and no longer as a subjective right. In fact, parental responsibilities are defined as a cluster of *powers and duties* attributed by the legal system to parents so that they can fulfil their *function* of caring for their children.

Under the terms of Article 1878 of the CC, 'it falls to the parents, in the interests of their children to care for their safety and health, provide support, oversee their education, represent them, even when still unborn, and administer their property'. Parental responsibilities are thus constituted as a cluster of powers and duties, including, particularly those of: *custody of the child; caring for the child's health; providing support; overseeing their education; representation; administration of the child's property* (Article 1878, No. 1 of the CC).

341. Doctrine usually divides the contents of parental responsibilities into two distinct groups: one relating to the person of the child and the other relating to his/her property.

It would seem that such rights and duties cannot be exhaustively listed. It would be almost impossible to supply a complete list that strictly included all the various rights and duties that make up parental responsibilities, because these necessarily vary in accordance with the particular needs of the child, his/her development and the real circumstances of the case. However, there are main vectors that can be highlighted, essentially those mentioned in Article 1878, No. 1 of the CC.

In addition to these main vectors, there are also some other rights and duties: the *right and the duty to declare the child's birth*;[538]: the *right and the duty to* name *the child*;[539] the *right to apply for a passport for the child, to consent to or refuse* that

536. Articles 13 and 36, No. 4 of the CRP.
537. Article 1896 of the CC.
538. Article 97, No. 1, a) of the Code of Civil Registry.
539. Articles 1875 and 1876 of the CC and Art. 103 of the Code of Civil Registry.

request; *the right to travel abroad with the child; the right to authorize or refuse to allow the child to travel abroad; the right to allow or to refuse to allow the child to emigrate.*

342. Parents, as holders of parental responsibilities, are the legal representatives of their minor children. The power of representation involves the exercise of all the child's rights and the fulfilment of all his/her duties, except for acts of a purely personal nature, which the child has the right to exercise personally and freely, and acts of administration relative to property that is not administered by the parents.[540]

Law No. 137/2015 of 7 September, entitles the partner of a father or a mother, living as a married couple or in a de facto union, to share the exercise of parental responsibilities over the partner's child whenever the father or mother is *the only* parent recognized by law. In addition, the Law allows this sharing of the exercise of parental responsibilities over the partner's child in case of death or other impediment of this progenitor and *the second* progenitor is unable to take those responsibilities.

The right and the duty to represent minor children in court falls to both parents as the child's legal representatives, except for those acts that the children can exercise personally and freely.[541] In order to bring suits, the agreement of both parents is required,[542] and in the case of a suit brought against a child that is a minor, both parents should be summoned to court.[543] In the event of disagreement between the father and mother as to the convenience of bringing a particular suit, it is up to the competent court to decide the conflict, upon application by one of the parents.[544] There may also be disagreement between the father and mother during a suit, regarding the direction to be taken by the proceedings; in this case, the trial judge, upon application by one of the parents, will decide how the minor should be represented in the suit.[545] Before deciding, the judge should hear the other parent, if only one of them applied for the judge's intervention, and the Public Prosecution Service. Then, with the child's interests in mind, the judge may attribute powers of representation of the child to only one of the parents, to a *padrinho civil* or to the Public Prosecution Service.[546]

343. In accordance with the Article 12 of the *Convention on the Rights of the Child*, Portuguese law establishes that the child may, in some cases, participate in processes concerning him/her. These provisions include: Article 1901 of the CC, which determines that the child should be *heard*, when there is disagreement between the parents on important matters relating to the exercise of parental responsibilities; Article 1931, No. 2 of the CC stipulates that a minor over 14 should be *heard* in court before proceeding with the appointment of a guardian; and Article 1984, a) of the CC makes it compulsory that any children over 12 belonging to a

540. Article 1881 of the CC.
541. Article 16, No. 1 of the Code of Civil Procedure.
542. Article 16, No. 2 of the Code of Civil Procedure.
543. Article 16, No. 3 of the Code of Civil Procedure.
544. Article 18, No. 1 of the Code of Civil Procedure.
545. Article 18, No. 2 of the Code of Civil Procedure.
546. Article 18, No. 3 of the Code of Civil Procedure.

future adopter should be heard; Article 45, No. 1 a) of Law No. 166/99 of 14 September; while the *Law of Educational Protection* establishes the child's right *to be heard*, officiously or when applied for, by the legal authority; Article 84, No. 1 of the Law of Protection and Promotion of Children and Young People in Danger demands that children as young as 12, or even younger, be heard when they have sufficient discernment to understand the meaning of the intervention for the promotion and protection of their rights by protection committees or by the court. Such imposition is no more than a way of putting into effect one of the main guiding principles of Article 4 of the Law of Protection and Promotion of Children and Young People in Danger, the principle of compulsory hearing; the child has the right to be heard, alone or accompanied by his/her parents or by another person chosen by him/her, and to participate in acts and in the definition of measures to be taken to protect his/her rights.

344. The duty to support minor children is included in the complex of parental responsibilities. It essentially involves the obligation of parents to provide for their children's upkeep. This may be defined as a relationship of obligation that is established, by force of law, between parents and children that are minors, in which the first ones occupy the position of debtors and the second ones, the position of creditors. Based upon the biological bond of parenthood, this obligation seeks to satisfy all the child's needs relating not only to his/her upkeep, but also to health, safety and education.

This obligation is substantiated in the assumption by parents of the task of providing for their child's upkeep, health, safety and education – in short, for all needs related to their growth and development. In fact, the parents' obligation to provide for their child's upkeep also involves provisions of a non-fungible and immaterial nature, such as daily care, in order to ensure the total harmonious development of the child on all levels, physical, intellectual and emotional.[547]

345. The obligation to provide for the upkeep of children that are minors falls equally upon the parents.[548] In those situations in which parents and child live together, since they are married[549] or live in de facto union,[550] the upkeep of the child is provided by both within the normal expenses of family life.

346. In situations where there has been family break-up, divorce, legal separation of persons and property, or declaration of nullity or annulment of marriage,[551] the question arises of how parental responsibilities should be regulated, particularly regarding the way each of the parents will fulfil their obligation to provide for the child.[552]

547. Article 1885 of the CC.
548. Article 36, No. 3 of the CRP and Arts 1874 and 1878 of the CC.
549. Article 1901, No. 1 of the CC.
550. Article 1911, No. 1 of the CC.
551. Article 1905, No. 1 of the CC.
552. Article 1906, No. 1 of the CC and single custody, Art. 1906, No. 2 of the CC.

347. In cases of single residence, the question becomes more complex. In fact, the conditions under which both parents must fulfil their legal obligations to provide for the upkeep of their child are not equal. While the resident parent continues to provide for the child's upkeep in a similar way to that prior to the break-up of the family, the other, the other parent does not do so in the same way. Instead, this parent will fulfil his/her obligation through the payment of a monthly sum of money, as maintenance provisions.[553] In cases of shared residence, the payment of such monthly sum should depend on the specific arrangements of time and responsibilities of each parent.

348. The amount of maintenance to be paid to the child is calculated in accordance with the child's needs and the parents' means. Regarding the child, it is important to stress that it is not only the child's primary needs that are in question (food, footwear, clothing, shelter, etc.). The aim of this obligation is to completely satisfy the needs in order for him/her to have a lifestyle in accordance with his/her social condition, aptitudes, state of health and age, and with a view to furthering his/her physical, intellectual and moral development. Two further factors should also be taken into account: first, the right of the child to maintain the standard of living that they had enjoyed before the break-up of the family; and second, the obligation of parents to provide similar conditions of comfort and a similar standard of living to what they themselves enjoyed.

349. Regarding the parents' means, it is important to highlight that, in assessing the possibilities of the parent that owes maintenance, the judge should take into account not only regular income from work, but also other possible sources of revenue, such as gratuities, future profits, Christmas and holiday bonuses. Capital returns are also included, such as rents, dividends from shares and bonds and also the value of property. If the parent is unemployed or has insufficient revenue to provide maintenance for the child, he/she may be required to sell his/her property. Thus, the parent is expected to sacrifice capital, if necessary, and within reason, since it is unacceptable that the parent should own a considerable amount of property yet fail to provide maintenance to the child, on the grounds that his/her income is insufficient

350. Underlying the obligation to provide maintenance is the fragility and state of dependency that characterizes childhood as a stage of life. This parental obligation towards their child is considered to be fulfilled when the child effectively acquires the capacity to support himself/herself, since, in principle, children that are minors are not in a condition to support themselves. However, Article 1879 of the CC takes into account the possibility that the minor might support himself/herself through working or through some other form of income, in which case the parents are no longer obliged to do so. Thus, the obligation to provide maintenance is extinguished, given the capacity of that child to provide for himself/herself. However, this possibility has to be understood in a very limited way so as not to force the child to assume premature work effort.

553. Article 2005, No. 1 of the CC.

351. Article 1896 of the CC establishes that parents may use the income from property belonging to their minor children in order to support costs arising from their upkeep, health and education, and also expenses relating to the needs of the other members of the family group, within reasonable limits, in homage to the notion of family solidarity. Parents, as holders of parental responsibilities, and because of this, enjoy the right to use the revenue from the property of their minor children in accordance with the order of priorities determined by law; thus, the child's needs regarding up-keeping, clothing, safety, health and education, come in first place, and only after these needs have been satisfied may the needs of other members of the family group be taken into consideration, within reasonable limits.

352. The obligation to provide maintenance comes to an end, in principle, when the child attains majority. The grounds for the obligation cease to exist at that time. Indeed, from that moment on, he/she is no longer subject to parental responsibilities.[554]

353. It is in the name of family solidarity that the law imposes upon parents, within reason, the obligation to provide support for their children, even after they have attained majority or have been emancipated by marriage, in order to enable them to complete their professional training in the time normally required for that effect.[555] In accordance with Article 1880 of the CC, there are three requirements that have to be fulfilled before parents can be obliged to provide maintenance and support the safety, health and educational costs of a child that has achieved majority: first, the child must not yet have completed his/her academic or professional training at the moment they reach majority; second, it must be reasonable to demand support from parents; and third, the child must complete his/her training in the time that is normally required. And the recently altered[556] Article 1905 (No. 2) specifies that the maintenance goes up to 25, unless the academic or professional training has ceased before or has been voluntarily interrupted, or if the obligation seems unreasonable.

354. Law No. 75/98 of 19 November and Law No. 164/99 of 13 May established a new scheme to insure maintenance payments. Whenever a parent does not pay, and the child has no means above minimum wages, a public fund takes the place of the debtor and starts paying. The public fund takes the place of the creditor and tries to get reimbursement from the parent.

Albeit some difficulties set by courts and public administration, this regime has been very helpful to the more needy.

Besides, substitution of the defaulting parent has proved to be quite ineffective, as most of the defaulting parents have neither assets nor money; or they simply cannot be found in order to make payment.

---

554. Article 1877 of the CC.
555. Article 1880 of the CC.
556. By Law No. 122/2015 of 1 September.

355. Parental obligation towards their grown-up children ends when they have fulfilled their aims; that is to say, when the children have the means to provide for themselves, or in other words, when they enjoy economic independence from their parents. This question of economic independence should be assessed case by case; in some situations, it will be reached following the completion of academic or technical/professional training, while in other cases, it will be necessary to complete an apprenticeship or traineeship first.

Chapter 8. Guardianship and Custody

§1. INTRODUCTION

356. Under the 1867 Code, only the father of a child had paternal power. Indeed, Article 138 of that statute established that (full) rights to paternal power and the exercise of those rights belonged exclusively to the father, with the mother considered merely as the collaborator of her husband. In 1966, with the new CC, there was an alteration in this traditional orientation, and, according to Articles 1879, 1881 and 1882 (in their original wording), paternal power became the prerogative of both parents; however, while the father and mother shared the power jointly, each of them had different specific functions to perform. This was altered by the 1977 Reform, which established the full bilateral exercise of parental responsibilities (by that time, still named paternal power) as a rule. Thus, parental responsibilities over a child born within wedlock, when paternity is legally established, belong to both parents and is exercised jointly by them both.[557] This conception of course conforms much more to the principle of equality between spouses.[558] Although the rule concerning parental responsibilities of Article 36, No. 3 of the CRP refers only to the maintenance and education of children, it should be understood as covering all aspects of the parent-child relationship.

It should be pointed out that civil law sought to 'extend' the principle of equality that now existed between married parents to unmarried ones, not only regarding the right to parental responsibilities but also its exercise. Thus, No. 1 of Article 1911 of the CC (in the wording introduced by Law No. 61/2008 of 31 October) establishes that, if the parents cohabit as if they were married, parental responsibilities would belong to both of them.

357. If a marriage has been dissolved by death of one of the spouses, then parental responsibilities belong to the surviving spouse;[559] therefore, upon the death of one of the parents, parental responsibilities pass to the other. This is also the case if the parents are not married but cohabit; if they don't, parental responsibilities must be regulated by a court decision.[560]

358. In the event of the death of both parents, a child that is a minor is, as a rule, subject to guardianship.[561] Guardianship is one of the ways of substituting parental responsibilities. The parents of the child may appoint a guardian (or guardians) in a will or other authentic or authenticated document, in the event of their death or incapacity.[562] If the parents have appointed more than one guardian for the same

557. Article 1901, Nos 1 and 2 of the CC.
558. Article 1671 of the CC.
559. Article 1904 of the CC.
560. Article 1912 of the CC.
561. Article 1921, No. 1, a) of the CC.
562. Article 1928 of the CC.

child, then only the first person named will exercise guardianship, unless the parents have indicated some order of precedence.[563] The guardian indicated by the parents should be confirmed by the Juvenile Court,[564] which will also oversee the exercise of guardianship.[565]

When a guardian has not been named by the parents, or if their choice has not been confirmed by the court, the judge shall appoint a guardian, after having heard the family council. The guardian shall be chosen from amongst the relatives (by blood or affinity) of the minor or from amongst those people that have cared for/are caring for the minor or who have shown some affection for him/her.[566] The law expressly allows for a minor that is 14 or older to be heard by the court on the issue of the appointment of a guardian.[567]

359. The legal role of the guardian is based upon parental responsibilities. Indeed, the guardian has approximately the same rights and obligations of the parents, which he/she should exercise with the diligence of a *bonus pater familias*.[568] However, the rights and duties of guardianship are not exactly the same as those that comprise parental responsibilities,[569] for the law establishes some restrictions upon it. Guardians may only use the revenue from their wards' property for the child's maintenance and education and for the administration of his/her assets;[570] guardians may not freely dispose of their wards' property,[571] rent or acquire property or rights belonging to the minor, hold credit or other rights against him/her,[572] celebrate any contracts in their ward's name that would oblige him/her personally to perform certain acts[573] or receive gifts or bequests from their wards, *inter vivos* or upon death,[574] under threat of those acts being considered null and void.[575] In their capacity as representatives of their wards, guardians also need the court's permission to perform certain acts,[576] and in the absence of such permission, those acts may be annulled,[577] unless they have been confirmed by the juvenile court.[578]

Amongst the rights enjoyed by guardians is the right to be remunerated for the exercise of its functions. The remuneration may be established by the parents in the act of appointing the guardian, or by the court, having heard the family council, and

563. Article 1929 of the CC.
564. Article 1925, No. 2 of the CC.
565. Article 1925, No. 1 of the CC.
566. Article 1931, No. 1 of the CC.
567. Article 1931, No. 2 of the CC.
568. Article 1935, No. 2 of the CC.
569. Article 1935, No. 1 of the CC.
570. Article 1936 of the CC.
571. Article 1937, a) of the CC.
572. Article 1937, b) of the CC.
573. Article 1937, c) of the CC.
574. Article 1937, d) of the CC.
575. Article 1939, No. 1 of the CC.
576. Article 1938 of the CC.
577. Article 1940 of the CC.
578. Article 1941 of the CC.

it may not exceed a tenth of the child's net income.[579] One of the guardian's responsibilities involves presenting a report of the ward's assets and liabilities,[580] and presenting accounts to the juvenile court when the period of guardianship comes to an end, or whenever this is demanded by the court;[581] guardians are also responsible for any injuries caused by their ward when he/she has been found guilty.[582]

360. Both parents exercise parental responsibilities during marriage.[583] This joint sharing of the responsibilities means that both parents must agree upon various matters concerning the person and property of their child. In accordance with the provisions of No. 2 of this precept, when parents are unable to agree on important matters (and only in relation to these matters), then the court will intervene, upon application by one of the parents. The court will, in the first instance, try to convince the parents to come to an agreement. If this proves impossible, then the court will decide the matter. Beforehand, however, the child (whatever the age) shall be heard by the judge, unless there are particular circumstances militating against it. This reflects the 'principle of participation in relation to the exercise of parental responsibilities' introduced by the 1977 Reform.[584]

The legal requirement that there be agreement between the parents as to the exercise of parental responsibilities concerning various aspects of their child's life does not mean that both parents must necessarily intervene in every act. Indeed, each parent may act alone, and the law will presume that they have the agreement of the other. However, this presumption does not function with regards to those acts for which the law expressly demands the consent of both parents (i.e., the bringing of actions representing a child that is a minor[585]) or regarding acts of particular importance.[586] The law does not stipulate what acts of particular importance are understood to be. Doctrine and jurisprudence have considered that they include: application for a passport, authorization for an operation, the decision to baptize the child or not, etc.

Regarding acts of normal importance, the absence of agreement between the parents may not be opposed to third parties in good faith.[587] Good faith is removed by the knowledge of a lack of agreement between the parents or if the act in question has particular importance.[588]

361. In the event of family break-up, through divorce, declaration of nullity or annulment of the marriage, or by the 'alteration of the matrimonial relationship in

579. Article 1942 of the CC.
580. Article 1943 of the CC.
581. Article 1944 of the CC.
582. Article 1945 of the CC.
583. Article 1901, No. 1 of the CC.
584. Article 1901, No. 2, *in fine* of the CC.
585. Article 12, No. 2 of the Code of Civil Procedure.
586. Article 1902, No. 1 of the CC.
587. Article 1902, No. 1, *in fine* of the CC.
588. Article 1902, No. 2 of the CC.

the sense of a slackening or relaxation of that relationship' through the de facto separation of persons and property, the question of parental responsibilities once again comes to the fore.

Legislators have understood the need for care in the regulation of matters resulting from divorce, declaration of nullity or annulment of marriage, legal separation of persons and property, or a de facto separation, particularly their consequences upon a child, and the judge is bound to protect the child's interests. Thus, in situations of conflict, the new system of parental responsibilities may result from a regulation drawn up by the parents by means of an agreement, subject to ratification by the court,[589] or it may result from court intervention, when parents are not in an emotional state that allows them to separate the question of marital conflict from the question of the exercise of parental responsibilities, when agreement seems unlikely, or when the agreement presented is not in the interests of the child. The regulations for the new way of exercising parental responsibilities are therefore drawn up, upon a judicial decision in keeping with the interests of the minor.[590] In order to ensure that the decision is in fact in accordance with the child's interests, the judge will hear the child over 12 years old as well as younger children that are able to understand the matters, taking into consideration the child's age and maturity. The presence of grandparents and other relatives may also be authorized,[591] or of any other person that may have shown affection or cared for the child. In consensual situations (i.e., divorce by mutual consent), the new system of parental responsibilities will result from parental agreement. In fact, spouses who intend to divorce by mutual consent are supposed to present to the Civil Registry Office,[592] together with their divorce application, some agreements: one relating to maintenance provisions for the spouse that requires it; another regarding the exercise of parental responsibilities over children that are minors; and another regarding the allocation of the family home.[593] The agreement about the exercise of parental responsibilities after divorce is sent to the Public Prosecution Service, who will declare, within thirty days, whether or not the agreement is in the interests of the children.[594]

Under the law, it is the child's interests that are of supreme importance to be promoted in processes concerning the regulation of parental responsibilities. Thus, this is the criterion that will have precedence in the judge's decision whether or not to ratify or establish the parents' agreement, and also in the Public Prosecution Service's analysis of the parents' agreement.[595,596]

362. The traditional solution was to award single custody of the child to one of the parents. The right and duty of custody would therefore belong exclusively to one

589. Article 1905, No. 1 of the CC.
590. Article 1905, No. 2 of the CC.
591. Article 35 of the of the General Regime of Civil Tutelage.
592. Article 12, No. 1, b), Decree Law No. 272/2001 of 13 October.
593. Article 1775, No. 2 of the CC.
594. Article 14, No. 4, Decree Law No. 272/2001 of 13 October.
595. *Ibid.*
596. Articles 1905 of the CC and 37 and 40 of the General Regime of Civil Tutelage.

parent; this meant that all the other rights and duties that comprised parental responsibilities would also belong exclusively to the resident parent with custody. This model has been reversed.

According to Law No. 61/2008 of 31 October, following a divorce, declaration of nullity or annulment of a marriage, or separation of persons and property, parents have joint parental responsibilities; they must act jointly in important matters,[597] and each of them has the right to act alone either on daily matters or in urgent cases.[598] This has been a major change in the Portuguese legal system.

The court may decide, however, that one of the parents may exercise parental responsibilities alone, subject to the best interests of the child.[599] The new Law No. 24/2017 of 24 May, added a provision to the CC (Article 1906 – A) to highlight the special cases of serious disagreements or domestic violence within the family, followed by a ban on contact between the parents or, in any case, where there is 'serious risk to the rights or safety of the child'. The law notes that these circumstances may endanger the interests of the child and thus may represent clear examples where the joint exercise of parental responsibilities will be inappropriate for the purpose of applying Article 1906 of the CC.

The parent with whom the child is currently or temporarily living may delegate his/her parental responsibilities with respect to daily matters in any other person.[600] This provision, as broad as it may be, is intended to support daily decisions made by the person with whom the parent is living with.

Law No. 137/2015, 7 September, has broadened the possibilities to exercise parental responsibilities by others than parents, particularly by stepparents and partners of the parent. Since 2015, in cases of impediment of both parents, the court may grant stepparents, the partners of the parent or even other family members the exercise of parental responsibilities regarding the child.[601] This kind of order may also be required in cases of death of both parents.[602]

363. The Law did not change much the way the court decides residence. The child may reside with one of the parents, while keeping the right to visit the other parent; or may reside with both on an alternate basis. The criteria for the court to choose the parent with whom the child will reside are currently the traditional ones; nevertheless, the law added that the court must bear in consideration which of the parents is more prone to promote and keep personal relations between the child and the other parent.[603]

The non-resident parent has at least the right to oversee the child's education and living conditions, thus keeping a check over the actions of the other parent.[604]

597. Article 1906, No. 1 of the CC.
598. Article 1906, No. 3 of the CC.
599. Article 1906, No. 2 of the CC.
600. Article 1906, No. 4 of the CC.
601. Article 1903 of the CC.
602. Article 1904 of the CC.
603. Article 1906, No. 5 of the CC.
604. Article 1906, No. 6 of the CC.

The new Law highlights the importance of the court to make decisions trying to always promote the sense of sharing responsibilities and the contact between the child and both parents.

364. Under the terms of Article 12 of the General Regime of Civil Tutelage, suits for the regulation of parental responsibilities are considered voluntary jurisdiction. This process, regulated in Articles 34–44-A of the General Regime of Civil Tutelage, falls under the Chapter III of General Regime of Civil Tutelage, alongside other civil tutelary procedures such as maintenance provisions due to minors. The procedure in question is characterized by the predominance of equity over legality. Indeed, the interest of the minor is the legal criterion that guides the decision in each case.[605] Judgments may also be freely modified: Article 42, No. 1 of the General Regime of Civil Tutelage, for example, establishes the possibility of a different solution being found, in the interests of the child, should the circumstances change; or, in the event that the parental agreement or even the final decision is not respected, either of the parents, the guardian and also the Public Prosecutor Service may apply to the court for a new parental responsibilities regulation. In fact, this is how it has been understood in doctrine and jurisprudence. Such procedures are not subject to appeal to the STJ. Article 34, No. 1 of the General Regime of Civil Tutelage allows the judge to order any inquiries that he/she deems pertinent in order to gain a better understanding of the child's interests and decide in accordance with this interest, thereby ratifying or not the parents' agreement as to the new way of exercising parental responsibilities, as the judge sees fit. He/she may also do the same in situations when the parental agreement was promoted by the judge at a meeting.[606] Within the ambit of these procedures, the court has at its disposal numerous instruments with which to freely investigate the facts and collect proof: these include inquiries into the social, moral and economic situation of the parents and the situation and needs of the child, and the possibility of ordering any medical and psychological tests that the court deems necessary.[607] Medical and psychological tests are in fact of enormous importance in more delicate cases in order to assess the real interests of the minor, owing to the type of data that they reveal. This way, the judge is better able to proceed to a correct interpretation of the child's interests.

365. In the case of a child born outside wedlock, when parenthood is only established in relation to one parent, it is that parent who has parental responsibilities. The law establishes this as a rule, and the full exercise of parental responsibilities belongs to the parent whose parenthood has been established.[608] If parenthood has been established for both parents, and they live together, the law determines that parental responsibilities belong to both of the parents as if they were married.[609] If

605. Article 1905, Nos 1 and 2 of the CC, and Arts 37, Nos 1 and 5, 40, Nos 1 and 3 of the General Regime of Civil Tutelage.
606. Article 37 of the General Regime of Civil Tutelage.
607. Article 38 of the General Regime of Civil Tutelage.
608. Article 1910 of the CC.
609. Article 1911, No. 1 of the CC.

the parents live apart, parental responsibilities may also be regulated by agreement according the rules that are applicable to ex-spouses living separate.[610]

366. In the past if the divorced parents wished to modify the parental responsibility agreements that they agreed at the time of the divorce, they needed to ask for the change in court. However, Law No. 5/2017 of 2 March, authorized the request for a change to be submitted and also approved by any civil registry office, provided that there is agreement between the parents. The same shall apply to parents who are married but separated de facto and to parents who have never been married.

§2. Adopted Children

367. In the case of adoption,[611] the adopted child acquires the status of son or daughter of the adopter, becoming part of the adopter's family alongside his/her descendants, from the transit in *rem judicatam* of the judgment. All family ties between the adopted child and his/her ascendants are thereby extinguished.[612] Consequently, the power and duties that comprise parental responsibilities will fully belong to the adopter or adopters, depending on whether it is a sole or joint adoption.

§3. Failure to Comply with the New System of Parental Responsibilities and Abduction of Minors

368. If one of the parents fails to observe the rules established by agreement or judicial decision for the exercise of parental responsibilities (i.e., rules concerning the residence of the child, contact rights, maintenance provisions, etc.), the other parent may, under the terms of Article 41 of the General Regime of Civil Tutelage, apply for the court to take the necessary steps to enforce the system that was established and punish the parent concerned with a fine, obliging him/her to pay compensation to the minor or to the other parent, or to both.[613] Upon such an application, the judge may summon both parents to a meeting[614] in order to encourage them to reach an agreement. This may result in an alteration of the parental responsibilities system established, so as to better adapt it to the interests of the child.[615] The judge may also decide to notify the parent who does not fulfil the duties to appear within a period of five days to make his/her allegations.[616] In this

610. Article 1912 of the CC.
611. Articles 1979 onwards of the CC.
612. Article 1986, No. 1 of the CC.
613. Article 41, No. 1 of the General Regime of Civil Tutelage.
614. Article 41, No. 3 of the General Regime of Civil Tutelage.
615. Article 41, No. 4 of the General Regime of Civil Tutelage.
616. Article 41, No. 3 of the General Regime of Civil Tutelage.

case, or if the parents, at the meeting, are unable to arrive at an agreement, the judge orders a summary inquiry, as well as any other procedures that he/she deems useful to make a decision upon the matter.[617]

The recourse to coercive measures, such as police intervention, particularly in matters relating to failure to respect contact rights, given the emotionally destabilizing effect this may have on the child, should be understood as a last resort, only to be used in situations where it is absolutely necessary, and as part of a joint action between magistrates, experts, social workers, etc.

369. If a child who is a minor runs away from the parental home or from the home the parents chose for him/her or is removed from it, application should be made to the court with jurisdiction in the area for the child to be returned. The same happens when the child has been legally entrusted to a third person or to an educational or welfare establishment.[618]

As regards the abduction of children by one of their parents (or by a third party) to another country, it should be noted that Portugal, by means of Decree No. 136/82 of 21 December, ratified the European Convention on Recognition and Enforcement of Decisions concerning Custody of Children and on Restoration of Custody of Children, concluded in Luxembourg on 20 May 1980, and approved, by Decree No. 33/83 of 11 May, the Convention on Civil Aspects of International Child Abduction, concluded in the Hague on 25 October 1980.

It should also be mentioned that, given the widespread emigration of Portuguese citizens to France, thereby establishing residence and family ties with French citizens, Portugal and France have also celebrated an agreement to promote legal cooperation in matters of child protection: the Luso-French Convention of Legal Cooperation concerning the Protection of Minors, approved by Resolution No. 1/84 of the Assembly of the Republic.

§4. General Principles Concerning the Award of Custody of Minors in Cases of Divorce, Declaration of Nullity or Annulment of Marriage or the Judicial Separation of Persons and Property of the Parents

370. With the 1977 Reform, Portuguese legislation established that the custody of minors, in the case of divorce, separation of persons and property, declaration of nullity or annulment of marriage, would be awarded in accordance with the principle of the best interest of the child.[619]

The best interest of the child, however, is a vague legal concept, and therefore requires further definition. The task of defining it, in the context of parental responsibilities suits, falls primarily to the judge, either by ratifying the parental agreement or by establishing a new system of custody by judgment. The judge, in performing this task of making manifest the interests of the child, has to take

617. Article 41, No. 7 of the General Regime of Civil Tutelage.
618. Article 49, No. 1 of the General Regime of Civil Tutelage.
619. Article 1905 of the CC.

account of various sub-criteria or factors, the child's preference, the age of the child, the non-separation of siblings, the parents' educational capacity, the principle of awarding custody to the parent that most favours the relationship of the child with the other, the quality and consistency of the child's affective relations, the continuity of the child's relationships, the identity of sex between child and parent, moral conduct, and religion, as well as the economic conditions, the professional and social life of each of the parents.

371. Custody of the child may be awarded to either parent, mother or father, or to both of them jointly, if there is agreement in this respect. Only in exceptional cases, particularly when there is danger to the safety, health, moral training and education of the minor,[620] will custody be awarded to a third party or to an educational or welfare institution.[621]

When the child has been entrusted to a third party or to some educational or welfare establishment, the powers and duties of parents now fall to them, in the performance of their functions.[622] Regarding the powers and duties that are not necessary for the proper performance of these functions, the court should pronounce on the issue of which parent shall exercise them.[623]

372. The process of regulation of parental responsibilities, as has already been mentioned, is included in that group of processes known as voluntary jurisdiction.[624] This is characterized by the principle of alterability of decisions or provisions resulting from them, as established in No. 1 of Article 987 of the Code of Civil Procedure. This rule translates into the possibility of modifying the resolutions proffered within these suits, since, given their nature, they cannot be considered irrevocable. Effectively, whenever justified by supervening circumstances, these decisions may be freely altered. Supervening circumstances are considered for this effect, and in accordance with the provisions of the second part of Article 988, No. 1 of the Code of Civil Procedure, to be both the circumstances occurring subsequent to the decision, and those that occurred previously, but which were not alleged by ignorance or for some other ponderous reason. Therefore, the decision regarding parental responsibilities may be altered. However, it should be mentioned that any alteration to the decision has to be grounded, and may be subject to the appreciation of the Appeal Court, should there be an appeal.

It is also important to mention that decisions about the regulation of parental responsibilities are not subject to appeal to the STJ. In fact, as laid down in No. 2 of Article 988 of the Code of Civil Procedure, appeal may not be made to the Supreme Court for any decisions proffered in the sphere of voluntary jurisdiction, according to criteria of convenience and equity. This applies whatever the value of the case in question.

620. Article 1918 of the CC.
621. Article 1905, No. 2 of the CC.
622. Article 1907, No. 1 of the CC.
623. Article 1907, No. 2 of the CC and Art. 40, No. 5 of the General Regime of Civil Tutelage.
624. Article 12 of the General Regime of Civil Tutelage.

§5. MORAL CONDUCT OF PARENTS

373. Fault in cases of separation or divorce has not been considered a relevant factor by doctrine and jurisprudence for awarding custody of minors and even less today in the context of a divorce system which is exclusively no-fault.

When the question of the custody of minors is discussed in court, allusions are frequently made to the sexual behaviour and moral conduct of the parents. According to doctrine, the court should distinguish the affective relationship of the minor with each of the parents from any judgments about moral and sexual conduct.

§6. HOMOSEXUALITY

374. Sexual orientation of parents should not be considered as a criterion in the custody decision.

It should be pointed out, however, that jurisprudence has not always seen the matter in this way. Indeed, the Lisbon Appeal Court, in a judgment of 9 January 1996, made the issue of custody directly depend upon the sexual orientation of one of the parents, removing the homosexual parent from the custody of the child. That parent then appealed to the European Court of Human Rights which, in a judgment of 21 December 1999, pronounced that the Portuguese court had unduly discriminated against the parent on the basis of their sexual orientation, in clear violation of Articles 8 and 14 of the European Convention of Human Rights.

§7. STATUS QUO

375. This means, essentially, attempting to avoid unduly disrupting of the child's life, since he/she will already have been profoundly affected by the separation of the parents. This principle is grounded on the need for the balanced and healthy development of the child. Therefore, considering the continuation of the child's affective and social relationships to be a criterion in the custody decision, the judge will tend towards the solution that will least affect the child's affective bond and will provoke less disruption in his/her everyday life. In accordance with this criterion, custody shall be awarded to that parent who has exclusively or predominantly cared for the child and who was responsible for his/her education until then.

I. Very Young Children

376. As regards the custody of very young children, the notion of maternal preference was traditionally very strong, grounded in the idea that the mother, for biological, psychological and social reasons, was more able to satisfy the physical and emotional needs of the child. However, this view has been slowly eroded. Indeed, it has been increasingly understood that a child may be cared for by someone other than the biological mother, such as the father or a third party that has been involved in the care and education of the child, with full view of his/her healthy development.

§8. The Child's Preference

377. The most important criterion under analysis is the best interest of the child. Today, the child is perceived as a subject of their own rights, whose autonomy gradually increases with age and with the development of capacities.[625] One of the recognized fundamental rights of the child is the right to freely express an opinion and to have this opinion taken into account in matters that concern him/her,[626] that is, the right to participate in decisions that affect his/her future. One of such decisions is precisely the regulation of the exercise of parental responsibilities.

378. The right of the child to have his/her opinion taken into account is mentioned in different rules in the Portuguese system.[627] The right to be heard in a legal procedure in more general terms has been addressed since 1999, by the Law of Protection of Children and Young People in Danger, that has adopted among its guiding principles the right to mandatory hearing and participation of the child, by him/herself or in the company of parents, guardian or person of his/her choice, in the procedures that deal with children in situations of danger.[628]

More recently, in the 2015, General Regime of Civil Tutelage, the sphere of the right of mandatory hearing of the child[629] has been enlarged. Indeed, it now applies to all legal these procedures that deal directly with the situation of the child in relation with his/her parents, guardians or carers.

Naturally, the experience of participating or being heard in a legal procedure will inevitably arouse complex feelings in the child and doctrine has discussed this issue, its risks and its uses as a suitable means to ensure the respect for the child's interests, and as an opportunity for them to express their own opinion and to participate actively in a decision that concerns them, and which will determine their present and future situation.

This discussion is cultural, by nature, and rooted in the image that the community holds of the child and of his/her role in that community at any given time.

379. The intervention of an expert does not remove the opportunity for the child to take part in the process.

---

625. Articles 5, 12 and 14, No. 2 of the Convention on the Rights of the Child, adopted by the United Nations General Assembly on 20 Nov. 1989.
626. Article 12 of the Convention on the Rights of the Child and Art. 3 of the Council of Europe's Convention on the Exercise of Children's Rights (signed in 6 March 1997, ratified in 31 March 2014 and in force since 1 July 2014).
627. Cf. Arts 1878, No. 2, 1885, No. 2 as to the exercise of parental responsibilities and, in the context of a legal procedure, cf. Arts 1901, No. 3, 1931, No. 2, 1981, No. 1, a), 1984, a) of the CC.
628. Article 4, j) of the Law of Protection of Children and Young People in Danger.
629. Article 4, No. 1, a), c), Arts 5, 35 of the Civil Tutelary Process Legal Regime.

380. Regarding the consequences of the hearing of the minor, it is necessary to clarify that this should not be seen as a deposition, given the complexity of the message. Hearing the minor means acting in accordance with the results of that hearing and recognizing the child's right to self-determination on matters that are of great importance for his/her life.

This sense of hearing means that the judge has the obligation to mention this step as grounds for the decision. While the hearing of the minor is not the only means the court may use to decide upon the question of custody, it is an extraordinarily important way of determining the interests of the minor, and of satisfying them. Thus, it would seem to be the judge's duty to mention if and to what extent he/she took the child's message into account.

§9. The Non-separation of Siblings

381. Another tendency or orientation of jurisprudence has been not to separate siblings in matters of child custody. By applying this principle, it is hoped to observe that other principle of maintaining the continuity of the child's affective and social relationships. Indeed, the child will already have had his/her life profoundly affected by the parental break-up and the leaving of one of them. In these circumstances, the separation of siblings and the distancing that this entails would further destabilize the child's life, depriving him/her of the company of siblings. Relations between siblings, particularly at moments of crisis, are reputedly essential for the normal balanced development of the child. Thus, the non-separation of siblings reduces feelings of loss and discontinuity in the child's affective and social relations, and will encourage the child to integrate into the 'new family' that is to be formed, also stimulating the spirit of mutual support and cooperation before the problems that this new life presents.

382. The application of this principle is not absolute. In exceptional circumstances, the interests of the children themselves may indicate the opposite solution.

§10. Religion

383. As a general rule, doctrine and jurisprudence do not consider religion to be a relevant criterion in the custody decision. The religious faith of one of the parents does not function as a reason for exclusion of that parent from the child's custody. Such exclusion would only be grounds when there are strong reasons to believe that it might cause physical or psychological damage to the child. Religion is therefore almost irrelevant as a criterion. However, it may be indirectly relevant to the custody decision. It may be that, during the hearing of the child by the judge in the context of the parental responsibilities suit, the expression of a particular religious faith may emerge which, if the child has sufficient discernment, should be taken into consideration. Thus, if the child expresses a preference for the parent that professes the same religion or for the parent that is more likely to respect the child's choice, then the court should take this into account. The court should also consider whether there has been prior religious education, seeking to make the decision that would allow the child to continue to be educated in the religion which they have till now been educated in.

§11. Relations with Siblings and Ascendants

384. Portuguese law expressly privileges the principle of the continuity of the child's affective relations, particularly regarding siblings and ascendants. Thus, Article 1887-A of the CC, introduced by Law No. 84/95 of 31 August, imposes upon parents the duty not to forbid children to contact siblings and ascendants, unless that prohibition is justified in the interests of the child.[630] Thus, the situation that existed during the marriage should remain after the separation.

Regarding the contacts of the child with third parties, some doctrine seems to be beginning to accept that, in exceptional circumstances, the judge could award contact rights or rights of correspondence to a third party, when this is in the child's interests.

§12. Special Representative of the Child

385. Portuguese law does not consider the possibility of the minor being represented in the process, particularly in parental responsibilities suits, by a special representative, different from their legal representative when it exists. In accordance with No. 2 of Article 16 of the Code of Civil Procedure, minors subject to parental responsibilities are represented in court by their parents.

However, some doctrine understands that the child may be represented in a suit by someone other than their legal representative, particularly in those situations where there is likely to be some conflict between the child's interests and those of the legal representatives. This special representative may be chosen by the minor himself/herself (from amongst those adults not involved in the conflict with whom they have developed a relationship of trust) appointed by the court. This possibility is indeed anticipated in Articles 3 and 4 of the European Convention on the Exercise of Children's Rights and in Article 12 of the Convention on the Rights of the Child.

630. Article 1887-A of the CC.

Part III. Matrimonial Property Law

Chapter 1. The Patrimonial Effects of Marriage Irrespective of the Property Regime Adopted

§1. Administration of Matrimonial Property

386. Article 1678 lays down the general rules governing the administration of a couple's property.

It is important to distinguish between the administration of personal property and community property.

Concerning *personal property*, the rule is easily expressed: each spouse manages his/her own property.[631]

There are, however, some exceptions to this rule. Thus, under the terms of No. 2 of this Article, one of the spouses may manage the property of the other: (a) in the case of movable property which, though belonging to the other spouse, is used exclusively as a work tool by the administering spouse;[632] (b) if the other spouse is absent or prevented in some way from managing it himself/herself;[633] (c) when the other grants him/her administrative powers, through revocable mandate.[634]

387. With regards to *community property*, the rule is basically one of joint administration;[635] spouses manage their community property together.

An exception to this principle is when ordinary administrative powers are granted to one or the other spouse;[636] this legislation is clearly aimed at streamlining the system, regarding acts that are performed with a certain frequency.

However, it has been argued that this rule of the individual exercise of ordinary administration should be avoided in the case of a company share that is community property of the couple, as a result of the matrimonial property regime adopted; similarly, it has been argued that a commercial establishment that is community property of the couple should also be exempt from the rules of administration laid out in Article 1678, No. 3.

631. Article 1678, No. 1 of the CC.
632. Article 1678, No. 1 subpara. e) of the CC.
633. Article 1678, No. 1 subpara. f) of the CC.
634. Article 1678, No. 1 subpara. g) of the CC.
635. Article 1678, No. 3, 2nd part of the CC.
636. Article 1678, No. 3, 1st part of the CC.

Other exceptions to that rule are cases of property which, though common, should be managed by one of the spouses, either because there is a special connection with that spouse, or because the other is absent or prevented from managing it themselves or has granted the spouse administrative powers through revocable mandate. Thus, though dealing with community property, No. 2 of Article 1678 attributes to each spouse exclusive administration: (a) of income received from their work, although property is common as a result of the matrimonial property regime in force in their marriage; (b) of royalties; (c) of community property that the spouse brought to the marriage or acquired after it for free or any substitute of it; (d) of property that has been given or bequeathed to both spouses excluding one of them from the administration, except in the case of property given or bequeathed on the account of the compulsory share of that spouse; (e) of community movable property used exclusively by him/her as a work tool; (f) of all the couple's property, if the other spouse is absent or prevented from managing it; (g) of all the couple's property or part of it, if the other spouse grants that power through revocable mandate.

388. Rules concerning the administration of a couple's property are mandatory; intended spouses may not agree upon different rules to suit themselves.[637] However, the granting powers of administration by mandate, which is unilaterally revocable, is admissible.

389. The powers of the administering spouse go beyond mere administration;[638] they include the power to dispose of community movable property or of his/her own property.

390. As regards responsibility for administration, the law distinguishes here between various types of situations that deserve special attention.

In cases in which the spouse has the right, by force of law, to manage property that is not his/her own – Article 1678, No. 2, subparagraphs a)–f) – the administrator is not obliged to provide accounts of his/her administration and is only liable for acts intentionally performed that may prejudice the couple or the other spouse.[639]

In the case of administration based on express or tacit mandate, Nos 2 and 3 of Article 1681 establish broad responsibility; as a general rule, the administrator of community property or of the personal property of the other spouse is obliged to provide accounts of that administration, through application of the rules of mandate;[640] the only difference is that the administrator is only obliged to provide accounts and reveal the balance of the previous five years. In addition, the administrator is liable for his/her acts and omissions under the general terms of failure to comply with his/her obligations. He/she also is liable for bad faith, in the case of the final part of Article 1681, No. 3; that is: he/she is liable for material losses even

637. Article 1699, No. 1, subpara. c) of the CC.
638. Cf. Art. 1682, No. 2 of the CC.
639. Article 1681, No. 1 of the CC.
640. Article 1681, Nos 2 and 3, and Art. 1161, subpara. d) of the CC.

if he/she has acted without fault;[641] he/she should make restitution for any profits that were not received but which would have been obtained by a diligent owner[642] and loses, in all cases, any amenities that he/she has made.[643]

When the administration has been so disastrous that the non-administering spouse runs the risk of losing what is his/hers, the law also provides the possibility of applying for a simple legal separation of property, under the terms of Articles 1767 onwards.

391. According to Article 1679, 'the spouse that is not responsible for the administration of the property is not prevented from making provisions in this matter, if the other is for some reason unable to do so, and if delaying this will result in losses'.

§2. Limiting the Rights and Powers of Spouses

I. Limitations

392. In the matrimonial property regimes involving community of assets, the consent of the other spouse is required for the following acts:

- the disposition of personal or community immovable property;[644]
- the encumbrance of personal or community immovable property through the constitution of rights in rem of use and enjoyment – *utendi* and/or *fruendi* – or warranty rights, leasing them, or the constitution of personal rights of enjoyment;[645]
- the disposition of a commercial firm, either a personal or a community asset;[646]
- the encumbrance or lease of a commercial firm, either a personal or a community asset;[647]
- the disposition of the family home;[648]
- the encumbrance the family home through the constitution of rights in rem of use and enjoyment – *utendi* and/or *fruendi* – or warranty rights, leasing it, or the constitution of personal rights of enjoyment;[649]
- the disposition of the right to lease the family home;[650]
- the disposition of personal or community movable property jointly used by the spouses in the household;[651]

641. Article 1269 of the CC.
642. Article 1271 of the CC.
643. Article 1275, No. 2 of the CC.
644. Article 1682 -A, No. 1, a), CC.
645. Article 1682 -A, No. 1, a), CC.
646. Article 1682 -A, No. 1, b), CC.
647. Article 1682 -A, No. 1, b), CC.
648. Article 1682 -A, No. 2, CC.
649. Article 1682 -A, No. 2, CC.
650. Article 1682 -B CC.
651. Article 1682, No. 3, a), CC.

- the disposition of personal or community movable property jointly used by the spouses as joint working tool or equipment;[652]
- the disposition of personal or community movable property that is not within their scope of administration;[653]
- the disclaimer of the succession – inheritance or legacies.[654]

393. When the matrimonial property regime involves a separation of property, the conjugal limitations are much narrower, being restricted to some of the acts mentioned *supra.*

The remaining acts, referred to in other subparagraphs, are permitted to either spouse.

II. Consent from the Other Spouse and Substitution

394. Conjugal consent for the performance of acts that legally require it should be specific to each of those acts.[655] This does not prevent the consent from being express or tacit, under the general terms.

Conjugal consent takes the form required for the respective transaction or legal act.[656] Normally consent is granted through the simultaneous intervention of both spouses in the transaction or legal act.

Article 1684, No. 3 anticipates the possibility of legal substitution of consent, when one spouse is not entitled to perform on his/her own a legal act that he/she deems necessary or convenient.

Substitution is admitted not only when it is 'impossible' for consent to be granted, but also in the case of an 'unjust refusal'. It falls to the applying spouse to prove not only that consent has been refused or is impossible, but also the advantage or necessity of performing the act.

In those cases in which one of the spouses performs an act for which the consent of the other is necessary and it was neither obtained nor judicially provided, the act will be voidable. The spouse who did not consent or his/her heirs can, within six months from the knowledge of the act, but never later than three years after its performance, demand the annulment of the act (Article 1687, No. 1 e 2, CC). When one of the spouses disposes or encumbers personal assets of the other without administration powers, this act is null and void (Article 1687, No. 4, CC).

652. *Ibid.*
653. Article 1682, No. 2 e 3, b), CC.
654. Article 1683, No. 2, CC.
655. Article 1684, No. 1 of the CC.
656. Article 262, No. 2 of the CC.

§3. LIABILITY FOR SPOUSES' DEBTS

395. Each spouse may *legally contract debts* without the consent of the other,[657] and it is understood that, for the purpose of determining the liability of the spouses,[658] the date upon which the debts were contracted is that when they originated.[659]

I. Debts for Which Both Spouses Are Liable

A. *Types of Debts*

396. Both spouses are liable for the debts mentioned in the various subparagraphs of Nos 1 and 2 of Article 1691:

- debts incurred, before or after the celebration of marriage, by both spouses, or by one of them with the consent of the other.[660] This involves debts contracted both before and after marriage, whatever the matrimonial property regime in force;
- debts incurred by any of the spouses, before or after the celebration of marriage, in order to cover the normal expenses of the household. It would seem reasonable that this rule should apply, by analogy, to de facto union; indeed, the de facto union may appear to creditors as an actual marriage, who would rely on the application of matrimonial rules. Namely, creditors would trust that the joint responsibility for debts would grant them access to both community assets and the assets of both 'apparent spouses' would pay for the debt;
- debts incurred during marriage by the administrator spouse, for the joint benefit of the couple, and within the limits of their power of administration.[661] In the practical application of this principle, it should be borne in mind that the administration normally falls to both spouses. This means that, in order to know if a particular debt contracted by one of the spouses should be considered as joint liability in the light of subparagraph c), it is necessary to begin by investigating whether that debt is connected with the property that this spouse has to manage;
- as to the concept of joint benefit, there are several notions that need to be pointed out. The first is that joint benefit is not presumed, except in cases where the law declares it.[662] The second is that joint benefit is gauged not by its result but by the purpose envisaged by the debtor that incurred the debt. If this purpose is the interest of the couple, the debt is considered to have been applied to the joint benefit of the spouses, even though, in reality, it may have resulted in losses. The joint interest of the couple may include not only material or economic interest, but also moral or intellectual interest;

657. Article 1690, No. 1 of the CC.
658. For example for the effect of Art. 1691, No. 2 of the CC.
659. Article 1690, No. 2 of the CC.
660. Article 1691, No. 1, subpara. a) of the CC.
661. Article 1691, No. 1, subpara. c) of the CC.
662. Article 1691, No. 3 of the CC.

- debts incurred by any of the spouses in the course of trade, except those that have not been incurred for the joint benefit of the couple.[663] The system is supplemented with the provisions of Article 15 of the Commercial Code: 'The commercial debts of the spouse that is a merchant are presumed to have been contracted in the exercise of his/her trade.' The spouse of the merchant may wish to remove the communicability of the debt. The first step to be taken to remove liability for a debt is to demonstrate that the debt was not contracted in the exercise of the debtor's business, contrary to what is presumed in Article 15 of the Commercial Code; that is, the debt, though commercial, was not contracted during the exercise of the business of the spouse who is a merchant. Subparagraph d) establishes a true legal presumption of joint benefit in favour of the creditor. Thus, unlike what happens in the system of the previous subparagraph, the creditor does not have to prove joint benefit. This presumption is not absolute, though. However, the fact of the spouses being de facto separated is not enough to show the absence of joint benefit. In truth, de facto separation does not prevent the businessman/woman from exerting his/her activity with the intention of joint benefit, supposing for example that he/she withdraws a maintenance pension for his/her spouse from the company's revenue. The debt is not a community debt if the spouses are legally separated;
- debts that encumber gifts, inheritances or legacies, when the respective property has become community property;[664]
- debts incurred before marriage by either of the spouses for the joint benefit of the couple, when the marriage is regulated by the matrimonial property regime of universal community of property;[665]
- debts that encumber community property;[666]
- debts that, when there is community of assets, encumber personal property, if they have been contracted in view of the respective return.[667]

B. Property To Be Used for the Discharge of Debts of Joint Liability

397. Debts for which both spouses are liable are discharged using community property, or in its absence or insufficiency, with the personal property of either of the spouses.[668]

The same Article 1695, Nos 1 and 2 establishes that (in the case of a debt that is to be discharged with personal property) the spouses' liability is joint and several when the matrimonial property regime is of community of assets, unlike the regime of separation of property. However, it is clear that conventional joint and several liability is not excluded here.[669] It should also be added that each spouse's portion of liability is not necessarily 50%; when debts were incurred in order to satisfy the

663. Article 1691, No. 1, subpara. d) of the CC.
664. Article 1691, No. 1, subpara. e), and 1693, No. 2 of the CC.
665. Article 1691, No. 2 of the CC.
666. Article 1694, No. 1 of the CC.
667. Article 1694, No. 2 of the CC.
668. Article 1695, No. 1 of the CC of the CC.
669. Cf. Arts 512 onwards of the CC.

normal expenses of family life, each spouse's liability should correspond to their duty to contribute to those expenses, under the terms of Article 1676, No. 1, that is, in proportion to the possibilities of each one.

II. Debts for Which Only One Spouse Is Liable

A. *Types of Debts*

398. These are almost all mentioned in Article 1692:

- Debts contracted by one of the spouses without the consent of the other.[670]
- Debts resulting from crimes or other acts committed by one of the spouses.[671] There is, however, the case of those facts, implying only civil liability, that are covered by the provisions of Nos 1 or 2 of Article 1691. This is particularly the case of indemnifications due for facts performed by the administrating spouse, within his/her powers of administration and for the joint benefit of the couple.
- Debts that encumber personal property of any of the spouses.[672] However, if as a result of the matrimonial property regime, all income is common, then the debts that were contracted with the prospective of returns are joint liability.
- Debts that encumber gifts, inheritances and legacies that regard personal property.[673]

B. *Property to Be Used in the Discharge of Debts for Which One of the Spouses Is Exclusively Liable*

399. The general rule is that of Article 1696, No. 1: these debts should be discharged using the personal property of the spouse that is liable, and secondarily, by his/her half of community property.

It has been discussed whether the property of the debtor spouse should be used to discharge those debts when the administration of that property is in the hands of the other. It would seem reasonable that it should not, at least when the law has entrusted the administration of that property to the other spouse (e.g., property that he/she uses exclusively as a work tool).

In keeping with Article 1696, No. 2, not only is the personal property of the debtor spouse used to discharge the debt, but also 'property that he/she brought to the couple or subsequently gratuitously acquired, and the respective returns on

670. Article 1692, subpara. a) of the CC of the CC.
671. Article 1692, subpara. b) of the CC.
672. Articles 1692, subpara. c), and 1694, No. 2 of the CC.
673. Article 1693, No. 1 of the CC.

that',[674] 'the product of work of the debtor spouse and royalties',[675] and 'property subrogated in the place of those referred to in subparagraph a)'.[676]

Although this property may be commonly owned, in view of the matrimonial property regime in force in the marriage, and considering that community property is only subsidiarily used in the discharge of personal debts, the law has in this case sacrificed the community property of the couple to satisfy the expectations of the creditor, who had trusted in the solvency of the debtor, in view of the property that he/she brought to the marriage and that acquired later through inheritance, gift or profits (which may be considerable) of his/her work or royalties.

III. Compensation Due for the Payment of the Couple's Debts

400. Article 1697, No. 1 regulates the case in which the property of one member of the couple has been used to discharge debts of joint liability to a greater extent than it should have. It does not matter that the overpayment has been voluntary.

In either case, the spouse that paid more than their due becomes entitled to compensatory credit from the other spouse; this, however, can only be demanded at the moment of distribution of the couple's property.

401. No. 2 of the precept regulates the opposite situation: when community property is used to discharge debts for which only one of the spouses is liable, which is what happens, for example, in the cases of Article 1696, No. 2. In this case, a compensatory credit will be due to the community property from the property of the owing spouse, to be taken into account at the moment of distribution of property.

§4. Contracts Between Spouses

I. Introduction

402. In the legal systems of Roman origin, the tradition of immutability of prenuptial agreements and of the associated property regimes has been widely associated with tight restrictions on the business capacities of the spouses. The permanence of such regimes meant that spouses did not have the opportunity to alter the composition of their estates through legal transactions involving transfer of ownership, which could lead to a result prohibited by law.

In addition, the hierarchy of conjugal roles did not seem to be compatible with other legal relations based upon equality, in which spouses had equal status, or those in which there was an inversion of the hierarchy, such as when the wife had the power of direction over her husband.

674. Article 1696, No. 2, subpara. a) of the CC.
675. Article 1696, No. 2, subpara. b) of the CC.
676. Article 1696, No. 2, subpara. c) of the CC.

Thus, in our law, prohibitions were established on purchase and sale, and on the setting up of companies; there were also restrictions on participation in companies, gifts between spouses, and work contracts.

As the principle of immutability gradually gave way before the need to adapt to modern property interests, and the status of spouses equalized, those restrictions gradually became meaningless, and were abandoned by various legal systems in successive stages, though not without some controversy and contradictions.

The 1977 reform of Portuguese law introduced the rule of legal equality between spouses, but it did not touch upon the traditional principle of immutability. This factor, allied to a feeling of distrust regarding the free exercise of private autonomy within the couple upon which the rule of immutability is based, justifies the maintenance of various restrictions to the freedom of contract between spouses.

II. Company Contract

403. Article 8, No. 1 of the Code of Commercial Companies[677] altered Nos 2 and 3 of Article 1714 of the CC, in the ambit of companies and non-commercial civil societies that take a commercial form. Today, 'the setting up of companies between spouses is permitted, as is their participation in companies, provided that only one of them assumes unlimited liability'.

The prohibition against setting up companies or participating in them with third parties was reduced to cases in which both spouses assumed unlimited liability for company debts.

III. Gifts

404. Gifts between spouses are not admitted unreservedly. For one, there is the fear that the gift may result in the ascendancy or influence of one of the spouses over the other; the fact of conjugal living, generally, and the feeling that property given as a gift 'stays in the family' may lead to one of the spouses benefiting the other without due reflection, jeopardizing the freedom and spontaneity of the act. Second, the interests of third parties, such as the couple's creditors, will also be against the possibility of them making gifts to each other, thus transforming community property into personal property or personal property into community property.

Our law permits gifts between spouses but considers them freely revocable, like testamentary provisions (a system which is not uncontroversial). Gifts, however, are prohibited in all cases in which the law imposes the matrimonial property regime of separation of property.

In addition, gifts between spouses may only have as their object the personal property of the donor.

---

677. Decree Law No. 262/86 of 2 September.

405. Gifts between spouses are forfeited if, in first place, the recipient dies before the donor, except if he/she confirms the gift in the three months following the death of the recipient.[678]

They are also forfeited[679] when there has been a declaration of nullity or an annulment of the marriage, but without prejudice to the principles of the putative marriage.[680] Thus, the gift is not forfeited if there was good faith on the part of both spouses, since the effects already produced are sustained upon that good faith; neither is the gift forfeited if only one of the partners acted in good faith, when he/she is the recipient.

Finally, gifts are forfeited in the event of divorce or separation, unless the donor determines that it shall pass to the common children of the spouses.[681]

IV. Purchase and Sale

406. Purchases and sales between spouses are null and void.[682]

This legislation results from the understanding that, if sales were valid, spouses could make true gifts to one another under the appearance of a sale, with which they could easily evade the principle of free revocability of gifts between spouses. As simulation of this kind is difficult to prove, frequently one of the spouses enriches himself/herself unjustly at the expense of the other; one of them is led to make what really are gifts to the other, but irrevocably, since they are disguised as sales. In addition, contracts imply the transfer of property, with an alteration of the spouses' estates, which constitutes a violation of the principle of immutability, broadly understood.

V. Other Contracts

407. The validity of the *contract* of *employment* was difficult to accept when the systems sanctioned the unequal status of spouses within marriage. It was above all strange that the husband should be subordinated to his wife; a contract such as this was considered null and void because it meant an 'inversion of roles'.

In a system based upon the legal equality of spouses, such as the present Portuguese system, it may still seem strange that a relationship of *subordination*, typical of the work relationship, is introduced into the relationship between spouses. The problem of the contradiction between the equality of spouses and the rule of subordination of labour is resolved by means of a distinction between family life, marital status and the professional relationship.

It seems, therefore that the constitution of a working relationship between spouses is valid, and governed by general labour laws.

678. Article 1766, No. 1, subpara. a) of the CC.
679. Article 1766, No. 1, subpara. b) of the CC.
680. Article 1647 of the CC.
681. Article 1791 of the CC.
682. Article 1714, No. 2 of the CC.

408. Neither does *loan* or *loan for use* seem to be prohibited between spouses. The reciprocal duty of cooperation, in the form of providing mutual protection and assistance, should be able to assume one of these concrete forms, before it becomes necessary for either of the spouses to resort to a third party.

The question seems clear, particularly if the spouses are married under the matrimonial property regime of separation of property. Some problems are raised when there is community of assets, however.

409. *Lease* between spouses is not prohibited, although it raises problems similar to those of loan and loan for use.

410. The opening of *bank accounts* has long been allowed for both spouses; however, it is recognized that accounts that may be operated by either spouse (joint partnership accounts) considerably disturb the normal application of the rules of family property law.

§5. End of Property Relations: Distribution of Property

411. Property relations between spouses cease with the dissolution, declaration of nullity or annulment of the marriage[683] or with the separation of persons and estate.[684]

After property relations have terminated between spouses, the distribution of the couple's property takes place.[685] This is also done if a simple judicial separation of property is decreed,[686] or if one of the spouses is declared absent[687] or bankrupt.[688]

Each spouse, or, in the case of dissolution of marriage by death, their heirs, will receive in the distribution their personal property and their half of the community property, after they have replaced anything they owe to that property.[689] This is what is established in Article 1689, No. 1.

412. The distribution of property, broadly accepted, consists of three basic operations: keeping apart personal property, as preliminary operation; the liquidation of community property, in order to establish the value of the community liquid assets, through a calculation of compensations and debts to third parties and between spouses; and the distribution itself.

In first place, a separation is made of the personal property of each spouse. The relationship of community property includes property and rights qualified as common by the rules of the matrimonial property regime that was in force during their

683. Article 1688 of the CC.
684. Article 1795-A of the CC.
685. Article 1689 of the CC.
686. Article 1770 of the CC.
687. Article 108 of the CC.
688. Article 201, No. 1, subpara. b), of the Code of Special Procedures for the Recovery of Companies and Bankruptcy.
689. Cf. Art. 1697, No. 2 of the CC.

marriage, apart from the exceptions stipulated in Articles 1719 and 1790. In principle, this is a simple uncontroversial description of community assets.

413. Compensations are a correction mechanism, a way of restoring justice, when, during the marriage, transfers took place between estates (the community estate and the two personal estates of the spouses), for instance, either because community funds were used to finance improvements in real estate that is personal property or to pay off a debt that was the exclusive liability of one of the spouses, or because the family home was acquired with the personal capital of one of the spouses, without subrogation being formalized, or because a debt belonging to both was discharged with capital of one of the spouses, etc. Compensations made at the moment of distribution of property are done at nominal value, not updated.

Debts owed by one spouse to the other should be discharged, first using the debtor spouse's moiety from the community property, and, if there is no community property or if it is insufficient, from the personal property of the debtor spouse.[690]

Article 1689, No. 2 makes provision for the discharge of debts to third parties.

Community property is used first to pay off joint debts and only afterwards personal debts; one of the essential purposes of community property (in addition to serving as the economic expression of the joint effort, which will be divided) is to guarantee liability for joint debts, characteristic of conjugal living.

Personal estates may be used to pay off all debts indifferently, both personal and joint, if the community property is not enough to pay the latter; but joint creditors are always in the most advantageous position, since they benefit legally from joint and several full liability established in Article 1695, No. 1.

414. The distribution of property itself is done, in principle, according to whichever matrimonial property regime was adopted, but there are some exceptions to this, stipulated in Articles 1719 and 1790.

Article 1719 allows spouses to agree, for the case of dissolution of marriage by death of one of the spouses when there are common descendants, that the property will be distributed according to the regime of universal community of property, even if the property regime adopted was different.

Article 1790 is also of great interest. According to this precept, in case of divorce (but also legal separation), none of the spouses may receive in the distribution of property more than they would have received if the marriage had been celebrated according to the regime of community of acquisitions.

415. The provisions of Articles 1105, 1793, 1731 and 2103-A of the CC are also of interest for the matter of distribution of property.

When spouses live in rented accommodation, Article 1105 allows them to agree as to which of them will be the lessee following a divorce or separation; and in the absence of an agreement, it allows the court to decide, taking into account the circumstances referred to here.

690. Article 1689, No. 3 of the CC.

Article 1793 covers the situation in which divorced or judicially separated spouses own their home, allowing the court to give the family home over to rent to either spouse, at their application, whether this be community property or property of just one of them.

416. Articles 1731 and 2103-A regulate the so-called preferential benefits. Before the negotiations between the spouses, leading to the fulfilment of each one's moiety of the community property (as is proper to a distribution of property transaction), the law itself reserves certain assets for one of the spouses, given the special connection that spouse has with them; in other words, this is a way of valuing the particular relationship between a spouse and a certain piece of property, and of providing a guarantee against the weak negotiating position of that spouse, who may not be capable of negotiating alone with the other interested party (or interested parties, heirs of the deceased spouse) the attribution of that property.

Article 1731 refers to spouses' work tools which, through the property regime in force, have become part of the community estate, thus recognizing the right of the spouse that has need of them for the exercise of his/her profession to be given priority at the moment of distribution of property, whatever the cause of it may be.

Finally, in the case of dissolution of marriage by death, Article 2103-A attributes to the surviving spouse the right to be given priority in the distribution of property regarding the right of residence of the family home and the right to use of the respective contents, with compensation due to the co-heirs if the value received exceeds that of their share of the inheritance and moiety, if that exists.

417. There has been discussion as to the validity of the promise of contract regarding distribution of property, drawn up during the marriage, usually when a divorce is pending, in order to come into effect immediately after the transit in *rem judicatam* of the sentence dissolving the marriage. Recent legal decisions have accepted it.

Chapter 2. Effects Dependent upon the Property Regime

§1. Prenuptial Agreements

418. A prenuptial agreement is an agreement between intended spouses designed above all to establish their matrimonial property regime.

Portuguese law does not yet permit spouses to alter the agreements that they made prior to marriage, nor does it permit new agreements to be drawn up after marriage. This is why they are called prenuptial agreements.

419. Two general principles dominate the matter of the content of prenuptial agreements: freedom and immutability.

In the first place, the intended spouses have the freedom to establish the matrimonial property regime, in the prenuptial agreement, either by choosing one of the regimes laid down in the Code or by stipulating what they want in this respect.

However, they do not only have the freedom to choose the matrimonial property regime.

The law itself shows that it is possible to include provisions that do not conform with the property regime, such as those regulated in Articles 1700 onwards.

This freedom allows them to include any transactions of either patrimonial or non-patrimonial nature.

Any clause is subject to appreciation of its validity, under the general terms; stipulations that violate mandatory rules of public policy or public morality, cannot be considered valid.

420. There are, however, some limits to the freedom of agreement.

The regulation of the succession as to the estate of a deceased spouse or of a third party may not be the object of a prenuptial agreement.[691]

Neither are clauses allowed that constitute 'an alteration of paternal or conjugal rights or duties'.[692]

Stipulations that imply an 'alteration of rules about the administration of the couple's property' are also not admitted.[693]

Subparagraph d) refers to the 'stipulation of communicability of property listed in Article 1733' which is strict personal property.

In addition, No. 2 of Article 1699 prohibits, in marriages celebrated by someone who has children, the stipulation of the matrimonial regime of universal community of property, referred to in No. 1 of Article 1722. This rule seeks to ensure the protection the children, guaranteeing that their parent keeps within his/her personal estate the property he/she brought to the marriage or gratuitously acquired and that is subrogated in its place; property that, therefore, will not be confused with the community property of the couple and shared with the other spouse, who, in the event of distribution of property, would take half and would also become a rival heir to the child.

691. Article 1699, No. 1, subpara. a) of the CC.
692. Article 1699, No. 1, subpara. b) of the CC.
693. Article 1699, No. 1, subpara. c) of the CC.

421. As regards the principle of immutability, Article 1714, No. 1 establishes that 'apart from the cases laid down by law, it is not permitted to alter either prenuptial agreements or legally established property regimes after the celebration of marriage'. It is not only the property regime *agreed* by the intended spouses that cannot be modified within marriage, but also the *suppletory* regime which, in the absence of any agreement, is applied by the determination of the law under the terms of Article 1717.

It is important to stress that the prenuptial agreement is only immutable from the moment of the celebration of marriage, and may be freely revoked or modified up to that date, under the terms of Article 1712.

422. Under the terms of Article 1710, prenuptial agreements are only valid if they are celebrated by public deed or drawn up before the registrar of the civil registry office, during the process of publication of notice of the marriage[694] and the spouses may adopt one of the property regimes typified in the law – universal community of property or separation of property. If, however, they wish to introduce modifications to either regime, under the principle of freedom, they will have to use the more solemn and traditional procedure of public deed.

Prenuptial agreements also need to be *registered* in order to have effects in relation to third parties.[695]

Article 191, No. 2 of the Code of Civil Registry should also be taken into account. According to this precept, if the record of the prenuptial agreement is drawn up at the same time as the transcription of a catholic wedding, its effects are *retroactive* to the date the marriage was celebrated, if it was transcribed *within seven days*.

The prenuptial agreement expires if the marriage is not celebrated within a year, or if, having been celebrated, it is declared null and void, or annulled under the terms of Article 1716.

§2. 'LEGAL' MATRIMONIAL PROPERTY REGIME

I. Cases of Mandatory Regime

423. There are two cases in which the law imposes the regime of separation of property. These are in subparagraphs a) and b) of No. 1 of Article 1720: marriages celebrated without being preceded by the process of publication of banns, and for anyone who is already 60 years old.

424. The rule of Article 1720, No. 1, subparagraph a), which comes from previous legislation, is applied to all marriages that have been celebrated without being preceded by the preliminary publication of banns, both those that have been legally

694. Article 189 of the Code of Civil Registry.
695. Article 1711, No. 1 of the CC and Arts 1, No. 1, subpara. e), and 191 Code of Civil Registry.

celebrated, catholic[696] or civil[697] marriages, and those that should have been preceded by the process of publication of banns but which were in fact celebrated without this process. The legislator clearly understood that the circumstances in which the marriage is celebrated in most cases legitimize the suspicion that one of the intended spouses had decided to marry for economic interest.

This is the same reason that ultimately justifies the solution of subparagraph b) of No. 1 of Article 1720. However this rule does not seem to be compatible with the Constitution. It creates a discriminatory situation by restricting fundamental rights and the autonomy of the person grounded on the age of the spouses. It puts in stake the principle of constitutional equality[698] of all citizens as well as the right to civil capacity.

II. Suppletory Regime

425. The suppletory regime, that is, the regime which applies in the absence of prenuptial agreement or if the agreement has expired, is invalid or without force, is that of community of acquisitions.[699]

A. *General Characteristics*

426. Under the regime of community of acquisitions, there is or there may be community property and personal property of each spouse. Property that is brought to the couple or acquired individually is not communicated; only property acquired onerously after marriage is community property. This is the general idea that defines the regime and basically corresponds to the idea that only that which expresses the collaboration of both spouses in the patrimonial effort of marriage will become community property.

Community property constitutes an estate to which, in view of its special nature, the law grants a certain degree of autonomy, and which belongs to the two spouses equally, but *en bloc*; it could be said that the spouses are both holders of a single right over it.

We said that community property constitutes an estate to which the law gives a certain degree of autonomy, in view of its special nature. However, in truth, the autonomy of community property is limited and incomplete, in comparison with the personal property of each spouse. In the first place, this is because community property *is not only used to discharge joint debts*, but also, though exceptionally, for personal debts. Certainly the law has intended community property to be used for the satisfaction of the couple's needs and for the payment of joint debts, considering it especially suited for these purposes; but the system is not rigid, since the law permits that, although subsidiarily, community property is used to pay off personal

696. Article 1599 of the CC.
697. Article 1622 of the CC.
698. Article 13 of the Portuguese Constitution.
699. Article 1717 of the CC.

debt.[700] In the second place, community property *is not the only way of discharging joint debts*, since the personal property of either of the spouses is also liable, though subsidiarily.[701]

Article 1730, No. 1 attributes to each spouse the right to half of the value of community property, both assets and liabilities, considering null and void all stipulations to the contrary; our law has rejected solutions adopted by other legal systems that admit the stipulation of unequal distribution of property clauses.

B. Personal Property

427. From the provisions of Articles 1722, 1723 and 1726–1729, it can be inferred that the following is personal property:

- Property that the spouses bring with them to the marriage.[702]
- Property that is bequeathed to the spouse as an inheritance or gift.[703]
- Property acquired within marriage by means of the exercise of a right that existed prior to marriage;[704] 'without prejudice to the eventual compensation owed to the community property'. Acquired property by virtue of a previous right, is considered to include: property acquired as a consequence of rights existing prior to marriage over unliquidated property that was distributed after the marriage; or property acquired through *adverse possession (usucapio)* grounded on possession that began before marriage; or also property acquired in the exercise of the right of preference grounded on a situation already existing on the date of the marriage.
- Property subrogated in place of personal property, taking its place.[705] There have been different solutions in courts for cases in which subrogation is indirect: when the acquisition of an asset and the loss of a previous asset proceed from different legal acts, or whenever the relationship between the value of these assets is not ostensive. The interpretation of Article 1723, subparagraph c) has always been controversial.
- Property acquired partly with the money or personal property of one of the spouses, and partly with community money or property, if the latter is worth more;[706] without prejudice to the compensation due to the property prejudiced by the application of the rule.
- Indivisible property acquired, in part, by one of the spouses, that already had another part in it;[707] without prejudice to the compensation due to the property prejudiced through the application of this rule.

700. Article 1696 of the CC.
701. Article 1695, No. 1 of the CC.
702. Article 1722, No. 1, subpara. a) of the CC.
703. Article 1722, No. 1, subpara. b) of the CC.
704. Article 1722, No. 1, subpara. c) of the CC.
705. Article 1723 of the CC.
706. Article 1726 of the CC.
707. Article 1727 of the CC.

- Assets acquired through ownership of personal property and which cannot be considered its 'fruit';[708] the natural gain or income derived from capital that is personal property is considered to be common, under the regime of community of acquisitions. This involves, for example, accessions or materials resulting from the demolition or destruction of personal property. If community property happens to be diminished by the application of this rule, it may be a compensation.
- Property considered personal by nature, through the will of the intended spouses, or by legal provision. The first group includes honorific distinctions or objects representing particular professional situations, such as diplomas, decorations, trophies and medals, like the moral copyright and personal correspondence, whose incommunicability is imposed as the expression of rights of personality. The second group includes property that was considered incommunicable in the prenuptial agreements. The third group includes all property to which the law has attributed the mandatory quality of personal property, such as indemnities for acts committed against the person of each of the spouses or against their personal property, or clothes and other objects of exclusive personal use of each spouses.[709]
- Pets that belonged to each spouse, when they entered into marriage.[710]

C. *Community Property*

428. It is basically Articles 1724–1726 that tell us what counts as community property:

- The product of the work of the spouses.[711] Property acquired instead of salaries, such as retirement pensions, should be considered as an integral part of community property.
- Property acquired within marriage that is not exempted by law.[712] This category includes, in principle, all property acquired onerously, while it is certain that sometimes property resulting from these operations will be exempt from community of assets and integrated into the personal property of the person who acquired it, e.g., through the mechanism of subrogation.[713]
- Although acquired through inheritance or gift, property that is bequeathed as a legacy or gift to the two spouses also forms part of community property[714] – a solution which is explained by the respect due to the will of the deceased, an habitual respect in this kind of free transaction.
- Profit and income from personal property and the value of improvements made to that property. The expression covers the 'natural' gains that result directly from

708. Article 1728, No. 1 of the CC.
709. Article 1733 of the CC.
710. This rule has been added by Law No. 8/2017 of 3 March.
711. Article 1724, subpara. a) of the CC.
712. Article 1724, subpara. b) of the CC.
713. Article 1723 of the CC.
714. Article 1729 of the CC.

the thing, spontaneously or through human action, and the income derived from capital, such as interests on a bank deposit, produced through the intermediary of a legal relation.[715]

- Movable property, except when there is proof to the contrary. Movable property may be personal or community, according to the general rules. However, in the case of property that is acquired frequently and without documentation, it is difficult to know if it is community property or personal property. The spouses will prove by any means possible that such property belongs to one estate or the other. The law presumes that it is community property whenever the spouses cannot come to a conclusion over a particular case.[716]
- Property that has been subrogated in the place of community property.
- Property acquired partly with the personal money or property of one of the spouses and partly with community money or property, if the latter is worth more; if a patrimony happens to be diminished by the application of this rule, there may be a compensation.

§3. Conventional Matrimonial Property Regimes

I. Regime of Universal Community of Property

A. General Characteristics of the Regime

429. The regime of universal community of property is characterized by the fact that the community property is 'constituted by all present and future property of the spouses that is not exempted by law'.[717]

The regime of community of assets is in force when it is stipulated by the intended spouses in the prenuptial agreement or in the document drawn up before the registrar of the civil registry office, and only in this case.

Article 1734 considers 'all provisions relative to the community of acquisitions applicable to the universal community of property'. According to the Code, considering that the regime of community of acquisitions is a suppletory regime, it is the only one that is tightly regulated in law. It is in relation to that regime that the law specifically enunciates the general provisions concerning the regimes involving community property, which are also applicable to the regime of universal community of property.

B. Community and Personal Property

430. Under the regime of universal community of property, 'all present and future property of the spouses that is not exempt by law' is considered community

715. Article 212, No. 2 of the CC.
716. Article 1725 of the CC.
717. Article 1732 of the Civil Code.

property.[718] Only that property exempted by law from the community is therefore personal, and mandatorily so, as we have seen.[719]

The list of personal property is basically that of Article 1733, No. 1 referred to in the section concerning the standard regime of community of acquisitions.

II. Regime of Separation of Property

A. *General Characteristics of the Regime*

431. There is complete and absolute separation between the properties of the spouses. Under the terms of Article 1735, each one retains ownership and enjoyment of all their present and future property, which they can freely dispose of as they wish. The separation is not only of property, but also of administrations, and the spouses maintain almost absolute freedom to manage and dispose of their own personal property.

432. The spouses' freedom is not entirely absolute because of some constraints laid down by law. Thus, the performance of acts that imply the total or partial deprivation of the family home requires the consent of both spouses;[720] the same applies to the movable property that is used jointly in the home life or as joint work tool, and the movable property belonging exclusively to the spouse that does not manage it.[721] In those cases, although the property belongs exclusively to one of the spouses, the owner may not dispose of it freely.

433. The regime of separation of property is mandatory in the two cases laid down in Article 1720, No. 1, and, as a regime of choice, when stipulated by the intended spouses in the prenuptial agreement or in the document drawn up before the registrar of the civil registry office.

B. *Personal Property of the Husband and Personal Property of the Wife*

434. There is no community property in this case, but of course there may be, and normally there will be property that belongs to both in a regime of joint ownership, and in relation to which each may apply for the sharing-out of the indivision at any time,[722] by means of a process of division of joint assets.[723] It should be noted that the law presumes co-ownership of movable property,[724] though it allows

718. Article 1732 of the CC.
719. Article 1699, subpara. d) of the CC.
720. Article 1682-A, No. 2 of the CC.
721. Article 1682, No. 3 of the CC.
722. Article 1412 of the CC.
723. Articles 925 onwards of the Code of Civil Procedure.
724. Article 1736, No. 2 of the CC.

intended spouses to stipulate clauses in the prenuptial agreement that make presumptions about their respective property,[725] the force of which extends to third parties but without prejudice to any proof provided to the contrary.

725. Article 1736, No. 1 of the CC.

Part IV. Succession Law

§1. Introduction

435. Succession *mortis causa* may be *intestate* or by will or by contract, depending on whether the ground of entitlement on which it is founded is the *law* or a *private act*. And depending on whether this act is a *will* or a *donatio mortis causa* (in the exceptional cases in which *donatio mortis causa* is permitted), the succession is by will or by contract. However, within intestate succession, broadly speaking, there is a further distinction to be made, between the situation of *necessary heirs* (who are the persons entitled to a reserved share (legitim) of the estate, that is not available for the person whose succession is concerned to dispose of) and of heirs in intestacy (the ones who inherit in the absence of forced heirs or, when they exist, within the limits of the disposable part of the estate).

436. Thus, there are four kinds of succession *mortis causa*: intestate in favour of necessary heirs, intestate in favour of legal heirs, by will and by contract.

437. Beneficiaries may be of two types. 'Heir is the person who succeeds the deceased in the totality or in a portion of his or her estate, and legatee the person who succeeds in specific assets or values.'

The legal criterion for the distinction between heir and legatee is grounded – in a manner of speaking – on the *determination* or *in determination* of the assets: the heir receives indeterminate assets whereas the legatee receives determinate assets.

Chapter 1. Intestate Succession

§1. The Opening of the Succession

I. Death (And Missing Persons and Absentees)

438. Death is the requisite for succession – certain death, certified death and presumed death. The legal declaration of death *in absentia*, from which derives presumed death, may be requested by the interested parties mentioned in Article 100, when ten years have elapsed after the last news was heard, or five years if the absent person has completed 80 years of age in the meantime (Article 114). However, being called to the succession in the case of presumed death is a resolvable calling, and it will be resolved whenever the absentee returns or is heard of. For further developments about this subject, see Part I, Chapter I, §3.

439. Death is generally proved by means of a death certificate taken from its registry within the Civil Registry's database.[726]

440. Death triggers the succession procedure. This procedure is a legal effect produced at a given moment. This is the moment in which the person whose succession is concerned dies. Succession begins with the death of the person, under Article 2031.

441. As to determining the place where the succession is initiated, Article 2031 prescribes that succession begins at the *last residence* of the deceased.

§2. The Heir (And Other Beneficiaries)

I. Capacity to Succeed

442. On the death of the deceased, not all the persons who are appointed by law, by contract or by will necessarily inherit. Indeed, there is a hierarchy of these different titles that determines the order by which the beneficiaries are designated. To hold a ground of entitlement that has priority in such hierarchy is, therefore, the first requirement to inherit. Schematically speaking, we may say that the hierarchy scale is as follows:

(1) Within the portion of the estate to devolve compulsorily to the heirs, come the forced heirs, who, under Portuguese law, are the spouse, the descendants, and the ascendants, according to the order and rules prescribed for the succession on intestacy, under Article 2133 and subsequent ones.[727]

726. Article 211 of the Code of Civil Registry.
727. Up to Art. 2157 of the CC.

(2) Next comes the heirs or legatees by contract. These come after the forced heirs,[728] but before the heirs entitled under a will. That is what may be understood from the legal solution to the conflicts that may arise between the appointment by contract and by will. The contractual appointment prevails over the testamentary one, regardless of being prior[729] or subsequent[730] to it.
(3) Then the testamentary heirs (or legatees), the people who the person whose succession is concerned designated as his/her beneficiaries in his/her will.
(4) According to the order prescribed in Article 2133, No. 1, come the heirs on intestacy referred to in this Article, who are designated by law to succeed the deceased. The legal designation is grounded on marriage,[731] kinship,[732] or even on a sovereignty relationship with the State.[733]

443. The second requirement is the *existence* of the beneficiary. The person appointed to the succession will have to exist as a *legal entity*, at the moment of the opening of the succession. This requirement expresses two different demands – those appointed to the succession (i) must *still* be alive at the time of the death of the person whose succession is concerned and therefore still hold *legal personality* at the moment of the opening of the succession; (ii) must *already* exist when the deceased died. This last requirement is that the beneficiary is already a *legal entity* at the moment of the opening of the succession. For an individual, this begins at birth, while for a juridical person, it begins with the recognition of the correspondent *substratum*. This demand raises a number of doubts in its application to concrete cases where there appears to be, and perhaps there is in fact, appointed persons who are not yet entities at the moment of the opening of the succession. Such are the cases of the succession of unborn children who have already been conceived (who may inherit on the account either intestate succession and succession by will or by contract), succession of unborn children not yet conceived (allowed to inherit when the appointment is made by will or by contract) and succession of corporate bodies not yet recognized (regarding whom succession by will is allowed).

444. The third and last requirement is the capacity to inherit. The incapacities to inherit are generally grounded not on any *natural*, physical or psychological incapacity of the heir or legatee, but on the idea of some unworthiness on the part of the person eligible for succession. The acts of the heir or legatee, which result in a disqualification by conduct, are described in the paragraphs of Article 2034.

Law No. 82/2014 of 30 December established that the criminal conviction for homicide of an heir may declare its status of *unworthiness* to succeed; otherwise, the court shall inform the Public Prosecutor of the criminal conviction and the Public Prosecutor will initiate a civil lawsuit in order to declare the *unworthiness* to succeed, whenever the convicted is the only heir.

728. Articles 1759 and 1705, No. 3 of the CC.
729. Articles 2311 and 2313 of the CC.
730. Article 1701, No. 1 of the CC.
731. Paragraphs a) and b) of the CC.
732. Paragraphs a), b), c) and d) of the CC.
733. Paragraph e) of the CC.

II. *Commorientes*

445. A particular aspect of the issue of the proof of death is the so-called problem of *simultaneous death*. It may happen that the person eligible for the succession and the deceased died in the very same accident, or on the very same day; in such cases, in order for the succession to take place, it must be proved that the prospective beneficiary outlived the deceased – even if for a minute, even if for an instant.

How does our law solve this problem?

The general principle is that the proof of the moment of death and hence the proof of pre-death is to be accomplished by all possible means. And what happens if no proof is produced? In such a circumstance, the legal presumption is that of simultaneous death. The deceased and his/her heirs or legatees will be presumed to have died at the same time, and the transfer of the estate or the legacy will not occur – as dictated by Article 68, No. 2. Its text contains a general principle of law that is valid for any form of succession.

III. Unworthiness to Succeed

446. Unworthy conduct on the part of the heir or legatee may assume several different forms: against the life of the deceased, in the form of a restriction of the person's liberty to make a will, acts against the will itself, or against the honour of the deceased or of his/her family, even if merely an attempt.[734]

447. It appears that Article 2036 does not intend that the lack of capacity to inherit to apply automatically; a lawsuit designed to obtain a disqualification by conduct, a declaration of unworthiness to succeed of the beneficiary is required. However, Article 2038, No. 1 allows for the reinstatement of the heir or legatee that was debarred from inherit, if the person whose succession is concerned *explicitly* rehabilitates him/her by means of a will or deed, notwithstanding his/her indignity having been judicially declared. And the law further allows for *tacit* rehabilitation when the testator, despite knowing of the cause of indignity, includes the unworthy beneficiary in the will; in such a case, the unworthy beneficiary may inherit within the limits of the testamentary disposition (No. 2).

448. Heirs benefiting from the legitim (forced heirs), as any other heirs, are subject to the general rules of Article 2034 and subsequent ones. Hence, they may be *declared unworthy*, if they commit any one of the acts described in the paragraphs of Article 2034.

Additionally, those heirs may also be *disinherited* by the person whose succession is concerned, if they commit any of the acts described in paragraphs a), b), and c) of No. 1 of Article 2166. These acts presuppose, as a rule, that the heir was condemned for having committed some crime against the person of the deceased, or against one of his/her close relatives, or that the heir refused to pay maintenance to the deceased or to his/her spouse.

734. Article 2034 of the CC.

Disinheritance must be part of a will, which must explicitly state the reason for it. The situation of the disinherited person is, for all legal purposes, equivalent to that of the unworthy heir.[735] However, he/she may *impugn* the disinheritance on the grounds of non existence of the alleged reason for it, during the two years subsequent to the date of the reading of the will.[736]

§3. The System of Descent

449. Intestate succession occurs not only in the *absence* of a will but also when the deceased did not 'validly and effectually dispose of the assets that he/she might dispose of after death, entirely or in part'.[737] Therefore intestate succession takes place when (i) *there is* no will; (ii) there is a will, but the testator only disposed of a *part* of his/her assets; (iii) there is a will, but it is not valid and was *declared null and void*; (iii) there is a will, but it is not *in force* because it was *revoked* or it has *expired.*

Under Article 2133, the heirs are called in the following order of precedence:

- Spouse and descendants.
- Spouse and ascendants.
- Collaterals.
- The State.

I. The Classes of Heirs

A. *Surviving Spouse and Descendants*

450. The fact that the law refers to the spouse in both paragraphs a) and b) of No. 1 of Article 2133 is clarified in No. 2 of the same precept: the surviving spouse is included in the first class of persons eligible for succession, unless the person whose succession is concerned dies without descendants, in which case he/she is included in the second category.

Consequently, if the spouse applies for succession alongside the descendants, the estate is divided by the first and the latter, under Articles 2139 and 2140. In the absence of a surviving spouse, the estate is divided by the descendants.[738] In the absence of descendants, a distinction must be made: if there are no ascendants either, only the spouse inherits; if there are ascendants, the estate is divided by the spouse and the ascendants, under Article 2142, No. 1, including the spouse alongside the ascendants in the second class of prospective beneficiaries.

735. Article 2166, No. 2 of the CC.
736. Article 2167 of the CC.
737. Article 2131 of the CC.
738. Articles 2139, No. 2 and 2140 of the CC.

451. At any rate, the spouse is not called to the inheritance in the following situations, described in Article 2133, No. 3: (a) if up to the moment of death of the person whose succession is concerned, the sentence of divorce or of separation had transited in *rem judicatam*; (b) if the sentence had been pronounced prior to that date, although it did not transit in *rem judicatam* until later; (c) if legal action was pending at the time the person whose succession is concerned died, but the sentence of divorce or separation was pronounced subsequently, under Article 1785. A fourth possibility has been recently introduced in the Portuguese legal system. Indeed Law No. 48/2018 of 14 August, allows the mutual renunciation of spouses to each other's inheritances when agreed upon in the prenuptial agreement. Since the spouse is a necessary heir, such possibility implies the renunciation to the legitim (reserved share). This is only allowed when the matrimonial regime is the one of separation of property (Article 1700, No. 3 of the CC) and it may be agreed under the condition of the existence of surviving heirs of any type (Article 1700-A, No. 1 of the CC). Such option, however, does not deprive the spouse from the possibility to demand maintenance from the inheritance (Article 1700-A, No. 2 of the CC) and is complemented by a right to remain in the family home (Article 1700-A, No. 3–7 of the CC). Additionally that 'donations made to the spouse who renounces his or her inheritance shall not affect the descendants' legitims, and therefore shall not be unlawful (inofficious), provided they are within the hypothetical share that would belong to the spouse if the spouse had not renounced their status as heir' (Article 2168, No. 2 of the CC). This new regime means two important changes in traditional Portuguese law: on the one hand, it reintroduces the 'renunciation pacts on future inheritance' that had been abolished some five hundred years ago; on the other hand, it represents the withdrawal of 'public order' rules in favour of establishing the status of legal heir by contract.

452. When the spouse applies for succession alongside his/her children, Article 2139, No. 1 is applicable. Partition between the spouse and his/her children is made per person, and the estate is divided into as many parts as there are heirs; the spouse's share, however, is never less than one-fourth of the estate.

453. When the deceased leaves no surviving spouse and only his/her children apply to the inheritance, the estate is divided by them in equal shares.[739] It is of no relevance that some of them were born in wedlock and others out of wedlock. Neither is it relevant that some children were born of the first marriage while others of the second marriage. If any of the children cannot or will not claim his/her share of the estate, the descendants will represent him/her, under the terms and with the consequences mentioned below.

454. Finally, when there are no descendants and the deceased has left no ascendants either, the spouse is appointed to inherit the whole of the estate.[740]

739. Article 2139, No. 2 of the CC.
740. Articles 2141 and 2145 of the CC.

B. Surviving Spouse and Ascendants

455. The spouse is included in the second class of prospective beneficiaries, alongside the ascendants, *when the person whose succession is concerned dies without descendants but leaves ascendants.*[741] The spouse is entitled then *two-thirds* and the ascendants *one-third* of the estate.[742]

456. In the absence of spouse, the ascendants are entitled to inherit the whole of the estate.[743]

457. Article 2143 must be taken into consideration as well. When spouse and ascendants apply for succession, if any of the ascendants cannot or will not claim his/her share, that share *accrues* to those of the other ascendants applying for succession; only, and only when there are no ascendants, will it be added to the share of the surviving spouse.

C. Collaterals

458. In the absence of spouse, descendants and ascendants, the siblings and, *representatively*, their descendants are summoned to inherit,[744] whatever the degree of family relationship.[745]

459. In the absence of spouse, descendants, ascendants, siblings, nephews and nieces, the other collateral relatives to the fourth degree will inherit. Regarding these collaterals, the so-called right of representation is not applicable, the closest relatives taking precedence over the more distant ones in any case;[746] and partition is always made *per person.*

D. The State

460. Finally, in the absence of spouse and all other possible relatives, the State is summoned to inherit,[747] having the same rights and duties as any other heir regarding the estate.[748]

After the non-existence of other people eligible for succession has been judicially recognized, the estate is declared in escheat and handed over to the State.

---

741. Article 2133, No. 2 of the CC.
742. Article 2142, No. 1 of the CC.
743. Article 2142, No. 2 of the CC.
744. Article 2145 of the CC.
745. Article 2145 of the CC.
746. Article 2147 of the CC.
747. Article 2152 of the CC.
748. Article 2153 of the CC.

II. Representation, Substitution and Right to Accrue

461. The beneficiary may be appointed directly or indirectly. Indirect appointment occurs when a person inherits instead of another who could not or would not apply for succession. Indirect appointment means that somebody may not be appointed to the succession because any of the requirements mentioned above was lacking, or because, after the appointment, he/she was has disclaimed the inheritance: the law will, consequently, appoint another person to take his/her place.

462. One of the forms of indirect appointment is the so-called right of representation. Under Article 2039, 'representation in the succession takes place when the law appoints the descendants of an heir or of a legatee to take his/her place, because he/she could not or would not claim the inheritance or the legacy'.

463. Another form of indirect appointment is direct substitution, also called ordinary substitution because it is the most common of the substitution forms. Article 2281 defines it as follows: 'The testator may replace the appointed heir with somebody else, in case the latter cannot or will not claim the inheritance: this is called direct substitution.'

464. The third form of indirect appointment is the right to accrue.

Article 2301 defines the concept of this right, according to which when two or more heirs inherit the totality or a share of the estate, whether jointly or separately, and any of them cannot or will not claim the estate, their share will accrue to the share of the other heirs in their totality or in their share.

III. Adoption

465. Adoption ceases the relationship that the child had with biological parents and establishes a new familial relationship with adoptive parents. The child takes the full position of a descendant to the first degree of the adoptive parents.

Chapter 2. Testamentary Succession

§1. Introduction

466. Portuguese law defines a will in Article 2179:

> 1. Will is the unilateral and revocable act whereby a person disposes of all, or part of, his or her assets, to have effect after his or her death. 2. The provisions of non-patrimonial nature permitted by law in a will are valid if they are part of a testamentary act, even if no provisions of non-patrimonial nature are contained in it.

467. A will is a *unilateral* act. The declaration is valid as soon as it is made, and it is not required to be communicated to a specific person. The will is complete when the declaration is issued in a form deemed sufficient by the law.

A will is a *personal* act. This means that the testator's mind must be expressed by himself/herself, and that no other person may act as his/her representative.

A will is an *individual or single* act. Under Article 2181, the same will may not include two or more persons.

§2. The Capacity to Make a Will

468. The presiding principle is that of full testamentary capacity, apart from the cases in which the law explicitly removes that capacity.[749] The persons without capacity for making a will are non-emancipated minors and the persons under custodianship when it is determined by Court decision.[750] Special incapacity to make a 'closed will' may be added in the case of those who cannot read.[751]

§3. Different Types of Wills

469. In terms of form, the most common are the public will and the closed will. The public will must observe the formal requisites of a deed, in the sense that it is an act performed by an official entity and not a private one.

The closed will is written and signed by the testator; it may also be written by somebody else and signed by the testator, or it may be written and signed by somebody else, but always at the request of the testator.[752]

The approval of the closed will by the Notary Public is a condition for its validity.[753] The requisite of the approval of the closed will by the Notary Public excludes

749. Article 2188 of the CC.
750. Article 2189 of the CC.
751. Article 2208 of the CC.
752. Article 2206 of the CC.
753. Article 2206, No. 5.

the validity of the so-called holographic will – a will that is simply written and signed by the testator, and which is legally accepted in some countries.

The closed will may be kept by the testator, the notary or a third party.[754]

470. Article 2210 and subsequent ones prescribe the special forms of a will – military, on board a ship or craft, in case of public calamity.

The validity of the will formulated in one of the special, simplified forms, expires two months after the moment the exceptional circumstances that justified it ceased to exist. Besides the rules of Article 27 of Regulation (EU) No. 650/2012, Article 65 of the CC allows for the formal validity of the will made in conformity with the law of the place where it was written, or with the law recognized by that place's rules on the conflict of laws, or with the personal law of the testator at the time of death or the personal law at the time the disposition was made. Nevertheless, No. 2 of the same Article prescribes the observance of any particular formal requirement mandated by the personal law of the testator.

Although only in very strict terms, it is legal to make dispositions *per relationem.* Article 2184 allows for the omission of certain aspects of the provisions in the text of the will. In other words, the testator may complete the testamentary provisions with manifestations of his/her intentions, which are explicit and different from the will itself, and to be found elsewhere. However, it is not simply about referring to another text; it is about completing the manifestation of the intention expressed in the will – for example, 'I bequeath to Antonio the assets mentioned on the list that is kept in the drawer of my desk.'

The first part of Article 2184 shows that a mere verbal expressing of intention, conveyed to somebody else, is not permitted as a way to complete the will. It would mean the nullity of that expression of intention for lack of the required form.

There is no difficulty in accepting a reference made to a public document, since it has the same formal value as the will.

§4. The Joint Will

471. 'Joint wills' are not allowed. It may happen that the validity of 'joint wills' made abroad by Portuguese citizens has to be evaluated in accordance with the law of that country. Courts usually hold that the prohibition of joint wills is a *formal* rule, and that a document written in conformity with the local law must, therefore, be recognized.[755] However, doctrine usually says that the prohibition deals with a *substantial* aspect of the will and, therefore, the applicable law is that of the personal law of the testator – the Portuguese law[756] which does not accept joint wills.[757]

754. Article 2209, No. 1 of the CC.
755. Article 65, No. 1 of the CC.
756. Article 62 of the CC.
757. Article 2181 of the CC.

§5. Revocation of a Will

472. Wills are freely revocable acts. The possibility of the will being revoked may not be renounced, out of respect for the testator's last intentions.[758] The revoking of a will is a manifestation of intention equivalent to that of the writing of a will.

There are usually three modalities of revocation: explicit, tacit and material ('real'). The last one results from the physical destruction of the will or from the fact that the testator alienated the legacy or transformed it into something of a different nature, form or designation.

§6. Provisions in a Will

473. The testator may use the will to make all kinds of provisions, both of personal and patrimonial nature.

A will is traditionally and fundamentally a patrimonial act; it focuses on the juridical relationships that are patrimonial in nature. However, wills have always been considered to be used for personal provisions.

It was doubtful whether wills might be used for personal provisions alone. Article 2179, No. 2 of the CC clearly resolves this issue in an affirmative sense.

§7. Restrictions

I. The Legitim

A. *Introduction*

474. Under Article 2156, the legitim or reserved share ('legítima') is the portion of the testator's assets of which he/she may not dispose of, because it is legally destined to the surviving *spouse*, *descendants* or *ascendants*.

The term 'legitim' (reserved share) may be used in two senses.

Article 2156 defines global 'legitim' or, more precisely, the non-disposable share of the estate. *Global* legitim and *non-disposable portion* of the estate are the same concept, although seen from different perspectives: the perspective of the heirs and the perspective of the deceased, respectively. The deceased has a non-disposable portion in his/her estate; the legal heirs have a reserved share, globally considered. '*Legitim*' is also used to describe the reserved share of *each* heir, that is, his/her personal *legal share*. If a person dies leaving two children and assets to the amount of EUR 60,000, the global reserved share is of EUR 40,000 and the reserved share of each heir is of EUR 20,000.

The surviving *spouse*, the *descendants* and the *ascendants* are the heirs entitled to this reserved share.[759]

758. Article 2311 of the CC.
759. Article 2157 of the CC.

475. Depending on the case, the legitim is half, two-thirds or one-third of the estate, but in order to make an estimate of the reserved share, the estate has first to be defined. The legitim is a portion of the estate; it is half, two-thirds or one-third *of what*?

The question is solved in Article 2162, under which the estimate of the legitim must take into consideration the existing assets belonging to the person whose succession is concerned at the time of his/her death, the donations, the expenses subject to the obligation to restore or account (hotchpot) and the obligations of the estate.

The legitim is half, two-thirds or one-third of a calculation made in such a way. This estimate, which is made according to what is prescribed in Article 2162, includes four distinct operations – evaluating the assets, deducting the obligations, fictitious restoring of donations and expenses subject to hotchpot, and imputation of gifts anticipating the legitim.

476. Article 2163 enshrines the principle of the intangibility of the legitim, prohibiting the testator to impose any charges on it (e.g., usufruct) or to define the assets that constitute it, against the heir's will.

B. Succession of Spouse and Descendants

477. When the spouse applies for succession alongside his/her children, the legitim of the first one and of the latter is two-thirds of the estate.[760]

When the deceased leaves no surviving spouse, and only his/her children apply for succession, their reserved share is half or two-thirds of the estate, depending on whether there is one child or two or more children.[761]

Finally, when the spouse does not apply alongside descendants or ascendants, his/her legitim is half the estate.[762]

C. Succession of Spouse and Ascendants

478. When, being there no descendants, the spouse and the ascendants apply for the inheritance, their legitim is two-thirds of the estate.[763]

When the deceased leaves neither descendants nor spouse, the ascendants' legitim is half or one-third of the estate, depending on whether the parents or the ascendants to the second degree, and subsequent ones, are called to the succession.[764]

760. Article 2159, No. 1 of the CC.
761. Article 2159, No. 2 of the CC.
762. Article 2158 of the CC.
763. Article 2161, No. 1 of the CC.
764. Article 2161, No. 2 of the CC.

D. Maintenance Provisions

479. The surviving spouse may apply for maintenance upon the assets left by the deceased spouse. The heirs will be charged according with the proportion of assets received by each of them.[765]

480. The surviving partner of a de facto union may apply as well, provided that the deceased person.[766]

§8. Interpretation of a Will

481. On interpreting wills, one must seek the meaning that appears to be in conformity with the genuine intention of the testator, even if evidence external to the will and disregarded by the addressee has to be gathered. Thus, a situation may arise in which the meaning is inaccessible for an ordinary addressee under the concrete circumstances of the will.

Article 2187, No. 2 excludes any meaning that does not appear to be acceptable in the context of the will.

765. Article 2018 of the CC.
766. Article 2020 of the CC.

Chapter 3. Acts *Inter Vivos* Related to the Estate

§1. DONATIO *MORTIS CAUSA*

482. Agreements as to succession are forbidden by law.[767] This prohibition is grounded on the idea that it guarantees that the deceased has the liberty to dispose of his/her property until the very last moment of his/her life. That liberty would be seriously restricted if such agreements were permitted; those agreements would be contracts, and, as such, would be *irrevocable*.

However, there are exceptional circumstances in which agreements as to succession are allowed – *donationes mortis causa*, between spouses and from third parties to spouses, concerning certain and determined assets, and of the whole or part of the estate.

Article 1700, No. 1, paragraph b), also allows for the instituting of an heir or the appointing of a legatee in favour of a third party, made by any of the spouses in the prenuptial agreement.

These provisions had been permitted by the Supreme Court's ruling of 16 December 1927, but doctrine was not unanimous about considering whether they had mere testamentary value (and were, thus, revocable) or were genuine contracts of inheritance (and, as such, irrevocable). Nowadays, the law makes a distinction between dispositions made in favour of undetermined persons, or of a specific determined person who is not part of the act as an acceptor (first case), and a disposition made in favour of a certain determined person who participates in the act as acceptor in a prenuptial agreement (second case). Both cases are regulated by law, in Articles 1704 and 1705, respectively. In the first one, the provision is merely testamentary, whereas in the second one the disposition is contractual in nature.

767. Article 2028 of the CC.

Chapter 4. Acquisition and Administration of the Estate and Partition

§1. The Acquisition

483. The acquisition of an inheritance only materializes through *acceptance* (or claim), that is, through an affirmative response to the appointment.

Articles 2062 and subsequent ones regulate the disclaimer of the estate by which the person summoned responds negatively. When the prospective beneficiary disclaims the estate, he/she is *deemed as not summoned* (except for representation purposes). It may be said that, as a rule, this notion is the basis for the definition of the effects of disclaimer, and they retroact to the moment of the opening of the succession, in the same way that those of acceptance do.[768]

§2. The Administration of the Estate

484. The *administration* of the estate may only raise questions until the moment of its full liquidation and partition, in other words, while the expenses are due or the estate remains undivided. Under Article 2079, the responsibility for the administration of the estate falls to the administrator (*'cabeça-de-casa')l*, and the subsequent Articles regulate who is to hold that responsibility, his/her powers, and in which cases he/she may be excused or removed from their office, and so on.

485. Under Article 2068, the estate is responsible not only for the debts of the deceased, but also 'for the funeral costs and for liabilities, for testamentary, administering, and liquidating obligations of the estate (…) and for the partition of the legacies'.

Heirs are liable for the 'obligations of the estate', under Article 2071, up to the value of the assets inherited. The liability of the heirs does not, under Portuguese law, cover *ultra vires hereditatis.*

486. Unlike heirs, legatees are not, in principle, liable for the obligations of the estate; their liability for those expenses is merely incidental and subsidiary.

In fact, the conclusion drawn from Article 2276 may be no other. Legatee are responsible for the *obligations of the legacies*, and not for the *obligations of the inheritance*. Legatees are liable for the *obligations* of the legacies within the amount of the legacies alone.

768. Article 2062 of the CC.

§3. PARTITION

487. Under Article 2101, No. 1, any of the co-heirs, or the spouse (when he/she is legally entitled to half of the community estate that results from marriage), have the right to claim the partition of the inheritance.

The partition may be voluntary or *by inventory.*[769] When the partition is voluntary it may be performed at a Notary or at a Civil Registry Office – in such case all the interested parties agree on it. In case (i) the parties do not reach an agreement, (ii) the Public Prosecution Service deems that the protection of a vulnerable person with diminished capacity requires acceptance by inventory, or (iii) by reason of absence or permanent incapacity of one of the heirs, occurs the partition by inventory.[770] Since 2013, this kind of partition occurs in the Notary Office.[771]

488. Under Article 2104, hotchpot ('colação') is the restoration that the descendants who wish to apply for succession have to make to the estate, regarding the assets or values given to them as gifts by their ascendant, so as to equalize the partition.

This institute is, according to common doctrine, founded on the *presumed will of the deceased*, who, on making a donation to one of his/her descendants, is not presumed to have wished to favour one to detriment of the others; his/her will is understood as having been a mere anticipation of the *hereditary share* of the *donee.*

The obligation to return falls to the descendants who are presumptive legal heirs of the donor, who wish to apply for succession and have not been discharged from returning the assets donated by the deceased.

Consequently, this obligation to return does not fall to the *ascendants* that wish to apply for succession of their descendant, alongside the spouse[772] or, in the absence of descendants or spouse, as beneficiaries to the entire estate:[773] since under normal circumstances, the donor will die after the beneficiary, the donation may not be presumed to be a mere anticipation of the latter's hereditary share.

The spouse is not under the obligation to return either, even when he/she is included in the first class of persons eligible for succession, under Article 2139, No. 1, after the 1977 Reform.

489. Donations and 'expenses' are subject to hotchpot, 'expenses' being patrimonial reductions that, because of not adding to the assets of the beneficiary, do not constitute donations, under Article 940.

769. Article 2102 of the CC.
770. Article 2102, No. 2 of the CC.
771. Law No. 23/2013, 5 March.
772. Article 2142, No. 1 of the CC.
773. Article 2142, No. 2 of the CC.

Selected Bibliography

AA.VV. (J. Figueiredo Dias, Dir.). *Comentário Conimbricense do Código Penal. Parte Especial.* Tomo I, 2nd ed., and Tomo II. Coimbra: Coimbra Editora, 2012, 1999.

AA.VV. (M.S. Costa Gomes, Coord.). *Estudos sobre a nova Concordata: Santa Sé – República Portuguesa.* Lusitania Canonica, 11, Lisboa, Universidade Católica Editora, 2006.

Abreu, J.M. Coutinho de. *Curso de Direito Comercial.* Vol. II – *Das Sociedades.* 5th ed. Coimbra: Almedina, 2015.

Andrade, J.C. Vieira. *Os Direitos Fundamentais na Constituição Portuguesa de 1976.* 5th ed. Coimbra: Almedina, 2012.

Antunes, H. Sousa. *Responsabilidade civil dos obrigados à vigilância de pessoa naturalmente incapaz.* Lisboa: Universidade Católica Editora, 2000.

Campos, Diogo Leite de. *A invenção do direito matrimonial. A institucionalização do casamento, Boletim da Faculdade de Direito da Universidade de Coimbra.* Vol. LXII. Coimbra, 1986.

Campos, Diogo Leite de. *Lições de Direito da Família e das Sucessões.* 2nd ed. Coimbra: Almedina, 1997.

Carvalho, Manuel Vilhena de. *O Nome das Pessoas e o Direito.* Coimbra: Almedina, 1989.

Casimiro, Fernando Simões. 'Os conceitos de família e núcleo familiar nos recenseamentos da população em Portugal'. *Revista de Estudos Demográficos.* no. 33 INE (2003): 5–21.

Coelho, F.M. Pereira. *Direito das Sucessões.* polycopied edition. Coimbra, 1992.

Coelho, F. Manuel Pereira & de Oliveira, G. (com a colaboração de R. Moura Ramos). *Curso de Direito da Família,* 5th ed., Coimbra, Imprensa da Universidade, 2016 (co-author with F.M. Pereira Coelho), DOI: http://dx.doi.org/10.14195/978-989-26-1167-9.

Coelho, F. Manuel Pereira & de Oliveira, G. (*com a colaboração de* R. Moura Ramos). *Curso de Direito da Família.* Vol. II – *Direito da Filiação,* Tomo I – *Estabelecimento da Filiação e Adopção.* Coimbra: Centro de Direito da Família/Coimbra Editora, 2006.

Cordeiro, A. Meneses. *Tratado de Direito Civil Português.* I – *Parte Geral.* Tomo III – *Pessoas.* Coimbra: Livraria Almedina, 2004.

Cunha, M.ªC. Ferreira da. 'Crimes sexuais contra crianças e jovens'. In *Cuidar da justiça de crianças e jovens. A função dos juízes sociais,* edited by AA.VV. (M.ª C. Sottomayor, et. al. Coord.). Coimbra: Livraria Almedina, 2003, 189–227.

Selected Bibliography

Dias, Cristina Araújo. *Do regime da responsabilidade por dívidas dos cônjuges.* Coimbra: Centro de Direito da Família/Coimbra Editora, 2009.

Dias, Cristina Araújo. *Lições de Direito das Sucessões.* Coimbra: Almedina, 2010.

Dias, Cristina Araújo. *Uma análise do novo regime jurídico do divórcio.* 2nd ed. Coimbra: Almedina, 2009.

Gersão, Eliana. 'As novas leis de protecção de crianças e jovens em perigo e tutela educativa: uma reforma adequada aos dias de hoje'. *Infância e Juventude,* no. 2/00 (April–June 2000): 9–47.

Guerra, Paulo. 'O Novo Direito das Crianças e Jovens – o verdadeiro recomeço'. *Infância e Juventude,* no. 03/01 (January–March 2001): 53–80.

Henriques, Sofia. *Estatuto patrimonial dos cônjuges.* Coimbra: Coimbra Editora, 2009.

Hörster, H.E. *A Parte Geral do Código Civil Português. Teoria Geral do Direito Civil.* Coimbra: Livraria Almedina, 1992.

Leite, Sofia. 'A união de facto em Portugal'. *Revista de Estudos Demográficos.* no. 33 INE (2003): 95–140.

Lima, F. Pires de & Varela, J. Antunes. *Código Civil Anotado.* Vol. I, 4th ed. Vol. II, 4th ed. Vol. IV, 2nd ed. Vol. V and Vol. VI. Coimbra: Coimbra Editora, 1987, 1992, 1995, 1997 e 1998.

Lopes, J. Seabra. *Direito dos Registos e do Notariado.* 7th ed. Coimbra: Almedina, 2014.

Marques, João P. *Remédio. Mudança de sexo o critério jurídico: o problema do 'paradigma corporal' da identificação-identidade sexual no registo civil.* Coimbra, [s.n.], 1991.

Martins, Rosa Cândido. 'Processos de Jurisdição Voluntária: Acções de regulação do poder paternal; Audição do menor'. *Boletim da Faculdade de Direito da Universidade de Coimbra* LXXVII (off-print). Coimbra, 2001.

Martins, Rosa Menoridade, *(In)capacidade e Cuidado Parental.* Coimbra: Coimbra Editora, 2008.

Mattoso, José. *História de Portugal.* Vols I, III, VI, and VII, Círculo de Leitores.

Máximo Mocica, F.M.B. & Serrano, M.L.M. *Código do Registo Civil anotado e legislação complementar.* 2nd ed. Lisboa: Editora Rei dos Livros, 2011.

Oliveira, Guilherme, 'Critérios jurídicos da parentalidade', in *Textos de Direito da Família para F. Pereira Coelho.* Coimbra: Imprensa da Universidade, 2016, 271–306.

Oliveira, Guilherme de. 'Um Direito da Família Europeu. Play it again, and again … Europe!'. In *Temas de Direito da Família.* 2nd ed. enlarged. Coimbra: Coimbra Editora, 2001.

Pinheiro, Jorge Duarte. *O Direito da Família Contemporâneo.* 3rd ed. Lisboa: AAFDL, 2010.

Pinheiro, Jorge Duarte. *O Direito das Sucessões.* Lisboa: AAFDL, 2010.

Pinheiro, Luís de Lima. *Direito Internacional Privado: Direito de Conflitos – Parte Especial.* 3rd ed. Coimbra: Almedina, 2009.

Pinto, Carlos Alberto da Mota. *Teoria Geral do Direito Civil.* 4th ed. (by Pinto Monteiro, A. e Mota Pinto, P). Coimbra: Coimbra Editora, 2005.

Pombo, João Robalo. *O registo civil na prática das conservatórias.* Coimbra: Almedina, 1996.

Ramos, Rui Moura. 'A protecção das crianças no plano internacional'. *Infância e Juventude*, no. 2 (April–June 1998): 9–38.

Ramos, Rui Moura. *Do Direito Português da nacionalidade*. Biblioteca Jurídica, Coimbra: Coimbra Editora, 1984.

Ribeiro, Geraldo Rocha, *A Protecção do Incapaz Adulto no Direito Português*. Coimbra: Coimbra Editora, 2010.

Rodrigues, A. Miranda & Duarte-Fonseca, A.C. *Comentário da Lei Tutelar Educativa* (reissued). Coimbra: Coimbra Editora, 2003.

Rodrigues, Hugo. *Questões de particular importância no exercício das responsabilidades parentais*. Coimbra: Centro de Direito da Família/Coimbra Editora, 2011.

Sampaio, Álvaro. *Código de Registo Civil anotado e comentado*. 4th ed. (with the collaboration of Amorim, M.) Coimbra: Almedina, 2011.

Silva, Filipa. 'Projecção das taxas de fecundidade específicas por idades no horizonte a longo prazo (2002–2050)'. *Revista de Estudos Demográficos* no. 32 INE (2002): 59–80.

Sottomayor, M.ª C. 'A responsabilidade dos pais pelos factos ilícitos praticados pelos filhos menores'. *Boletim da Faculdade de Direito da Universidade de Coimbra* LXXI (1995): 403–468.

Sottomayor, M.ªC. *Regulação do exercício das responsabilidades parentais nos casos de divórcio*. 5th ed. Coimbra: Almedina, 2011.

Sousa, Rabindranath Capelo. 'A Constituição e o direito das sucessões'. In 'Estudos sobre a Constituição'. *Livraria Petrony*, 1977.

Sousa, Rabindranath Capelo. *Lições de Direito das Sucessões*. Vol. I. 4th ed. Coimbra.

Telles, I. Galvão. *Introdução ao Estudo do Direito*. Vol. II. 10th ed. (updated). Coimbra: Coimbra Editora, 2000.

Torres, Anália Cardoso. *Divórcio em Portugal, Ditos e Interditos*. Oeiras: Celta Editora, 1996.

Varela, J. Antunes. *Alterações legislativas do direito ao nome*, 'Revista de Legislação e Jurisprudência', year 115, 1982–1983; year 116, 1983–1984; year 117, 1984–1985; year 119, 1986–1987.

Varela, J. Antunes. *Direito da Família*. Vol. I. 5th ed. Livraria Petrony, 1999.

Vítor, Paula Távora, *A Administração do Património das Pessoas com Capacidade Diminuída*. Coimbra: Coimbra Editora, 2008.

Xavier, Rita Lobo. *Recentes alterações do regime jurídico do divórcio e das responsabilidades parentais*. Coimbra: Almedina, 2009.

Selected Bibliography

Index

The numbers here refer to paragraph numbers.

Index

Index

Index

Made in the USA
Monee, IL
13 September 2026

62974287R00136